"The authors of this book contend that ˹ competing views on a particular topic, ther͙ tary models to gain an appreciation of a variety of productive vantage points. They serve readers well by presenting a collaboration of perspectives that together unpack an understanding of Genesis One that is more robust than any single approach can achieve. Their clear writing and their literary, cultural, and theological sensitivity provide a multidimensional expansion of interpretative insights that not only enrich our view of the creation narrative but suggest ways that we can finally move beyond some of the persistent squabbles that have divided Christians."

—John Walton,
Professor of Old Testament, Wheaton College,
author of *The Lost World of Genesis One*

"In *The Manifold Beauty of Genesis One*, Davidson and Turner persuasively describe the literary beauty and rich theological message of the opening chapter of the Bible. Genesis One proclaims that God created everything, but its message goes much deeper and further in scope. Davidson and Turner masterfully unpack Genesis One to reveal seven interlacing and complementary layers of meaning. This book is a must-read for everyone who wants to know Scripture, and therefore God, better."

—Tremper Longman, III,
Professor Emeritus of Biblical Studies,
Westmont College

"In *The Manifold Beauty of Genesis One*, Gregg Davidson and Kenneth Turner attempt what rarely occurs in biblical studies. Instead of devoting their energies to debunking interpretations of Genesis One with which they disagree, and then triumphally claiming the higher ground, they seek to capitalize on the strengths of divergent points of view to create a more colorful, variegated, and nuanced understanding. Approaching the biblical creation account from a thoroughly orthodox and evangelical perspective, they offer guidance in both substance and tone for pastors and lay readers. Some may not agree with some of their interpretations, but all should welcome this invitation to conversation and reflection on a rich text that has engaged scholars and ordinary people for thousands of years."

—Daniel Block,
Professor Emeritus of Old Testament, Wheaton College

"What a friendly and helpful book Gregg Davidson and Kenneth Turner have given us! With a clear commitment to Scripture, solid knowledge of their subject, and a gentle manner, they have offered us many ways to enrich our understanding of Genesis One and to quell our fears of its 'conflict with science.' They handle objections thoughtfully and persuasively, and they even provide discussion questions after each chapter. This should serve the church well."

—C. John Collins,
Professor of Old Testament,
Covenant Theological Seminary

"Gregg Davidson and Kenneth Turner have written a superb book devoted to understanding the riches and beauty of Genesis One and its wide-ranging implications. They show how this opening and foundational chapter to Scripture is richly textured, multi-layered, and theologically robust. It is a feast for mind and heart!"

—Paul Copan,
Professor of Philosophy and Ethics (Pledger Family Chair),
Palm Beach Atlantic University

"This work is an undertaking of monumental implication. This multi-layered approach to interpreting the Bible's creation narrative challenges the reader by painting a picture of God's creative communication that is greater than merely the sum of existing views, which so often examine only limited aspects of Scripture. *The Manifold Beauty of Genesis One* offers a fuller appreciation for the God who desires to capture his image-bearers' attention and invite them into a deeper devotion. The hopeful result is both a renewed sense of awe for the believer and a more irenic disposition to conversations over science and faith."

—Steve Douglas,
Pastor of Groups and Adult Ministries,
The Grove Church, MN

"Davidson and Turner have accomplished their aim of demonstrating to the general Christian reader—in a clearly written way—the rich tapestry of different meanings inherent in Genesis One. But they have done more. By including many possible understandings, 'none widely departing from the rule of faith' (in Augustine's words), they encourage readers to weigh the biblical evidence for themselves as responsible vessels of the Holy Spirit. Along the way, they show how disagreement on interpretation need be no barrier to fellowship in the truth. Furthermore, by setting the creation story in the context of a messianic biblical theology, their book serves as an introduction to understanding the whole Bible message. All in all, this is a significant achievement, and highly recommended for every serious Christian."

—Jon Garvey,
author of *God's Good Earth* and *The Generations of Heaven and Earth*

"In theological and seminary circles, the creation account of Genesis has been presented and interpreted throughout history in a multitude of ways, each side with their own pros and cons. But what if instead of choosing a side, there existed a rarely acknowledged harmony to those well-published views? The authors of *The Manifold Beauty of Genesis One* provide a worthwhile volume to scholars and laypeople alike as they engage in such an essential and multifaceted aspect to the Christian faith."

—Foster Gullett,
missionary, MTW—Italy

"*The Manifold Beauty of Genesis One* gives the reader a concise presentation of where evangelical scholarship is now concerning the opening chapter of the Bible. It presents seven different approaches to interpreting the creation account. This one feature makes the book a worthy purchase. However, Davidson and Turner go beyond merely surveying current interpretations. They show that—like overlapping tiles of a roof—these approaches collectively serve as complementary themes, which in turn reinforce the unified message of Genesis One."

—Ken Keathley,
Senior Professor of Theology,
Southeastern Baptist Theological Seminary

"With so many polemical books about the Genesis creation account, the grace you will find in this one is refreshing! Jesus promised that the Spirit would teach the church as a community (John 16:13; the 'you' in that verse is plural). This book models confidence in that promise, bringing together various insights from differing exegetes who share a high view of Scripture. The result is a book that genuinely advances the conversation. But more importantly, it sets a Christlike tone of fraternity that is too often missing from creation debates. May God use this work to enrich the church, as a communion of saints, in their worship of the Creator!"

—Michael LeFebvre,
pastor, author of *The Liturgy of Creation*

"As a pastor and church planter, many of my conversations with both Christians and non-Christians inevitably turn to the Genesis creation story. With so many perspectives and interpretations, it can be difficult to know which is the 'right' one. Davidson and Turner free us from this narrow way of thinking, and provide a better way forward. They help us to see that the different perspectives on the Genesis story aren't competing with each other, rather they are part of a rich multi-layered understanding of God and his creation. This book is an invaluable tool for pastors and ministry professionals. It helps us to better understand the Genesis story, and explain it to others. Comprehensive and illuminating, this book belongs in every pastor's and church's library."

—Mario Russo,
pastor, church planter in Germany

"In contrast to singular and contentious readings of the creation accounts in Genesis 1 and 2, here is a book that explores multiple levels of meaning in these inexhaustible texts. Drawing on ancient Christian commentary and more recent exegetical studies, Davidson and Turner exhibit the theological richness of Genesis 1 and 2. In the process they illustrate the deep connection between creation and the entire drama of Scripture, while inspiring the reader to celebrate the one God who is both Creator and Redeemer."

—J. Richard Middleton,
Professor of Biblical Worldview and Exegesis,
Northeastern Seminary

"If Scripture is authoritative and inerrant in all that it teaches, how do we make sense of the many conflicting ways that Genesis is understood? Which one of the many readings of Genesis One is correct? To this false choice, Davidson and Turner respond that Genesis is an ancient text, rich with manifold layers of beauty. Many interpretations are, in fact, correct at the same time, each one resonating with a different layer of meaning. Turning from the cacophony of falsely conflicted interpretations, we are invited to worship in a symphony of many interpretations true and held together. The book samples the melodies of seven layers, but we should wonder about and search for layers in Genesis beyond just these. Disagree with the particulars if you must, but—in calling the church to recover the multifaceted beauty of Scripture—this book rightly affirms the diversity of many faithful readings. In reading Genesis together, we find that our diversity is a strength, not a weakness. As declares the Lausanne Covenant, our diversity '[discloses] to the whole Church ever more of the many-colored wisdom of God.'"

—S. Joshua Swamidass,
Associate Professor of Laboratory and Genomic Medicine, Washington University,
and author of *The Genealogical Adam and Eve*

"Davidson and Turner have managed to pull together a most helpful combination of approaches to the reading of Genesis One. They have shown how these approaches collectively contribute to a fuller understanding of its meaning. This approach to the reading of the first chapter of the Bible has tremendous potential for helping us in the ongoing discussion over the relationship between the first chapter of the Bible and modern science. The authors help us see that we can and must allow the Bible its own concerns as we bring it to bear on our concerns about God, people, and the world of science."

—Richard Averbeck,
Professor of Old Testament and Semitic Languages,
Trinity Evangelical Divinity School

"The effect of our modern society is to obscure Genesis 1 in clouds and storm, leaving a mountain few dare to climb. Happily, Gregg Davidson and Kenneth Turner have braved its heights, and returned with some of the most helpful biblical insights that I have seen. They present a rich, multidimensional perspective that remains entirely faithful to Scripture. Anyone seeking to understand the biblical account of creation should adventure into *The Manifold Beauty of Genesis One*. A compelling read for the expositor and novice alike."

—Fletch Matlack
Senior Pastor,
Immanuel Baptist Church, NY

"*The Manifold Beauty of Genesis One* is a deep, patient, reverent unfolding of Scripture that relates to the creation event. This is a book that thoughtful students of Scripture will not only learn from, but rejoice over. I wish I had it years ago to give to people who asked me about Genesis! I thank God it is available to thinking Christians now, and look forward to giving away many copies."

—Paul Lundquist,
former Wycliffe linguist,
missionary, pastor

The
MANIFOLD
BEAUTY
of
GENESIS
ONE

A Multi-Layered Approach

Gregg Davidson & Kenneth J. Turner

The Manifold Beauty of Genesis One: A Multi-Layered Approach
© 2021 by Gregg Davidson and Kenneth J. Turner

Published by Kregel Academic, an imprint of Kregel Publications, 2450 Oak Industrial Dr. NE, Grand Rapids, MI 49505-6020.

The Hebrew font, NewJerusalemU, is available from www.linguistsoftware.com/lgku.htm, +1-425-775-1130.

The illustration on page 53 is under Creative Commons licensing, and is in public domain.

ISBN 978-0-8254-4544-6

Printed in the United States of America

21 22 23 24 25 / 5 4 3 2 1

I believe in God the Father Almighty, maker of heaven and earth, and in Jesus Christ his only son our Lord; who was conceived by the Holy Spirit, born of the virgin Mary, suffered unto Pontius Pilate, was crucified, dead, and buried. He descended into hell; the third day he rose again from the dead; he ascended into heaven, and sits on the right hand of God the Father Almighty. From there he shall come to judge the living and the dead.

I believe in the Holy Spirit, the holy catholic church, the communion of saints, the forgiveness of sins, the resurrection of the body, and the life everlasting.

—*The Apostles' Creed, second century* A.D.

ABOUT *the* AUTHORS

KEN TURNER

Dr. Turner is professor of Old Testament and biblical languages at Toccoa Falls College in northeast Georgia. His free time is largely spent attending his kids' soccer games and speaking at apologetics conferences. His interest and involvement in origins stems from his undergraduate degree in physics and math, his interaction with college and high school students, and his involvement in the homeschool world. On issues that can sometimes be contentious, he has a keen desire to ensure Christians have accurate information, helping to foster intellectual honesty and irenic dialogue.

GREGG DAVIDSON

Dr. Davidson is a professor and department chair of geology and geological engineering at the University of Mississippi. His day job includes research in geochemistry and hydrology, with lots of time spent in the cypress swamps of Mississippi. His dissertation at the University of Arizona included many hours in the same radiocarbon lab that dated the Dead Sea Scrolls and the Shroud of Turin. He describes his upbringing as the odd and wonderful product of having two preachers for grandfathers and a biologist for a father, raised to uniquely appreciate God's written word and natural world. Later concern over misconceptions about both science and the Bible led to many articles and books, and speaking engagements across the United States and several continents. His books include the full-color, multiauthored *Grand Canyon: Monument to an Ancient Earth*; *Friend of Science, Friend of Faith*; and, just for fun, a science fiction trilogy. More at GreggDavidson.net.

OTHER BOOKS *by the* AUTHORS

GREGG DAVIDSON

Nonfiction

Friend of Science, Friend of Faith
The Grand Canyon: Monument to an Ancient Earth (coauthored)

Fiction

The Mulapin Trilogy
Shadows of the End
Princes and Principalities
Though Nations Rage

KEN TURNER

Habakkuk (commentary)
The Death of Deaths in the Death of Israel: Deuteronomy's Theology of Exile
For Our Good Always: Studies on the Message and Influence of Deuteronomy
(coedited)

CONTENTS

ACKNOWLEDGMENTS

Writing a book is both harder and more rewarding than originally conceived. It is never a one-man endeavor—or even two-man in this case! We owe a debt of gratitude to many, going back long before the beginning of this project, who have encouraged, prodded, and challenged us in our thinking—teachers, students, friends, colleagues. Above all, we offer our deep appreciation and thanks to our families. Our wives in particular have been our champions and our soulmates, helping us find balance between time with family and hours set aside to research, write, and travel.

Valuable critiques of early drafts were provided by many: Richard Averbeck, Kieran Clements, Lee Dearing, Joel Duff, Sy Garte, Jon Garvey, John O'Haver, Kristine Johnson, Kenneth Keathley, Michael LeFebvre, Paul Lundquist, Melvin Manickavasagam, David Schreiner, Bryan Sims, Joshua Swamidass, and Joel Woodruff. Several Toccoa Falls College students, enrolled in an upper-level class on Genesis, also read and gave helpful criticism. We believe this book is immensely better for the honest feedback and suggestions we have received. Of course, we own any and all remaining weaknesses and errors.

We would be remiss if we did not acknowledge the fantastic staff of Kregel. Their initial enthusiasm never dampened, even during a series of delays, largely due to the COVID-19 pandemic. They exhibited great patience and skill in bringing the final manuscript to fruition. We would not have wanted to work with anyone else on this project.

Finally, we thank our great God and Savior, who has inspired and sustained us throughout. Our desire is that he is exalted as this book helps others delve more deeply into his word and grow in admiration of his creation.

INTRODUCTION

The Many Layers of Genesis 1

*T*he opening chapter of the Bible tells an amazing story. It draws on the oldest of stories, likely repeated in various forms across generations by ancient orators before being recorded for the fledgling nation of Israel. Though ancient in origin, its message has spread across the globe and permeated the consciousness of even the most technologically advanced cultures. It touches on the deepest of human questions about where we came from, how we are related to others from distant times and lands, the nature and character of the material world, and, most importantly, who is responsible for bringing the world into existence.

In modern times, however, the richness and beauty of this story is too often overwhelmed by acrimony, with verbal wars fought over the appropriate interpretation of the text. The conflict would be easier to understand if the battles were principally between those who believe in the inspiration of the Bible and those who do not, but it isn't that simple. The discord runs deep within the ranks of those who hold to the authority and divine inspiration of the Scriptures. Even among those who self-identify as biblical inerrantists, views can radically differ, with fortified theological trenches dug to separate Christian from Christian. Churches have split and friendships have been lost over disagreements on how this singular text should be understood.[1]

It is our belief that much of this conflict derives from a failure to fully embrace what the church has long affirmed about the nature of the Bible as a

---

1. A personal friend even experienced a divorce driven by a shift in understanding of Gen. 1.

whole. When reading beyond Genesis, many Christians have recognized the Bible is not a one-dimensional script, but often contains layers to its message—layers that will sometimes be apprehended only after the third or tenth or hundredth visit. Gregory the Great, an early pope and theologian, captured this sense well in his study of Job, describing the Bible as "a river in which a lamb could walk and an elephant could swim."[2] He recognized some themes in Job that were obvious from a superficial reading, and some that could only be plumbed by careful study, approaching it from multiple perspectives.[3]

Few Christians would disagree with Gregory's assessment of Job or of the Bible in general.[4] Yet when it comes to Genesis, the discussion suddenly changes. If listening in on a typical conversation over the proper understanding of the creation story, one may come away with the impression that there is *one and only one* way to understand it. Moreover, there is often an accompanying sense of urgency, that to get it wrong on Genesis 1 is to get it wrong on all of Scripture.[5] To truly believe the Bible means to betroth oneself to the one true meaning, forsaking all others. Borrowing from Tolkien, the faithful seek to find the One Interpretation to Rule Them All.[6]

But what if we approached Genesis 1 with the same search for *richness*—that it too may contain *layers* of truth, each complementing and expanding on the others? Is it possible that more than one angle or emphasis or theme could be simultaneously valid? We are not suggesting something mystical or some sort of free-for-all in which a passage can mean something different for every reader. On any biblical subject, there will never be a shortage of interpretations that are simply wrong, whether because of logical inconsistencies or human bias overprinted on a biblical text. So what exactly do we mean by layers of truth?

As an illustration, consider this example from God's creation. Suppose that we explore a mineshaft and come across a beautiful mineral formation.

---

2. Gregory the Great, *Moral Reflections on the Book of Job*, 1:53.
3. It was common in medieval times to consider Scripture from four perspectives or senses: historical sense, allegorical sense, moral sense, and anagogical sense (pertaining to the afterlife or ultimate things). Wikipedia, s.v., "Allegory in the Middle Ages," https://en.wikipedia.org/wiki/Allegory_in_the_Middle_Ages.
4. The evangelical Lausanne Covenant affirms that the Holy Spirit "illumines the minds of God's people in every culture to perceive its truth freshly through their own eyes and thus discloses to the whole Church ever more of *the many-colored wisdom of God*" (emphasis added). Section 2: "The Authority and Power of the Bible" (cf. Eph. 3:10).
5. The seven days of creation extend a few verses into Gen. 2. As we will note later, we use "Genesis 1" as shorthand for Gen. 1:1–2:3.
6. *Interpretation* is used in the common sense here as a single thread of understanding or meaning. More explanation follows later in the Introduction.

Upon examination, we find that it is composed chiefly of the elements calcium and fluorine, with pinkish crystals taking the shape of interconnected cubes. A scratch test demonstrates that it is harder than calcite and softer than apatite. All this contributes to identifying the mineral as fluorite. This characterization represents one layer of truth—one that excludes competing options such as misidentifying it as quartz, or errant claims that it is made of lead and silicon.

But something surprising happens when we consider this sample in a different light. Not metaphorically speaking, but literally—a different *light*. If held under shortwave ultraviolet light (invisible to the human eye), the pink crystal suddenly glows blue! The mineral is phosphorescent, absorbing ultraviolet light and emitting it back as a visible shade of blue. Our previous identification does not suddenly become false because of this new discovery. It is still true that it is made of calcium and fluorine. It is still shaped in cubes. And it is still genuinely pink under normal light. It is still fluorite. But under the new light, another layer of truth about this mineral becomes evident. It is an understanding we would never have discovered without looking for it. The example could be extended even further, for varieties of fluorite exhibit even more colors under *longwave* ultraviolet light, and may even display yet another color when heated (thermoluminescence). Each represents a different layer of truth that expands our understanding and appreciation of this mineral.

LAYERED TRUTH IN SCRIPTURE

A critical aspect of our mineral example is the *complementary* nature of each discovery. Blue coloration under one light does not challenge or negate pink coloration under another frequency of light. If asked whether our fluorite crystal is pink or blue, we might playfully answer *Yes!*

We find an analogous principle at work in Scripture. Two examples follow—one looking forward to a promised messiah and one looking back to events from Israel's history.

Example 1: Isaiah's Messiah

Early in the book of Isaiah, the prophet speaks of a messiah who will come as a conquering king. A child will be born who will sit on the throne of David, establishing his kingdom forever (Isa. 9:1–7). The description of this coming king includes breaking the rod of the oppressor, burning up opposing armies as fuel for a divine fire, and dividing the spoil. Such words were likely the reason why many of the Jews expected Jesus—if he was truly the Messiah—to take up the sword against Rome, and why the mother of James and John asked that her sons be seated to Jesus's right and left in his coming kingdom.

The misunderstanding of the true ministry of Jesus came, in part, from focusing on only one of the messianic layers in Isaiah. Reading ahead, the same prophet speaks of a gentle servant who will not raise his voice in the street, or snuff out a smoldering wick until justice is established on earth; a man who will be a light to the Gentiles, opening eyes that are blind and freeing captives from prison (Isa. 42:1–9). And still another layer is revealed in the well-known "suffering servant" passage of Isaiah 52:13–53:12. Here we find a description of the Messiah lacking physical beauty, despised and rejected, a man who would know suffering and pain, who would be crushed by God for our iniquities and cut off from the land of the living.

Isaiah was not confused whether the Messiah would come as conquering king, gentle healer, or propitiatory sacrifice. All are true, each representing a different layer of understanding, leading to a deeper, richer understanding of how the Messiah did and will yet come.

Example 2: Sarah and Hagar, history and analogy

A second example draws attention to different perspectives from different biblical authors on the same set of characters and events: Sarah and her maidservant Hagar. In Genesis, God promises a son to Abraham, but his wife Sarah is barren.[7] Not trusting things to change, especially given her advanced age, Sarah gives Hagar to Abraham to produce a son on her behalf (Gen. 16). Years later, Sarah herself conceives and gives birth to her own son (Gen. 21). At one level (one layer), this is a simple narration of historical events and interactions with God in Israel's past. At another level, it provides a moral lesson that God is faithful and sufficient to fulfill his promises, even when it seems impossible to us. Still another layer is God's intention of setting a people apart for himself, starting with the intentional selection of Abraham and Sarah.

But what if someone were to suggest that while this story is indeed historical, we can also now understand it *allegorically*? You might protest that it cannot be both, until being reminded that the "someone" we speak of is the apostle Paul (Gal. 4:21–31). Without denying the historical nature of the text, Paul nonetheless ascribes a deeper, symbolic meaning to the story, saying "this may be interpreted allegorically: these women are two covenants"

---

7. Abraham and Sarah's names were still Abram and Sarai at this point in the story (Gen. 16).

(Gal. 4:24).[8] Hagar (the slave woman) represents the old covenant, and her son represents children born according to the flesh (the present Jerusalem). Sarah (the free woman) represents the new covenant, and her son represents the children born of promise (the Jerusalem above). Thus, the same story conveys different layers of truth: historical, moral, *and* symbolic. Each layer of understanding adds to the richness of the text.

With all this in mind, we will explore a series of possible layers of truth derived from the opening chapter of Genesis. No layer will be presented in competition with the others, as is commonly found in books with titles like *Four Views on [insert theological issue]*. Rather, they are presented as *complementary* perspectives. One might think of these layers like overlapping tiles on a roof. In one sense, each tile is independent of the others. A single tile exists on its own as something real and genuine. But one tile does a poor job of shedding rain. When joined with others, the entire structure beneath is sheltered from the storm. The image of overlapping tiles serves as an apt metaphor for a second reason. While each layer will draw out something unique from the creation story, the textual or archaeological support for one layer will sometimes also serve to support another. Arguments used to defend each layer will overlap.

We said *possible* layers above, for we will not suggest or argue with certainty that *every* detail of *every* layer we describe was intended by the original writer or by the ultimate Author. You may find as you read that some of the layers or their parts resonate with your understanding of God's character and written Word, while finding others less convincing. Our primary thesis, that Genesis 1 contains layers of truth, is not dependent on all of our proposed layers being accepted, or that every element within each layer be affirmed. It is not an all-or-nothing proposition. The manifold beauty of the text should be apparent even if only a subset of the layers is embraced. In a similar vein, we make no claim that the layers we present exhaust all possibilities.

CULTURAL CONTEXT

A common theme through each layer in this book will be to understand the text through the eyes of the original audience.[9] One of the surest ways to misinterpret

---

8. Biblical scholars disagree whether Paul's use of the word *allegoreo* in Gal. 4:24 fits the technical sense of allegory, typology, or something else. The point we make of multiple layers of understanding is not dependent on resolving this question.

9. The original audience when Genesis was written was the nation of Israel, beginning at the time of the exodus and Mount Sinai. Some parts of the Pentateuch are clearly post-

Scripture is to assume its writers were guided by cultural norms equivalent to our own. If this does not strike you as intuitively obvious, consider for a moment the expected result of spending a month in a foreign land, assuming that everyone you encounter will conform to the cultural nuances of your home country. New and lasting friendships with the locals will not be a likely outcome!

The culture into which the Old Testament was written was part of the ancient Near East (abbreviated to ANE throughout this book). The language of the Bible embraces the time and place of its writing, with no attempt to normalize wording for distant lands or future civilizations. In the pages of Scripture, angels armed for battle do not arrive in mechanized vehicles with automatic rifles, but ride in chariots and carry swords (e.g., 2 Kings 6:17; Num. 22:23). A business transaction does not end with a handshake or a signature, but with a sandal removed and exchanged (Ruth 4:7–8). A young widow with no children is not encouraged to remarry and start again, but to move in with her brother-in-law to raise up children in her departed husband's name (Gen. 38:6–11).

In short, the Bible does not bend itself to match the sensitivities and nuances of *our* culture. God spoke to his people in the context of their own time and their own place.[10] If we wish our understanding of Scripture to grow, the onus is on us to put ourselves into the mindset and worldview of that original audience, recognizing that there will be times when modern, culturally infused standards forced on the Bible simply do not work.

ADDRESSING CONCERNS

The preceding paragraphs may raise some concerns for cautious readers regarding our assumptions and motivations. We have an appreciation and respect for these concerns, as we also wish to honor the inspired authority of the biblical text. The most common concerns are identified by category below, with our explanations and assurances.

For all times and peoples?

When we stress the importance of understanding the Bible from the perspective of the original audience, are we suggesting the Bible was not written for all

---

Mosaic (such as Moses's obituary), with some scholars arguing for updates extending into the period of exile. Our references to the "original audience" are largely the same for the people of Israel at the time of Moses and up through the exile.

10. A common expression to this point, popularized by OT scholar John Walton, is that the Bible was written *for* us, but not *to* us.

times and all peoples? What about the *perspicuity* of Scripture—the doctrine that says the central message of the Bible is clear for all readers at all times? To answer, the doctrine of perspicuity, or clarity, of the Bible pertains to the fundamental message of salvation.[11] The need for and path to God's forgiveness and redemption is not occluded in cryptic language or the nuances of an ancient culture. It is clearly expressed for all who read with an open heart. The doctrine makes no claim, however, about the clarity or ease of understanding of the Bible as a whole. If the intention of every passage of Scripture leapt from the page upon the first reading, there would be no point to seminary degrees or even personal Bible study. Scripture is simple to understand in some places and more difficult in others. More to the point of this book, it may be that one layer of understanding is indeed easily apprehended from a cursory reading of a text, but a sense of the richness and depth of the same text may come only after years of study.

Dependence on archaeology

Much of what we know about ancient Near Eastern culture has come from archaeological discoveries in the last two hundred years. If we draw on those discoveries, will we be inferring that a true understanding of Genesis was lost to most of the history of the church until the discovery of the ruins of ancient libraries? At a broad level, we can answer that none of the presented layers are entirely new. While the development or details of some layers came to fruition only in recent times, the underlying premise of each finds ancient support in the history of Jewish and Christian interpretation. Regarding the more recent developments, we return to the subject of perspicuity. Aspects of Genesis critical to our understanding of God's sovereignty, our sinful condition and need of redemption, and God's continued interest in his creation are evident even from a superficial reading. A greater knowledge of ancient Near Eastern culture does not *replace* all previous understandings of the text, but it does serve to refine and *enhance* understanding. In some respects, this can be compared to a traveler to the Holy Land who returns with a greater appreciation of the biblical stories, now able to place events in the context of a landscape visibly seen. The trip was not essential to understand the basic

---

11. Westminster Confession 1.7: "All things in Scripture are not alike plain in themselves, nor alike clear unto all: yet those things which are necessary to be known, believed, and observed for salvation, are so clearly propounded, and opened in some place of Scripture or other, that not only the learned, but the unlearned, in a due use of the ordinary means, may attain unto a sufficient understanding of them."

truths of Scripture, but perspective may be enhanced by a physical visit to the land.

Influence of surrounding nations

There are some who argue that the stories and laws of the Bible are borrowed adaptations of older stories and laws from the dominant cultures surrounding Israel. Is that where this book is leading? The answer is no. At no point will we argue that Israel simply borrowed ideas from their neighbors. We will periodically take note of *shared* cultural experiences that can in turn help us see things that were likely obvious to the original audience but are easily missed by a modern reader. We will revisit this subject with repeated reminders of our approach and intention.

Inerrancy and interpretation

The Chicago Statement on Biblical Inerrancy, article 18, affirms that "the text of Scripture is to be interpreted by grammatico-historical exegesis, taking account of its literary forms and devices, and that Scripture is to interpret Scripture."[12] While not an inspired document, the Chicago Statement is nonetheless viewed by many evangelicals as a standard for assessing the legitimacy of a biblical interpretation. It is thus understandable that some will ask where we stand on this statement. The short answer is that both authors concur with this statement, even affirming it annually as part of the membership requirements for the Evangelical Theological Society.

A longer answer is warranted, however, to understand what the statement means. It is helpful to see how this article is explained later in the same document. Under the heading "Infallibility, Inerrancy, Interpretation," the writers explain, "Scripture is inerrant, not in the sense of being absolutely precise by modern standards, but in the sense of making good its claims and achieving that measure of focused truth at which its authors aimed." In other words, Scripture is without error in all it intends to teach. The biblical authors were free to use literary devices and contemporary methods of accounting that may run contrary to modern expectations, without charge of error.

The later Chicago Statement on Biblical Hermeneutics, article 15, adds "the necessity of interpreting the Bible according to its literal, or normal,

---

12. International Council on Biblical Inerrancy, "Chicago Statement on Biblical Inerrancy," art. 18.

sense."[13] The definition of *literal* is then defined: "The literal sense is the gram-matical-historical sense, that is, the meaning which the writer expressed. Interpretation according to the literal sense will take account of all figures of speech and literary forms found in the text."[14] In this context, *literal* is under-stood more as *literary*, rather than its common *literalistic* use, where a text simply means what the words say.[15] The writers of both statements affirm that when considering literary genre, poetic or rhetorical devices, figures of speech or historical context, the proper interpretation may mean something very different (and more correct) than a superficial reading of the words.[16] Each layer we present in this book is consistent with and conforms to this understanding of biblical inerrancy.

Another point of potential confusion arises over the use of seemingly straightforward terms such as biblical *interpretation* and *meaning*. Among evangelical theologians, a biblical passage is understood to have one primary intended interpretation or meaning, with multiple themes, motifs, nuances, or layers possible that combine in support of the unified message.[17] Chris-tian laity, however, frequently use *interpretation* (or *meaning*) interchange-ably with terms like *themes* or *layers*. More than one "interpretation" may thus contribute to the overall intended message. These conflicting defini-tions present a challenge for a book aimed at a broad Christian audience. In short, we affirm there is an intended, unified message to Scripture, both in its parts and as a whole. The layers in this book are not presented as competing interpretations. They are presented as complementary themes that contribute to and reinforce the unified message of Genesis 1. Wherever we refer to nuanced meaning or interpretation, the intention is consistent with this affirmation.

---

13. International Council on Biblical Inerrancy, "Chicago Statement on Biblical Hermeneutics," art. 15. The Chicago Statement on Biblical Hermeneutics is not as widely affirmed among evangelical theologians as the Chicago Statement on Biblical Inerrancy.

14. International Council on Biblical Inerrancy, "Chicago Statement on Biblical Hermeneutics," art. 15.

15. Under "Formal Rules of Biblical Interpretation," part B, the exposition goes on to say, "that is, by asking what is the linguistically natural way to understand the text in its historical setting." International Council on Biblical Inerrancy, "Chicago Statement on Biblical Hermeneutics."

16. As a lighthearted example, shouting, "Heads up!" anywhere in the United States results in most people ducking their heads *down* in order to avoid being struck by an approaching airborne object.

17. International Council on Biblical Inerrancy, "Chicago Statement on Biblical Hermeneutics," art. 18.

Motivation

A final anticipated concern relates to the perceived motivation of the authors. Is this book really just a clever ploy to dismiss the historical veracity of the Bible or to make the creation story palatable for those looking to merge the Bible with modern scientific theories of origins? To the best of our ability to answer truthfully and honestly, the answer is no. While each of us has written elsewhere on the intersection of science and the Bible, this book approaches Genesis free of any obligations or deference to science. There are no scientific arguments or assumptions in these pages. Examples from nature may be called on for illustrations, such as our fluorite mineral above, but we will not draw on any scientific evidence to aid our understanding of the Bible.

There will be some who will nonetheless object, insisting the various perspectives presented would never have been considered if we had not given attention to the prevailing scientific theories of the day. To this we readily acknowledge that observations in God's natural creation have raised questions that drive us to look more deeply at God's written Word. The richness discovered, however, is contained within the Bible itself, independent of the truth or falsehood of any scientific theories. Ultimately, consistent with the Chicago Statement on Biblical Inerrancy, the defense of each layer relies on Scripture to understand Scripture.

OUR HOPE

Our hope for this book is twofold. The first is that it will contribute to your appreciation of the grandeur and beauty of the creation story. The second, by virtue of recognizing that the proper understanding is not limited to a single perspective, is that the church will experience greater unity, dropping unhealthy squabbles that undermine its mission. Our hope is that Christians will spend more time in discussions about their *favorite* layers (plural) and less time bickering over which view (singular) should kick all the others out of the theological nest.

DISCUSSION QUESTIONS

1. What do you think about a biblical text containing more than one layer in its interpretation? Where is this helpful? How might it be dangerous or wrongheaded?

2. What do you know about current Christian debates about creation? Have you found these more helpful or hurtful to the mission of the church?

3. What other concerns come to mind as you approach this book? How do you hope those concerns will be addressed?

A MODEL APPROACH

What Can Be Learned from a Genealogy?

G enesis 1 is history. This may seem like a straightforward statement, but it turns out not to be easily defined or constrained. In our Western mindset, "history" has a narrow definition, equated with a journalistic rendering of events in sequential order. But Israel, standing at Mount Sinai thousands of years ago, was not part of nor bound by Western culture. More importantly, *God* is not part of or bound by the literary standards of the postindustrial age. If we want to genuinely understand Scripture, it is imperative that we draw our assessment of what it means to be historical *from* the Bible, rather than bringing a set of predetermined rules to the biblical text.

The purpose of this chapter is to show how a passage of Scripture—one that may seem to be a plain and straightforward documentation of history—can be rich in literary devices and theological nuance. We will take what some might think of as the most straightforward of all possible biblical texts—genealogies—as our example. More space will be given to this subject than one might initially think necessary, as it will serve as a model for our subsequent approach to the creation story.

There is no shortage of genealogies in Genesis or the Old Testament that could be tapped, but the parallel genealogies of Jesus recorded in Matthew and Luke provide a unique opportunity to recognize literary devices at work that would not be as obvious in a single reported lineage. It is particularly fitting to start with the genealogy in Matthew. A deeper look at the opening of the New Testament sets the stage for an investigation of the opening of the Old Testament.

We will start by first drawing attention to well-known peculiarities within and between the two genealogies. This is not to suggest there are any unresolvable errors, but the peculiarities act as an impetus for looking at the text more closely for what lies underneath. From there, we will look at how these genealogies have been intentionally structured to assist with memory, harness important symbols, and challenge theological misconceptions.

PECULIARITIES

Matthew 1: Missing names and inconsistent counting

The book of Matthew starts with the genealogy of Jesus, affirming fulfillment of prophecies that that Messiah would come from the offspring of Abraham, through the line of Judah, and laying claim to the promise to David that his son would sit forever on the throne. At first glance, nothing may seem particularly odd. The list includes forty-one names, starting with Abraham and ending with Jesus. The genealogy closes with verse 17: "So all the generations from Abraham to David were fourteen generations, and from David to the deportation to Babylon fourteen generations, and from the deportation to Babylon to the Christ fourteen generations."

If expecting a straightforward historical listing, free of literary devices or liberties taken with the bare facts, problems arise when counting names and when comparing the list to the Old Testament account. First, three groups of fourteen should add up to forty-two, not forty-one. From Abraham to David, fourteen names are listed. From David to the deportation (Jeconiah), fourteen more names are given. From the deportation to Jesus, only *thirteen* additional names are listed. A second problem is discovered by going back into the Old Testament to find the same lineage. Matthew's genealogy from David to the deportation is missing four of the generations identified in the Old Testament.

Each name in Matthew's list is identified as the father of the next name. Traditional explanations will note that "the father of" (*gennao*) can also mean "the ancestor of," so generations may be skipped without error.[1] The word for "generation" (*genea*) likewise is used elsewhere in Scripture to refer to broadly grouped individuals as well as to parent-child relationships. These explanations are not sufficient by themselves, however, because Matthew is explicit about the total number of generations. He does not just identify lineage; he states a specific *number* of generations. It is a number that undercounts the actual list of ancestors.

---

1. Russell, "Genealogy of Jesus Christ"; France, *Gospel of Matthew*, 27.

Luke 3: Two dads and a lot more names

The genealogy of Jesus in Luke goes all the way back to Adam, passing through Abraham and David in accord with Matthew 1. But after David, the lineage diverges. Rather than going through Solomon as it does in Matthew 1, it goes through David's son Nathan. The two genealogies converge again at Joseph, the adopted father of Jesus.

A traditional resolution of the mismatch is that Matthew's lineage is through Joseph and Luke's is through Mary. If the text is straightforward history, however, devoid of literary license or liberties, problems remain. The first problem is not the father of Jesus per se, for there are appropriate "wiggle words" used to get around the question of Jesus's immediate predecessor. In Matthew, Joseph is not identified as the father of Jesus but as "the husband of Mary, of whom Jesus was born" (Matt. 1:16). Likewise, in Luke, Jesus is "the son (as was supposed) of Joseph" (Luke 3:23). The problem arises with the father of Joseph. Matthew says the father of Joseph was Jacob (Matt. 1:15); Luke says the father of Joseph was Heli (Luke 3:23). Two dads!

An additional difficulty is in the number of generations. From David to Jesus, Luke's list has a lot more names than Matthew—50 percent more. While this *could* be literally true, it requires a low-probability scenario in which all the names in Luke's list were born to young fathers, allowing for more generations, and all the names in Matthew's list were born to old fathers, resulting in fewer generations over the same period of time.[2] Something odd is afoot.

A DEEPER LOOK

Claims that such peculiarities represent historical errors are not defensible. The high importance that Jews placed on genealogies would have ensured that actual mistakes were quickly corrected. The records are written intentionally and with purpose. We will explore three layers of that intentionality.

Literary devices: structured for memory

Without frequent reminders of God's providence, faithfulness, mercy, and justice, we become easily consumed by daily cares, distracted by imagined threats (and shiny objects), and myopic in our view of life—thinking only in terms of our own struggles and immediate needs. God, mindful of our

---

2. To fit 50 percent more names into the same period of time, a literal reading requires that the men in Matthew's genealogy were 50 percent older, on average, when siring their sons relative to the fathers in Luke's genealogy.

frailties, helps us to remember in innumerable ways.[3] The pages of Scripture are filled with tools and instructions designed for this purpose. Some are explicit in recalling past events, such as the annual observance of Passover or the more frequent celebration of Communion. Songs are likewise overt in their creation to aid lasting memory. The Song of Moses (Exod. 15) and the Song of Deborah (Judg. 5) are poetic renditions of real events, fashioned and sung through generations to ensure that the children of Israel, and Christians today, would not forget the marvelous things God accomplished for his people. The Psalms were also written as songs, with a large number labeled "for the choir director" and some including instruction on the type of musical instruments that should accompany the lyrics.[4]

Subtler methods of aiding memory are found in the structure of narratives, making use of rhyme, wordplay, and poetic sequences that state and then revisit themes in parallel or reverse order (called a chiasm), or historical summaries interspersed in later stories. Highlighting just one of these methods, a wordplay may take two words that sound nearly the same but have very different meanings to draw attention to a point. In Jeremiah 1:11–12, God told the prophet he had planted an almond tree (*shaqed*) as a symbol that God was watching (*shoqed*) to ensure his word would be fulfilled. The word association (in the original language) makes the intended point easier to remember.

We find the use of memory devices even in a biblical list of ancestors.[5] Consider how the names in Matthew 1 are divided and numbered. A long list is easier to remember if divided up into equal blocks, with easily recalled categories for each grouping or readily recognized linkages leading from one to the next. In Matthew, the list is divided into three groups of equal size with hinges between them representing pivotal names or events in Israel's history: King David and the exile (the deportation). To maintain equal numbers on either side of those hinges, four names were left out of the middle set, with David used both to end the first set and begin the second set to yield a consistent fourteen.[6] This may seem awkward to modern readers, but with

---

3. A study of "remember" (or "do not forget") in Deuteronomy alone would show the importance of this concept (e.g., Deut. 4:9, 23; 5:15; 6:12; 7:18; 8:2, 11, 14, 18; 9:7; 15:15; 16:3, 12; 24:9, 18, 22; 32:7).
4. Stringed instruments (Pss. 4; 6; 54; 55; 61; 67); flute (Ps. 5).
5. Russell, "Genealogy of Jesus Christ."
6. Alternately, Jeconiah may be counted twice to end the second set and start the third set. Some commentators note David's name appearing twice in Matt. 1:17 as support for counting David twice rather than Jeconiah; e.g., Russell, "Genealogy of Jesus Christ."

repetition, even young children can memorize a list using these tools with barely a notice of inconsistency in double counting a name at only one hinge.

As clever as the construction may be, it still makes many Christian readers uneasy to see anything identified within a biblical historical account that isn't strictly literal. If the writer claims there are fourteen generations between each historical hinge, and there are actually more than fourteen in one group and less than fourteen in another, does that not represent a technical error—an *untruth*? The question may be understandable, but it reflects a superficial understanding of inerrancy.

The fundamental principle of inerrancy is more nuanced than just a belief that the Bible is true and free of error. It requires wrestling with what defines *error*. For example, consider the use of metaphor, hyperbole, symbolism, and dreams. Each makes use of words or descriptions that are not true in a literalistic sense. Few Christians would argue that Solomon's lover had teeth that actually looked like a herd of sheep (simile: Song 4:2), that there are as many descendants of Abraham as sand on the seashore (hyperbole: Gen. 22:17), or that cows actually ate each other in Egypt (symbolism and dreams: Gen. 41:4). Yet we believe these verses are nonetheless true. As we noted in the Introduction, what we really mean when we say the Bible is inerrant is that it is free of error in its *message*—in all it intends to teach. The writers of Scripture were free to use literary devices without a reasonable charge of error.

In Matthew's genealogy, the message—its *purpose*—is communicating the genuine ancestry of Jesus, starting from Abraham and running through Judah and through David. Jesus is truly the offspring of Abraham through whom "all the nations of the earth [shall] be blessed" (Gen. 22:18; cf. 12:3). Jesus is an actual descendent of Judah, to whom Abraham prophetically declared, "The scepter shall not depart from Judah, nor the ruler's staff from between his feet" (Gen. 49:10). And Jesus is of the kingly line of David, through Solomon, to whom God promised, "Your house and your kingdom shall be made sure forever before me. Your throne shall be established forever" (2 Sam. 7:16). The latter is particularly important, because, from a material perspective, there was a time when it seemed as if God's promise had failed. The line of kings appeared to end with Jeconiah and the deportation. But Jesus was coming—the *eternal* king!

Accommodating cultural norms, challenging theological error
Most Christians know of the promise God made to David mentioned above. David would always have a son to sit on the throne. Jesus is the ultimate

fulfillment of that promise with a pedigree documented in Matthew 1. Fewer are aware of the apparent conundrum of the curse of Jehoiakim. After many generations of wicked and unfaithful kings, the Davidic line of kings was cut off. Two declarations, both made by Jeremiah, seem at odds:

> For thus says Yahweh: David shall never lack a man to sit on the throne of the house of Israel. (Jer. 33:17)

> Therefore thus says Yahweh concerning Jehoiakim king of Judah [descendant of David]: He shall have none to sit on the throne of David. (Jer. 36:30)

The apparent tension may be resolved in the juxtaposition of the two genealogies.[7] Jesus traced his biological lineage through Mary back to David's son Nathan. This ancestry is not subject to the curse of Jehoiakim, whose biological lineage on the throne was cut off.[8] Yet through *adoption*, Jesus also traced his lineage from Joseph back through the kingly line to Solomon and David. The power of adoption underlies the entire gospel message, whereby non-Jews may be grafted into the family of God and granted full rights and privileges of children of the King (Rom. 8:12–9:13; Gal. 4:1–7).

For those who concur with the artistry in resolving blessing and curse, it may nonetheless seem puzzling that Luke did not just record Mary's name instead of Joseph's. Why create an apparent error with two genealogies claiming different fathers for Joseph? The answer follows the oft-repeated reminder that the Bible was written *for* us but not *to* us.[9] The Gospels were written *to* the people of first-century Judea and the larger Roman Empire. Luke accommodates the common custom of that age of associating a person's genealogy with the father even if then tracing the *maternal* grandfather's lineage, with no sense of error.[10]

This is an important recognition, for it reminds us that the truth claims of the Bible should not be measured against the literary norms of a culture two thousand years removed. In modern historical accounts, if a statement is not

---

7. Walvoord and Zuck, *Bible Knowledge Commentary*, 1176.
8. Alternately (or additionally), others have noted God's ability to redeem from a curse. Jeremiah 22:24–30 speaks of Jehoiakim's son as a signet ring torn from God's hand. Generations later, Hag. 2:20–23 uses similar language to say God will make Zerubbabel (a decedent of Jehoiakim) like a signet ring. Schreiner, "Zerubbabel, Persia, and Inner-biblical Exegesis."
9. For example, Miglio et al., *For Us, but Not to Us.*
10. A related OT example is found where Jair is called the "son of Manasseh" (Num. 32:41; 1 Kings 4:13), but is actually the son of Manasseh's granddaughter (1 Chron. 2:21–23; 7:14).

literally accurate, the truth of the whole account is suspect. Using that rubric, neither genealogy would be considered true. Yet God inspired each account to be written in accordance with and even embracing the cultural norms of the day.

The message of the Bible never attempts to step out of the culture into which its message was delivered, with the critical exception of when a *cultural* norm conflicts with a *theological* truth. An example may be found, conveniently, within the context of the same genealogies. While both Matthew and Luke follow the convention of naming the father in their genealogies, Matthew's list breaks with convention in naming not only five women but women with tainted histories. Tamar posed as a prostitute with her father-in-law. Rahab was a Canaanite prostitute. Bathsheba was the subject of David's adultery. Ruth was a foreigner from the hated nation of Moab. And Mary was pregnant out of wedlock. Inclusion of these names challenged the theological foundations of three different cultural norms: only men were significant in God's kingdom, only the noble or morally pure were worthy of mention, and God's grace extended only to Jews.

Symbolic use of numbers: meaning that supersedes arithmetic value

In Western culture, we are not used to numbers having a particular symbolic meaning. In the ancient Near East, the symbolic use of numbers was ubiquitous and carried over into New Testament times. We find an explicit reference to numerical symbolism in Revelation 13:18, where "the number of a man" is stated as 666. Six represented something that does not reach perfection. Seven represented perfection. Critically, the symbolic meaning of a number may supersede its arithmetic value.

The genealogies of Jesus make rich use of the number seven. Matthew's list consists of three groups of fourteen (2×7) from Abraham to Jesus. Luke records a continuous list from God to Jesus with a total of seventy-seven names (10×7), and two sets of twenty-one names (3×7) for the sequence that departs from Matthew's record. The presentation in multiples of seven, coupled with the imbalance in the number of names from David to Jesus in the two accounts, and with names known to be missing from Matthew's list, all contribute to tell us that the intention was not a simple identification of all members in the lineage of Jesus. The intention was richer and deeper.

IMPLICATIONS

The ancestry of Jesus through David and Abraham is real. It is historical. It is *true*. At the same time, the records freely employ literary devices and accommodate or challenge cultural norms in ways that may run counter to modern literary expectations. Old Testament scholar Sandra Richter notes that while the genealogies were derived from archival records, "they have been placed into a narrative context, and, therefore, have been overlaid with theological and narrative functions as well."[11] These functions communicate truths that would be missed if we stopped short at the literal meaning of words and ignored the culture into which the message was delivered.

Given what theologians have observed in the opening pages of the New Testament, it should come as little surprise if we find similar literary devices and cultural structures at work in the opening of the Old Testament. There is no theological requirement for such a parallel to exist, but it would be remarkably poetic.

In the genealogies, we started with the observation that they contained peculiarities if we expected straightforward, numerically focused records of Jesus's ancestry—oddities that drive the curious reader to deeper study. We can do the same with Genesis 1, looking to see if something more than a straightforward (literalistic) reading is intended.

EXAMPLES IN GENESIS 1

We don't need an exhaustive analysis of Genesis 1 at this stage. A few examples of peculiarities can be sufficient to indicate the intention is more than communicating a sequence of events. We have picked out three to briefly elucidate.

Separation of light and dark—twice

In Genesis 1:14–18, the sun, moon and stars are created in day 4 for the express purpose of governing the day and night, and "to separate the light from the darkness." But 1:3–5 states that light and dark were already separated back in day 1. It may be argued that the separation occurred in day 1 followed by the creation of celestial bodies in day 4 to *govern* that separation, but this requires a departure from the "plain" or "literal" reading. The actual wording of 1:14–18 says the celestial bodies *brought about* the separation of light, making day 4 seemingly redundant.

Separation of light from the absence of light?

There is great spiritual significance to God's separation of light from darkness. Light illuminates. Darkness obscures. The English expression "to bring to light"

---

11. Richter, *Epic of Eden*, 50.

captures the idea well. Thievery, lying, slander, oppression, murder, and other manifestations of evil cannot survive when all is fully revealed and brought to attention—that is, when it is brought into the light. But what about a literalist understanding with a *physical* separation? This proves more problematic, because it actually has no physical meaning. Light has a physical existence made of energetic photons that can be identified and measured.[12] Darkness is not a substance, or entity, or even a force that can be isolated. It is simply the *absence* of light.

By analogy, consider a jar of beans set before you. They are poured out onto the table and you are given a simple instruction: separate beans from the absence of beans. You object, "That has no meaning; the absence of something is not an independent 'something'!" Which is exactly the point. Something wonderful is expressed when God separates light from darkness—something much deeper than a physical act.

Evenings and mornings on a sphere

The long-recognized problem of three evenings and mornings with no sun is not just the absence of a light source.[13] The earth is a sphere. When it is day on one side of the planet, it is simultaneously night on the opposite side—perpetually. A rotating planet is half day and half night at the same time. The experience of transition from evening to morning is only possible if standing at a particular location as the planet rotates relative to a fixed light source. For the first three days, no human or animal had yet been created anywhere on the planet, and there was no designated light source. The answer that God was the light does not work, as it requires that (1) he was *not* light before day 1, (2) he was not omnipresent thereafter, isolating his brilliance in one spot, and (3) he simultaneously served as the sole observer from a fixed spot on the earth while placing his light off to one side where the sun would eventually be. The suggestion that the first three evenings and mornings are figurative expressions of literal twenty-four-hour days is equally untenable as it requires a figurative interpretation to defend a literal interpretation.

THE INTRIGUE GROWS

The list above could continue, but it doesn't need to.[14] It only takes a few "peculiarities" to suggest that there may be an underlying richness to the text that

---

12. Photons are simultaneously particles and energy waves.
13. Wrestling with the meaning of days prior to the presence of a sun goes back long before scientific challenges (e.g., Augustine, *Literal Meaning of Genesis*).
14. Internal conflicts that arise from a literalistic reading are described in more detail in Davidson, *Friend of Science, Friend of Faith*, 57–67.

is more than just a journalistic record. A quick look at what Hebrew scholars have discovered with the use of the number seven adds to our intrigue.[15]

- The days of creation are seven (6 + 1).
- The initial declaration (Gen. 1:1) consists of seven Hebrew words.
- The second declaration (Gen. 1:2) of being formless and void and God's spirit hovering consists of fourteen words (2 × 7).
- Phrases through the days of creation occur in multiples of seven:
  - "it was so" and "it was good" (7 times each)
  - firmament/heaven and earth (21 times each; 3 × 7)
  - God (35 times; 5 × 7)
- The summary statement of God's work creating the heavens and the earth and the blessing of the seventh day (Gen. 2:1–3) is made in thirty-five words (5 × 7).

Something fascinating and wonderful is at work in this text. Just as we learned that the Bible is full of riches even in something as seemingly mundane as a genealogy, so we have reason to expect that a seemingly straightforward list of a series of days may also contain wisdom and beauty that goes deeper than a simple sequence of events. It is a beauty we can only expect to see with study and an openness to God's Spirit.

NUTS AND BOLTS

As we get ready to dive into Genesis, a few "nuts-and-bolts" notes are warranted to avoid confusion. First, the creation story of Genesis 1 spills over a few verses into the second chapter. Repeated use of the full verse reference becomes unwieldy. We will henceforth refer to Genesis 1 as shorthand for Genesis 1:1–2:3.[16]

Second, readers will find some variability in whether a layer is limited to Genesis 1 or expands into the second story of Adam and Eve in Genesis 2–3. The focus of this book is on Genesis 1, but some layers require the expanded view to fully flesh out the perspective.

---

15. Davis, *Biblical Numerology*, 103–24, 136–37; Godfrey, *God's Pattern for Creation*, 32–33; Cassuto, *Commentary on the Book of Genesis*, 12–17; Hill, "Making Sense of the Numbers of Genesis"; Hyers, "Narrative Form of Genesis 1," 208–15.
16. Some theologians argue that Gen. 2:4 (or 2.4a) is the end of the first story rather than the beginning of the second. Our shorthand of Gen. 1 may be considered to apply to either option.

Third, we have chosen to retain the divine name of God (Yahweh) where found in biblical quotations.[17] Most English Bibles substitute "LORD," using small caps, in place of Yahweh. This is not the same word translated as "Lord" (*Adonai*). The subtle difference in representation (LORD vs. Lord), with a much bigger difference in meaning, is missed by most readers.

Last, we need to describe how we have addressed the work of others who have advocated for the views represented in each layer. In a typical *Four Views of...* book, each chapter would strive to fully describe a position, with elements in conflict with other views identified and defended. In this book, each layer is presented as *complementary* with all the others—no conflict to identify or defend. To accomplish this, we have drawn on the perspectives of various advocates, expanding on some themes and stripping out elements deemed nonessential that create conflict with the others. Each layer may thus be said to be "inspired by" or "derived from" the work of one or more advocates, rather than fully representing the position they defend.

With these notes out of the way, we are ready to launch. In keeping with the biblical significance of the number seven, we humbly present the manifold beauty of Genesis 1—in seven layers.

---

17. The proper name of God is often written as YHWH (יהוה), reflecting the fact that the vowels guiding pronunciation are missing in the original Hebrew. "Yahweh" is the most common full rendering.

DISCUSSION QUESTIONS

1. Does use of literary devices and cultural accommodations invalidate the historicity of the genealogies?

2. Why would the Bible accommodate cultural norms that God knew could be misunderstood by future generations?

3. What does biblical inerrancy mean? Does everyone use the same definition? How does inerrancy address the oddities observed in the genealogies of Jesus?

LAYER 1

Song

שִׁירָה

(*shirah*, "song")

*Where were you when I laid the foundation of the earth . . .
when the morning stars sang together
and all the sons of God shouted for joy?*
(*Job 38:4, 7*)

*T*he opening line of the Bible makes two grand statements. One, there was a beginning. The universe did not always exist. The history of earth and the cosmos does not extend infinitely into the past. There was a definitive moment in which it began.[1] Two, that beginning owes its existence to a singular, omnipotent deity, identified later in the text as Yahweh—a name rich in meaning, signifying a God who is self-existent, self-defining, and ever-present.[2]

In the next phrase (Gen. 1:2) we are told that the world was *tohu wabohu*, usually translated as variations of "formless" (*tohu*) and "empty" (*bohu*). Emptiness is the easier term to understand, though it does not simply mean the absence of material items. It includes the sense of things missing that would normally be expected to be present. As an example from our own language and experience, we think of a house with no people or furniture as being empty, even though we know that it is not truly devoid of material substance. It is filled with the atoms that make up the air, specks of dust drift about the rooms, insects and spiders occupy its corners and crevices, and microorganisms thrive on every surface. The things we think *should* be there,

---

1. Scholars disagree whether Gen. 1:1 explicitly teaches the doctrine of creation from nothing (*ex nihilo*), though clearly other biblical passages do (e.g., Col. 1:16; Heb. 11:3). The expression "heavens and the earth" is a statement of totality; *everything* that is—the world as we know it—was created by God. See Averbeck, "A Literary Day," 9–12.
2. The Hebrew, *Yahweh*, is a variant of the verb "to be" (*hayah*). The name first appears in Gen. 2:4, specifically identifying the creator as the God of Israel who redeemed his people from Egypt. For more on the meaning of the name, see Turner, "Exodus," 84–86.

however, are absent. In spite of the abundant molecules and microbes, it is an empty dwelling.

Formlessness is more nuanced. To be without form, in the Hebrew sense, includes lacking purpose, function, order, or meaning. Consider an analogy of a painter preparing to create a work of art. Before ever putting brush to pallet, a decision must first be made regarding the substrate. Will it be a wall for a mural, cold-press paper for a watercolor, or stretched canvas for an oil painting? The selection entails consideration of the *purpose* of the work, how it will *function*. What will be its *form*? Once selected, the painter now has a substrate, but it is empty—a blank surface that awaits *filling* with colors, textures, patterns, and images. God, as the ultimate Artist, recognized the need not only for things to fill empty spaces but also for those spaces to have purpose, order, and function.[3]

As God prepares to form and to fill, a curious statement is made. In the darkness, God's Spirit moves over the face of the deep, over the waters. Note that this comes *before* the first creative act of day 1. The presence of a world shrouded in darkness and encased in a primordial sea is not preceded by the familiar command "let there be," nor is it declared to be good. Modern readers struggle with this description, for it seems out of place. God speaks of something that is present that he must have brought into being, yet it precedes the events of the first day of creation.

The description becomes less troublesome when we give attention to the culture into which the story was first spoken. Among the nations of the ancient Near East, origin stories told of the pre-creation condition as a great landless sea that gave rise first to the gods, who were then responsible for the creation, often by accident, of humans. In some accounts, the primordial sea was represented by a god of chaos that had to be conquered by the other gods before land and order could be established.[4] Genesis 1:2 takes hold of this cultural notion and applies it as a powerful word picture. The great deep—without solid foundation or mortal life—represents a disordered and empty waste. It was ripe with potential awaiting God's creative command, but it was not good. It was a condition that agents of darkness and chaos would wish to

---

3. The phrase *tohu wabohu* is also employed in Jer. 4:23 in a context in which God looked at the corruption of the land and spoke of it as returning to a disordered, purposeless condition (lacking form), devoid of meaningful life (empty). We will revisit this understanding in subsequent layers.

4. For example, Tiamat was the primordial god of chaos in Babylonian mythology. More detail on ancient Near Eastern creation myths is provided in Layer 3 ("Polemic").

regain and reinhabit. Even after creation was complete, the sea continued to represent a source of potential chaos in Hebrew thinking. It was the home of the great sea monsters, Leviathan and Rahab,[5] and the source from which the evil beasts arose in the apocalyptic visions of Daniel and John (Dan. 7; Rev. 13). It was this condition of darkness and disorder and emptiness that God's Spirit surveyed, subduing and bringing forth light and order and substance.

A FRAMEWORK

The fascinating manner in which all this is presented is too often overlooked by modern readers. It is so much more than a sequence of events. In English, we miss the use of wordplay in the introduction—the rhyming of *tohu* and *bohu*, followed immediately with a description rich in metaphor. The watery abyss, possibly employing another wordplay with the similar sound of *tohu* and *tehom* (the deep), embodies the problems of darkness and disorder and emptiness. The subjugation of chaos, of creating order and function, and of filling the emptiness, is unfolded in the subsequent verses in a striking literary framework (table 1). The first three days address the *formless* problem (*tohu*), followed by three parallel days that address the *empty* problem (*bohu*).

TABLE 1. PARALLEL STRUCTURE OF THE DAYS OF CREATION			
creation of heavens and earth (1:1)			
A. *tohu* (formless)		**B.** *bohu* (empty)	
1	A1. realm of x. light y. dark	4	B1. filling with x. sun y. moon and stars
2	A2. realm of x. sea y. sky	5	B2. filling with x. fish y. birds
3	A3. realm of x. land y. then plants	6	B3. filling with x. animals y. then humans[6]
completion of heaven and earth (2:1–3)			

---

5. Leviathan: Ps. 104:26; Isa. 27:1. Rahab: a powerful sea monster in Jewish folklore, referenced in Job 9:13; 26:12; Ps. 89:10; Isa. 51:9.

6. Days 3 and 6 each have two phases of creative acts, noted in the table as creation of item x, *then* creation of item y.

Days 1–3: solving the formless problem with realms or domains:

- Day 1: God begins solving the issue of formlessness (*tohu*), first fashioning the realms of light and dark. It is the realm of light that will give purpose to eyes, and the cycles of light and dark that will serve as the foundation for tracking the passage of days, of seasons, and of years.
- Day 2: God gives form to the realms of sea and sky. These paired realms serve the function of being the eventual home and playground of fish and fowl, a means by which ships may transport goods, and the system in which water will rise and fall and water the earth.
- Day 3: God gives form to the terrestrial realm, followed by a second phase of work to add plants. Plants are not a separate "foliage realm," but are an intrinsic part of land that is suitable for creatures to inhabit.

Days 4–6: solving the empty (*bohu*) problem with parallel days of filling:

- Day 4: God fills the realms of light and dark with the sun, moon, and stars.
- Day 5: God fills the realms of sea and sky with fish and birds.
- Day 6: God fills the terrestrial realm with animals, followed by a second phase of work to create humans.

DETAILS

Genesis 1 does not just tell of a God who made *things*; he made the very realms in which things can exist. The parallel structure of days 1 through 3 with days 4 through 6 is even more apparent if we look at the poetic pattern of phrases and repetition of statements (table 2).

TABLE 2. REPEATING PATTERN OF PHRASES IN PARALLEL DAYS			

1	(a) God said, "Let . . ." (b) And there was . . . (c) God saw that . . . was good (d) There was evening and morning	4	(a) God said, "Let . . ." (b) It was so (c) God saw that it was good (d) There was evening and morning
2	(a) God said, "Let . . ." (b) It was so (c) (d) There was evening and morning	5	(a) God said, "Let . . ." (b) (c) God saw that it was good (d) There was evening and morning
3	(a) God said. "Let . . ." (b) It was so (c) God saw that it was good (a) God said, "Let . . ." (b) It was so (c) God saw that it was good (d) There was evening and morning	6	(a) God said, "Let . . ." (b) It was so (c) God saw that it was good (a) God said, "Let . . ." (b) It was so (c) God saw . . . it was very good (d) There was evening and morning

- *Light from dark, twice.* The first three days start with the separation of light from dark in day 1 (1:4). We find light and dark separated *again* at the beginning of the second group in day 4 (1:14), with the additional mention of objects (sun, moon, stars) to complete or bring about the separation. The wording is awkward if intended to be read as a straightforward sequence of creative acts, for it would imply that the separation of day 1 was ineffective. Viewed as a literary device of parallel days, however, the wording links the two days seamlessly with the filling completing the task of forming, together serving to separate light and dark.

- *Sequence of repeated phrases.* Within each of the days of creation, the general pattern is:

    (a) God said, "Let . . ."; (b) it was; (c) God saw it was good; (d) there was evening and morning.

  Days 1 and 4 follow this pattern exactly. Days 2 and 5 exhibit this pattern while each omitting one element. Days 3 and 6 each include two sets of the *a-b-c* sequence before completing with the *d* element.

This structural framework sets up day 3 as a climax of the days of formation, and day 6 as the climax of the days of filling.

- *Omissions and declarations of "good."* Even the seemingly imperfect alignment of phrases described above—missing phrases in days 2 and 5—has the appearance of careful literary structure. The declaration that the creation was good is repeated seven times.[7] Seven is well known in Hebrew literature as the number of perfection or completion. Within the setting of a human workweek, only six of the days come with the declaration of "good." It would have been simple enough to get to seven with one mention each creation day and adding another to day 7, or with the double declaration on day 6. Instead, we find double declarations on day 6 *and* back on day 3, further emphasizing these days as each culminating their respective objectives of filling and forming. The usage of seven total references is preserved by leaving it out of day 2. Notably, the gap in the repeating structure is matched by a gap in the parallel day 5, where "it was so" is left out.[8]

- *Wording of opening and closing stanzas.* The six days are bracketed with another set of parallel stanzas:
  > In the beginning, God created the heavens and the earth. (1:1)
  > Thus the heavens and the earth were finished, and all the host of them. (2:1)

  The second stanza is divided into two parts that align with the two sets of triad days. "Heaven and earth" matches the creation of realms (days 1–3); "and all the host of them" matches the creatures that fill those realms (days 4–6).

Recognition of literary devices and the unique grouping of creation days into triads is not a new discovery. Augustine (fourth and fifth centuries) is well known for his conclusion that the description of the first three days of creation were clear indicators of the literary nature of the text.[9] The parallel

---

7. Many others have noted the intentional usage of numbers in the creation story. For example, Davis, *Biblical Numerology*, 136–37; Godfrey, *God's Pattern for Creation*, 32–33; Cassuto, *Commentary on the Book of Genesis*, 12–15; Hill, "Making Sense of the Numbers of Genesis"; Hyers, *Meaning of Creation*, 74–79.
8. Parallel phrasing with offset or mismatched omissions is also found in Hebrew poetry (typically within consecutive lines), where it is referred to as *elliptical parallelism*.
9. Augustine, *Literal Meaning of Genesis*; See also Letham, "Days of Creation from Origen

arrangement of days into two sets of three was noted by Thomas Aquinas (thirteenth century),[10] with fuller development by theologians over the last two hundred years. In modern writing, this understanding has been referred to as the framework view (a literary framework of two sets of parallel days) or as variants of "forming and filling."[11]

GENRE: POETRY, NARRATIVE, OR . . . ?

The wordplay of *tohu wabohu*, imagery of chaos and the great deep, parallel structuring of the days of forming and filling, and intentional use of the number seven all contribute to yield a text that seems remarkably poetic. Most Hebrew or Old Testament scholars, however, are reluctant to classify Genesis 1 as a Hebrew poem. The text exhibits a rich use of poetic *elements*, but is said to fall short of the *form* of poetry. Thus, scholars often describe Genesis 1 with in-between terms such as *exalted prose, poetic dimension, semi-poetic, poetic-style, poetic-shaping, blend of prose and poetry*, and even *literary art*.[12] Others go a bit further and use identifiers such as *liturgy, hymn*, or *song*.[13]

So how can a text contain rich use of poetic elements (wordplay, imagery, parallel structures) and not be considered a poem? The most common answer is that it does not match the particular form of poems found anywhere else in the Old Testament. Classical Hebrew poetry is known for its terseness and its type of parallelism in which brief stanzas are linked to play off of one another.[14] A good example is found in Genesis 1:27:

---

to the Westminster Assembly"; Allert, *Early Christian Readings of Genesis One*; Young, "Contemporary Relevance of Augustine's View of Creation."

10. Thomas Aquinas, *Summa Theologica*, I, q. 70, art. 1.

11. For example, Herder, *Spirit of Hebrew Poetry*; Noordtzij, *Gods Woord en der Eeuwen Getuigenis*; Ridderbos, *Is There a Conflict between Genesis 1 and Science?*; Blocher, *In the Beginning*, 39–59; Kline, "Space and Time in the Genesis Cosmogony"; Futato, "Because It Had Rained"; Irons and Kline, "Framework Interpretation"; Godfrey, *God's Pattern for Creation*, 51–53; Longman, "What Genesis 1–2 Teaches," 105.

12. Exalted prose: Young, *Studies in Genesis One*, 82; Collins, *Genesis 1–4*, 44. Poetic dimension: Fee and Stuart, *How to Read the Bible Book by Book*, 27. Semi-poetic: Copan and Jacoby, *Origins*, 73. Poetic-shaping: Patterson, "Genesis 1:1–2:3." Blend of prose and poetry: Blocher, *In the Beginning*, 32; Hummel, "Interpreting Genesis One," 177; Rankin, *Genesis and the Power of True Assumptions*, 203. Literary art (or artistic, literary representation): Gonzalas, "The Covenantal Context of the Fall," 7n37; Waltke with Fredricks, *Genesis*, 78.

13. Liturgy or liturgical: LeFebvre, *Liturgy of Creation*, 6, 113–14; Weinfeld, "Sabbath, Temple, and the Enthronement of the Lord," 510; Hymn: Copan and Jacoby, *Origins*, 76; Polak, "Poetic Style and Parallelism," 4; Wenham, *Genesis 1–15*, 50." Song: Richter, *Epic of Eden*, 98; Keller, *Reason for God*, 97.

14. For a readable introduction to parallelism, see Longman, *How to Read the Psalms*, 97–110.

So God created man in his own image,
>   in the image of God he created him;
>   male and female he created them.

Genesis 1 as a whole does not follow this formula.

Some further downplay the significance of poetic elements of Genesis 1 by emphasizing features that are common in Hebrew prose and generally lacking in poetry. One example is the frequent use of words that express a specific sequence: something happened, *then* something else happened, *then* something else.[15] Such observations serve as the basis for claims that Genesis 1 falls firmly within the realm of straightforward prose, and thus should be considered historical narrative.[16] What is often lacking in the latter arguments is that while Genesis 1 may be distinct from classical Hebrew poetry, it is also distinct from normal Hebrew prose. On this subject, Wycliffe Bible translator and linguist Robert Longacre notes,

> Nowhere else in the Hebrew Bible do we find an actor repeatedly referred to by a noun phrase which is not reduced to anaphora carried by the third person form of the verb. "And God did/said" occurs no less than thirty-one times in chapter 1 and 2:1–3. In ordinary narrative style we would not [for example] tell the story with multiple mention of his name: "And Abraham did A. Then Abraham did B. Then Abraham did C. Then Abraham did D." etc. The sonority and dignity thus attained by repeating the name of the Divine Actor have no parallel in any other passage of Biblical Hebrew.[17]

Longacre continues with observations of the peculiar use and repetition of phrases like "let there be," before concluding, "Whether we want to call

---

15. In technical discussions of the "*waw*-consecutive," the Hebrew letter *waw* attaches to the front of a word as a conjunction (e.g., "and" or "but"). When attached to certain verb forms, it often functions to indicate sequence of the mainline verbs (McCabe, "Critique of the Framework Interpretation," 216–23; Boyd, "Statistical Determination of Genre in Biblical Hebrew," 650–51; Beall, "Reading Genesis 1–2," 49).
16. Other elements in Gen. 1 more typical of prose include the use of definite articles and direct object markers.
17. Quoted in Presbyterian Church in America, "Report of the Creation Study Committee," 2347n113. Anaphora is the use of a word referring to or replacing a word used earlier in a sentence, to avoid repetition—for example, saying "he" instead of multiple repetitions of a person's name.

such diction and discourse structure a poem or not is somewhat arbitrary; it is certainly unusually elevated style and probably *sui generis*."[18]

Sui generis is a Latin phrase meaning "of its own kind." No other Hebrew text, inside or outside the Bible, is quite like Genesis 1—it is *unique*. The fact that it does not fall neatly within the form of either traditional Hebrew poems or historical narratives should make us hesitant to declare that it must be understood strictly as one or the other (see box 1). Such efforts are too often driven by cultural presuppositions brought to the text before ever starting a serious analysis. How much better to recognize the beauty of the text as it is—a genre of its own. This sense is captured well by a nineteenth-century Scottish cleric, Gilbert Rorison, who pondered the question of how "attributes of narrative prose" could be drawn from "the oldest and sublimest poem in the world."[19]

One can imagine the ancient storytellers, in their singsong voices, orating this age-old story.[20] A magnificent hymn. The first song. A song echoed by the writer of Job, relating God's admonishment of Job and his friends: "Where were you when I laid the earth's foundation? . . . While the morning stars sang together?" (Job 38:4, 7 NIV).[21] C. S. Lewis may have had just this sense when he wrote of the creation of Narnia in *The Magician's Nephew*. The children Digory and Polly exit a magical pool to find themselves in a new world that cannot rightly even be called a world, for it is initially dark and formless and empty. Somewhere, a voice begins to sing. The ground itself seems to rise up and sing back in reply, and they soon see it is Aslan, the great Lion, bringing form to Narnia and filling it with life. The stars join in the song, creating a celestial harmony in joyful response to their assignments.[22]

---

18. Quoted in Presbyterian Church in America, "Report of the Creation Study Committee," 2348n113.
19. Rorison, "The Creative Week," 288, quoted in Collins, *Reading Genesis Well*, 175.
20. In 1782, Johann Herder referred to Genesis 1 as "the most ancient poetry of nature" (*Spirit of Hebrew Poetry*, 49).
21. Copan and Jacoby note, "Most leading scholars of the OT recognize Gen. 1 as a magnificent hymn attesting to the oneness and magnificence of God" (*Origins*, 76).
22. Lewis, *Magician's Nephew*, chap. 8.

BOX 1: SCHOLARS AND EXEGETES ON THE GENRE OF GENESIS 1 [23]

"Is it prose or poetry? The choice is a gross oversimplification." —Henri Blocher

"If you have read Genesis 1, you know that the chapter could easily be described as poetry, or even as a song." —Sandra Richter

"I think Genesis 1 has the earmarks of poetry and is therefore a 'song' about the wonder and meaning of God's creation." —Timothy Keller

"It has been clearly shown that the dividing line between prose and poetry is not fixed and sharply defined but that elevated or impassioned prose may approximate very closely to poetry, especially that it is often marked by that basic characteristic of Hebrew poetry, balanced repetition or parallelism." —Oswald Allis

"The language type is not the same as the literary form; it aligns more with the style and register axes. That is, a piece of writing that has the literary form of a prose narrative can use ordinary, scientific, or poetic language types; knowing the literary form does not settle all the most important interpretive questions." —C. John Collins

"Hymnic Features [of Genesis 1]: The creation account is pre-eminently dominated by a number of formal poetic elements." —Frank Polak

"Gen. 1 is not normal Hebrew prose either; its syntax is distinctively different from narrative prose. [Other scholars have] pointed to poetic bicola or tricola in Gen. 1, while admitting that most of the material is prose. It is possible that these poetic fragments go back to an earlier form of the creation account, though, as Cassuto observes, 'it is simpler to suppose . . . the special importance of the subject led to an exaltation of style approaching the level of poetry' . . . Gen. 1 is unique in the Old Testament. It invites comparison with the Psalms that praise God's work in creation (e.g., 8, 136, 148) or with passages such as Prov. 8:22–31 or Job 38 that reflect on the mystery of God's creativity. It is indeed a great hymn, setting out majestically the omnipotence of the creator, but it surpasses these other passages in the scope and comprehensiveness of vision." —Gordon Wenham

WHAT ABOUT HISTORY?

If we say that Genesis 1 is poetic—a song of creation—is this a backhanded way of identifying it as mythology?[24] Is the creation story not to be considered

---

23. Blocher, *In The Beginning*, 32; Richter, *Epic of Eden*, 98; Keller, *Reason for God*, 97; Allis, *Five Books of Moses*, 109; Collins, *Reading Genesis Well*, 72; Polak, "Poetic Style and Parallelism," 4; Wenham, *Genesis 1–15*, 50.
24. Among historians and literary scholars, *myth* does not necessarily mean anti-historical.

historical? Is it not really *true*?[25] If you find yourself asking such questions, back up for a moment and consider why someone would suggest that poetic equals fictional. There is no rule that says history can only be related through straightforward or dry prose. As simple examples of poetic history in Scripture, consider the Songs of Moses (Exod. 15) and of Deborah (Judg. 5). In the first, we find a song (poem) telling of the drowning of the Egyptian army at the hand of God. In the second, we find another song that recounts the victory of Israel over Sisera, the commander of the Canaanite army. Broader swaths of Israel's history are similarly presented in the Psalms (e.g., 78, 105, 106, 107, 114). Genuine history is not diminished or invalidated by being recounted in poetic form.

Recognizing the poetic nature of the songs does warn us, however, against overreach in the meaning we attach to specific descriptions. It would be a mistake, for example, to argue Moses believed God piled the waters of the sea by blowing air from physical nostrils (Exod. 15:8), or that the stars of heaven literally fought against Sisera (Judg. 5:20). In Genesis 1, we read of real history—a real and true creation of ordered and purposeful realms, and a real and true filling of those realms with created things. At the same time, care should be taken before assuming that the literary structure of six days constrains the time or manner in which God physically created.

Genesis 1 may be thought of truly as a marriage of history and poetry. A glorious hymn of creation. The *firstborn* of songs.[26]

CHALLENGES AND RESPONSES

Objection 1: The parallel structure of Genesis 1 fails on closer examination.

Some authors have challenged the existence of a parallel structure (days 1–3 aligned with days 4–6), arguing that the luminaries of day 4 were placed in the heavens of day 2 (not day 1), and fish from day 5 were placed in the seas of day 3 or the water made prior to day 1 (not in the "waters below" of day 2).[27]

We use it here in the popular sense of an ancient story of the deeds of fictional gods.

25. This concern is represented well by a quote from Alexander McCaul (1799–1863): "If the first chapter of Genesis be poetry, or vision, or parable, it is not historic truth" ("Mosaic Record of Creation," 198).

26. "Firstborn" does not always mean first in time. Jesus is called the firstborn from the dead in Rev. 1:5, indicating preeminence, even though not the first in time (e.g., the widow's son in 1 Kings 17 or Lazarus in John 11).

27. Gentry, *As It is Written*, 169–86; Grudem, *Systematic Theology*, 300–304; Mortenson, *Searching for Adam*, 142–43.

Whether these represent genuine misalignments depends on which parts or themes of each verse are deemed central.

We unpack this in table 3, which is similar to table 1, but with excerpts from each day and key Hebrew words included. If attention is only given to *placement* of the luminaries in day 4, then perhaps an argument can be made against a parallel with day 1 because the expanse (*raqia'*) into which the luminaries were placed was made in day 2. If we are considering *purpose*, however, the parallel is strong. Day 1 and day 4 both serve to separate light from dark and day from night.

The objection of aligning the water of day 2 with the fish of day 5 is that the seas (*yammim*) are not named until day 3. But if we again give attention to *purpose*, the expanse (*raqia'*) in day 2 was made in order to separate the waters on the earth from the waters above the dome (or expanse) of the sky, giving rise to the realms of ocean and sky. This is consistent with the structure and word choice of the fifth day. Day 5 begins with fish filling the waters (*mayim*) and birds flying across the surface of the heavens (*shamayim*). The parallel structure thus proves to be robust.

TABLE 3. EXCERPTS FROM EACH DAY IN GENESIS 1 WITH KEY HEBREW WORDS.[28]	
Gen. 1:1–2 God created the heavens [*shamayim*] and earth [*'erets*] . . . hovering over the face of the waters [*mayim*]	
Day 1, Gen. 1:3–5 Let there be light . . . God **separated the light from the darkness**. God called the light day, and the darkness he called night.	Day 4, Gen. 1:14–19 Let there be lights in the expanse [*raqia'*] of the heavens [*shamayim*] **to separate the day from the night**.
Day 2, Gen. 1:6–8 Let there be an expanse [*raqia'*] . . . [God] separated the waters [*mayim*] that were under the expanse from the waters that were above . . . God call the expanse heaven [*shamayim*]	Day 5, Gen. 1:20–23 Let the waters [*mayim*] swarm with swarms of living creatures, and let birds fly above the earth across the expanse [*raqia'*] of the heavens [*shamayim*].
Day 3, Gen. 1:9–13 Let the waters [*mayim*] under the heavens [*shamayim*] be gathered together . . . God called the dry land earth [*'erets*], and the waters that were gathered together he called seas [*yammim*].	Day 6, Gen. 1:24–26 And let them have dominion over the fish of the sea [*yammim*] and over the birds of the heavens [*shamayim*] and over the livestock and over all the earth [*'erets*] . . .

28. Heavens (*shamayim*), earth (*'erets*), expanse (*raqia'*), waters (*mayim*), seas (*yammim*).

Objection 2: Poetic understandings of Genesis 1 are driven by attempts to harmonize Scripture with science.

We already touched on this in the introduction, but it is worth revisiting here. Some charge that any poetic or figurative understanding of the days of creation is driven by efforts to reconcile Scripture with science, not by an unbiased analysis of the text itself. This is a curious claim, given that theologians pondered the appropriate literary understanding of Genesis 1 long before apparent conflicts were raised by scientific observations. Early church fathers like Origen (third century) and Augustine (fifth century), both staunch believers in the authority of the Bible, wrote of the figurative nature of the days of creation.[29] Augustine argued that God brought all of creation into existence at the same instant, illustrated in figurative days aligned to a human workweek. This perspective came more than a thousand years before challenges would arise from the scientific observations of Copernicus, Galileo, Hutton, or Darwin.

What about the understanding outlined in this layer? The rhyming words and parallel days aligned under *forming* and *filling* would have been recognized by the original audience (who spoke Hebrew), but we don't have contemporaneous commentaries to probe how this influenced their understanding. Our theological assessments are predominantly from Western Christian writers many centuries and languages removed from the original story. Among these, focused attention on the literary structure of parallel days arose mostly within the last century, fleshed out by Arie Noordtzij, Henri Blocher, Meredith Kline, Lee Irons, and others. Were these theologians unduly influenced by the claims of science?

Answering this only requires reading what a few of them actually wrote. Lee Irons and Meredith Kline, early champions of the framework view, explicitly disavowed some scientific theories of origins, particularly evolution. While acknowledging that the study of God's natural world could legitimately raise questions to drive us back to his written word for a deeper look, they insisted that the only acceptable rationale for adjusting an interpretation of a biblical text was the text itself. Speaking for himself and for Kline, Irons wrote, "We reject as invalid any interpretation of Scripture which achieves harmony with natural revelation at the price of sound exegesis."[30] These scholars felt no compulsion to shoehorn Scripture into the scientific paradigm of their day. The beauty they saw in the literary structure of Genesis 1 was driven by the text.

---

29. Origen, *De Principiis* 4.16; Augustine, *Literal Meaning of Genesis*; see also Young, "Contemporary Relevance of Augustine's View of Creation."
30. Irons, "Framework Interpretation," 11.

DISCUSSION QUESTIONS

1. Does recognition of poetic language in Genesis 1 cast doubt on its historicity? Must readers choose between poetic and historical options?

2. What do you think was the intention of the parallel structure of phrases in days 1 through 3 and days 4 through 6 (tables 1–3)?

3. Had you heard of the framework view before? Does it make sense to you (even if you don't agree with it)?

4. What concerns do some have about the view expressed in this layer? How have the authors addressed these concerns?

5. The objection about the alignment of days (Objection 1) got a bit technical. Can you summarize the objection and the authors' response in your own words?

6. More than one third of the Bible consists of poetry.[31] What does this suggest about God's view of art or creative expression?

---

31. Duvall and Hays, *Grasping God's Word*, 346.

LAYER 2

Analogy

דְּמוּת

(*demut*, "likeness")

And [Jesus] said, "The kingdom of God is as if a
man should scatter seed on the ground."
(Mark 4:26)

he writers of Scripture had many ways of communicating truth. Using varied forms of analogy to draw comparisons between the natural and spiritual realms turns out to be one of the more common techniques.[1] If we think about this for a moment, it should be obvious that this is not just a literary convenience—but a necessity. We are finite creatures limited in spatial awareness to three dimensions, fixed in a narrow window of time that moves only in one direction, and subject to the confines of our biology. How are such creatures to comprehend a being or a realm unconstrained by time or space or biology? The nature and workings of God can only be communicated by imperfect comparisons. While his being and his ways are not ours, there are nonetheless similarities that are of instructive or illustrative value.

ANALOGIES IN THE BIBLE

The Bible is filled with analogies. Recall how many times Jesus stood before his disciples or a gathered crowd and offered a parable, starting with, "The kingdom of God is like," followed by a description of something familiar to listeners. Matthew 13 provides a string of examples in which the kingdom of God is *like* a tiny mustard seed that grows large (vv. 31–32), *like* leaven

---

1. Analogy, explaining or illustrating one thing by comparison to another, may be expressed by many different literary tools including simile, metaphor, allegory, and typology (or archetypes).

spreading through dough (v. 33), *like* a hidden treasure discovered (v. 44), *like* a pearl of great price (vv. 45–46), or *like* a net cast into the sea (vv. 47–50). None are intended to fully explain the spiritual kingdom, but each comparison—each analogy—provides a window of insight into the workings of God.

The gospel of John often drops the "one is like the other" motif and seems to tell us that the heavenly *is* what we are familiar with. Jesus declared himself to *be* the bread of life (6:35), the door (10:9), the light (8:12), the path (14:6), the good shepherd (10:11), and the true vine (15:1). Though dispensing with the comparative language that suggests one is *like*-but-not-*exactly*-the-other, there is no serious confusion thinking that Jesus was announcing himself to be baked, wooden, glowing, paved, tending actual sheep, or growing grapes from his arms. Each statement is a metaphor that makes use of our earthly experience to comprehend the heavenly reality. These simple statements help us see Jesus as the source of life (bread), the entryway to heaven (door), the illumination of truth, knowledge, and understanding (light), the route by which life is lived most fully (path), the caretaker of our lives and church (shepherd), and the origin of spiritual sustenance and blessing (vine).

In still other passages of Scripture, we might miss the analogy altogether if we don't pay attention. The wording does not always declare one thing to *be* or to *be like* another. The tabernacle, the blood of sacrifices, and the throne of David are just a few examples of earthly structures, practices, or concepts— each with contemporary practical purpose—that also correspond to or represent greater spiritual realities.[2] The earthly tabernacle provided a picture of the heavenly temple (Exod. 25:9; 2 Chron. 5–7; Heb. 8:5). God's presence could not be truly contained within the confines of a tent, but one was nonetheless used to illustrate God's desire to dwell among his people while also being unapproachable in his holiness. Earthly sacrifices were pictures of the heavenly sacrifice that God himself would provide. The blood of an animal had no capacity in itself to remove sins, yet it served as a powerful illustration of the role that Jesus, the Lamb of God, would play in reconciling men and women to God (Lev. 1–7; John 1:29; Rev. 5). David's throne is a picture of God's heavenly throne, where Jesus sits at the right hand of God the Father (Pss. 45:6; 89:36; Acts 2:30–35; Rev. 5).

---

2. The theological term for these examples is *typology*: something familiar is described as a *type* of what is less familiar or what is yet to come. That which "fulfills" the *type* is called the *antitype* (e.g., Christ).

And recall from the Introduction that even a historical account can simultaneously serve as an analogy to something on a higher spiritual plain. In Galatians 4:21–31, the apostle Paul refers to the history of Sarah and Hagar and their sons in Genesis 16, saying this can now also be understood *allegorically* as representing children of the promise and children of the flesh.[3] He was not negating the historicity of the story, but overprinting a figurative layer of understanding on the historical text.

With such precedent, it should not raise any theological eyebrows when it is argued that the creation story is likewise both historical and analogical. In fact, the Sabbath commandment of Exodus 20:8–11 instructs us to think this way. "Remember the Sabbath day. . . . Six days you shall labor. . . . For in six days Yahweh made heaven and earth, the sea, and all that is in them, and rested on the seventh day."[4] Israel was to consider the creation week as a model—by way of analogy—for the human rhythm of work and rest. An overarching analogical understanding of Genesis 1 is thus an ancient perspective, with affirmation in the covenant at Mount Sinai.

UNPACKING THE ANALOGY

In the absence of a relational, cognitive creature such as a human, there was no obvious need for God to spread his creative actions over a period of days.[5] God is not constrained by the hours available in a span of time. He does not tire or lose sight of his objective in the dark.[6] The division into days was inspired with an instructive purpose that goes well beyond a simple description of a sequence of events. The comparison of the days of creation with the human workweek provides unique instruction about the character of God—

---

3. Allegory is a type of analogy, a story told with characters and situations intended to represent/illustrate an abstract truth or lesson (e.g., moral, spiritual, political).
4. Interestingly, the rationale in Deuteronomy's version of the Sabbath command (Deut. 5:12–15) is a different analogy: recalling the slavery in Egypt (presuming little rest offered) and Yahweh's gift of Sabbath rest following the exodus.
5. This layer is not dependent on choosing between a literal or literary understanding of the sequence of days. We do concur, however, with C. John Collins's assessment that God's days are like but not the same as ours, lending weight to a literary reading (consistent with the whole of this book). For a description of how the days of creation are similar yet also different from ours, see Collins, "Reading Genesis 1–2 with the Grain."
6. Augustine argued in the fifth century that it was more likely that God created everything instantaneously, with the division of days used as a divine literary device for the benefit of humankind (Augustine, *Literal Meaning of Genesis* 10.21). In fact, the whole discussion of God's relationship to time is mind-boggling. Is God in time, outside of time, or both? This is not the place to pursue this question, but it prompts additional questions about the purpose of the creation week.

what *he* values and, therefore, what *humans* should value. It also sheds light on what it means to be created in the image and likeness of God.[7]

Though humans do not appear until day 6 of the creation week, the entire story is laid out with them in mind. The recounting parallels what our own experience will be in work, creativity, reflection, rest, and worship, each mirroring the character of the Creator and his relationship with creation.[8]

Work is good

In our culture, a common goal of employment is to squirrel away enough of our earnings to *stop* working, preferably sooner than later. Work is a burden. Leisure is the endgame. We long to live the life of the independently wealthy who sip their cocktails at exclusive ocean resorts, touring the world in private jets and living in mansions with servants to cater to every whim. But a very different view of work is portrayed in the creation story.[9] The divine work-week of Genesis 1 is not described as an onerous task. At the close of most of the days, God considered what he had done and each time "saw that it was good." We commonly think of this statement as an assessment of the quality of his product for the day—works of beauty that functioned as designed—but it is likely that the statement also includes the act of work itself. The *process* of creation, *working* toward completion, was also good. Work is not a result of sin. Work predates sin. Work was part of the creation mandate given to Adam to "work . . . and keep" the land (Gen. 2:15). Work is *good*.[10]

We are designed to work. The old phrase, "An idle mind is the devil's playground," derives from a common sense that our very nature includes a need to work. Depression, fractured families, and social unrest are common problems where unemployment rates are high, not only because of lost income, but also from interfering with a basic human need to engage in meaningful

---

7. The Bible does not spell out exactly what it means to be created in God's image. Theologians have made arguments for *resemblance* to God, *representation* of God's authority on earth, being *relational* in nature, or a combination of all three. See Collins, *Did Adam and Eve Really Exist?*, 93–95. The views expressed in this layer are not tied to one particular understanding.
8. We are not pitting sequential days here against the parallel days of Layer 1. Both structures are present, each for its own purpose (see Objection 2 under Challenges and Responses).
9. For a helpful resource on the theology of work, see the Theology of Work Project website, https://www.theologyofwork.org/.
10. Collins, *Reading Genesis Well*, 165–66; LeFebvre, "Adam Reigns in Eden," 30; Sandra Richter notes that work is not a curse but *fruitless* work is a curse (Richter, *Epic of Eden*, 111).

tasks—*to work*.[11] Adam's curse, "by the sweat of your face you shall eat bread" (Gen. 3:19), is not a curse resulting from having to work but from the weariness and uncertainty that come from our toils. The expression "sweat of the brow" is found in other ancient Near Eastern sources as an idiom for fear that one's efforts will come to naught, not just evidence of hard labor.[12]

This does not mean that we must strive incessantly to make money, or that one can never retire from a profession, or that a good Christian should feel guilty for taking a vacation. What it does mean is that as a matter of normal routine, our lives are to be filled with productive use of our time and talents. Retirement for the Christian should not be cessation of work but a transition from one type of work to another.[13] No longer needing to pursue an income may free a believer to help look after grandchildren, invest time in volunteer efforts, or spend more time in unpaid ministry.

Order from disorder

In its initial condition, the material world was formless, empty, and occluded in darkness (Gen. 1:2). Curiously, the existence of this primordial soup precedes day 1. Each of the six workdays of creation starts with, "And God said." The first occurrence, the start of day 1, comes in verse 3, following the hovering of God's Spirit over the face of something already there.[14]

While it is clear from verse 1 that God is the author of all, the structure of the story suggests that the real work of creation was not bringing energy and atoms into existence. The origin of the raw materials of the cosmos almost doesn't even bear mentioning, as it must be inferred from the opening line. Rather, the *real* work of creation, commencing on day 1, was bringing order and purpose to a disordered and purposeless condition. God took the dispersed components of the incipient cosmos and *ordered* them, separating out day and night, sun and stars, earth and sky, land and sea, plants and animals, woman and man.

---

11. This layer was written in the midst of the COVID-19 pandemic. Part of the emotional impact of this crisis has been caused by constraints placed on the ability to spend time in productive work.
12. Fleming, "By the Sweat of Your Brow." See also Richter, *Epic of Eden*, 111.
13. Piper, *Rethinking Retirement*.
14. Most theologians think day 1 starts with v. 3; for a good defense, see Collins, "Reading Genesis 1–2 with the Grain," 84. Outliers include starting day 1 in v. 1 (e.g., Lyons, "Genesis 1:1–3") or v. 2 (e.g., Sailhamer, "Genesis," 54–58). Regardless of which verse starts day 1, there is still a focus on ordering and purposing.

The garden into which humans were placed was good. Yet in the midst of a pre-fallen state, the garden needed tending. In Genesis 2:15, we read that "God took the man and put him in the garden of Eden to work it and keep it." Note that it does not say Adam was put in the garden to relax and enjoy its natural bounty. He was put there to work. "Work and keep" may be construed to include multiple functions, one of which was to bring order to the wild beauty of the garden—the work of a farmer or gardener.[15] Though we are not told what manner of horticulture was in play, we can imagine pruning to increase blooms, concentrating flowers into artistic beds, shaping of shrubs into attractive hedges, planting fruits and vegetables in more accessible plots, or guiding the flow of water for irrigation. We again see the value placed on work, with an emphasis on that which brings order.

We reflect one aspect of the image of God today when we act as caretakers, ruling as wise stewards over the natural creation, continuing the work of the garden.[16] This may be manifested in innumerable ways, cultivating crops and extracting resources in ways designed to sustain the environment for future generations, building or repairing homes and highways, or even cutting the grass and trimming hedges. To this we can add societal order. We bring godly order when we work to mitigate against the chaos of corruption and crime, when we establish and enforce laws for the peaceful governing of a nation, when we impose reasonable structure on our worship services, and when we train respectful interaction within a home.

Celebration of creativity

An analogy is periodically drawn in Scripture between God and a human potter (Isa. 29:16; 45:9; 64:8; Jer. 18:1–12; Rom. 9:21). The earthly potter takes a lump of clay and shapes it, slowly and intentionally, into a vessel designed for a particular purpose. The work of a talented potter may also be an object of beauty. Though the word for potter is not used in the creation story, the imagery of God as divine Potter is hard to miss. Following the creation of light in day 1, the Lord spends each subsequent day forming and shaping previously created earth materials into works of beauty and purpose. God took the formless mix of rock and water and air, and separated them into the earth

---

15. We will get to priestly roles associated with "work and keep" in Layer 5 ("Temple").
16. Collins, *Reading Genesis Well*, 88. A growing theological movement, called "creation care," seeks to emphasize and inculcate the Christian responsibility to steward God's creation. Evangelical examples include Bouma-Prediger, *For the Beauty of the Earth*; Moo and Moo, *Creation Care*; Sleet, *Serve God, Save the Planet*; Wirzba, *From Nature to Creation*.

below and the heavens above. He called to the inanimate dust of the earth to give life to plants that reproduced in verdant and fruitful abundance. He again spoke to the earth to give rise to the crawling creatures on the land. In the next chapter, Adam was not created by a simple word but, like all other life, was fashioned from the earth (Gen. 2:7, 19).[17]

None of this was necessary if the objective was simply to produce humans in a functioning universe. If the end product was all that God had in mind, a single word would have been sufficient. *Poof*—and it was so. But the story tells us that God delighted not just in the completed project but also in the creative expression along the way. This ties directly back to the message that work is good. Creativity is a form of work. Creativity, when done with acknowledgment of the author of our talents, is good.[18]

Creative talents are not just biological accidents. They are gifts from God. We see this explicitly in Exodus 31, where Bezalel and his artisans were filled with the Spirit of God to design beautiful works of gold, silver, and bronze, in cutting jewels for setting, and in carving wood to adorn the temple. Artistic expression is an outgrowth of being made in the image of the ultimate Artist, modeled in the creation story.

There is a godly sense in which we can look at our own creative work and also declare it to be good—taking pride in the work of our hands. This is different from being *prideful*, or *arrogant*. Arrogance comes from thinking our talents are somehow of our own making—that we owe no debt of gratitude and are not responsible to God for how we employ those gifts. True humility is not found in self-debasement or hiding creative authorship, but in our open profession of gratitude to God for the gifts he has bestowed.

Work, reflection, and refreshment

Consider the act of rest. A typical sermon from Genesis 1 will note God's provision for resting at least one day out of seven, but rest is found in more than just the seventh day. It is built into every day of the creation story. We see this in the seemingly odd ending of each day, which does not say there was *morning and evening*, one day, but *evening and morning*. This is not explained by a peculiarity of how Hebrew culture identified the passage of a

---

17. The word for "potter" in Jer. 18:2 is from the same root as the verb used in Gen. 2:7 for God "forming" of man from the dust of the ground (*yatsar*); it is also the same verb for forming the animals in v. 19. Egyptian texts describe the deity (Khnum or Ptah) fashioning people out of potter's clay (Currid, *Ancient Egypt and the Old Testament*, 70).
18. For an accessible book on a biblical view of the arts, see Ryken, *Art for God's Sake*.

full twenty-four-hour day—as if the day began at sunset—but to the nightly rest after daily labor.[19] Each "evening and morning" is a mini-Sabbath—the time people reflect on their accomplishments and sleep, rejuvenating their bodies in preparation for the next day of work. Days are not piled one after the other in incessant activity but are broken into intervals constrained by the hours of daylight, each separated by a time of rest and enjoyment of the day's accomplishments. In the creation story, God does not wait until the end to declare his work good, but does so *daily*. The workweek is modeled with God stopping to reflect on each act of forming or filling, and declaring it to be good. The night is allowed to pass before work once again commences.

Finishing out six days of daytime work and nighttime rest, we find God declaring his work to be more than good. It is *very* good (Gen. 1:31). It is not just that the work is now done, nor that it has culminated in the creation of humans. It is an assessment of the process as well as the product. The action of work was good. Each interval of rest and reflection was good. Altogether, it was *very* good.

For God's people, work is good—even essential—but that is not all there is. As with all gifts from God, we can warp it into something that turns the original purpose against itself. The glutton takes a pleasurable, life-giving gift and turns it into an assault on personal health and mobility. The sex addict takes a gift designed to wondrously bond a husband and wife, and turns it into an empty physical act that erodes the capacity for genuine love. The workaholic, routinely burning the midnight oil, never taking a holiday or weekend off, is not doing a good thing. It is not work "as to the Lord" (Col. 3:23). It is not a reflection of the Creator. It is a gift misused, warped to defraud others of our time, damaging our health, and robbing joy found in quiet reflection.[20]

Beyond daily rest: Sabbath rest

The culmination of the creation workweek is not just an extended day of rest or of reflection. It is something more. Many have noted that the seventh day,

---

19. Collins, "Reading Genesis 1–2 with the Grain," 86–87. On the difference between a "proper day" (running from sunrise to sunset) and a full twenty-four-hour day (running from sunrise to sunrise) in OT times, see LeFebvre, *Liturgy of Creation*, 16–18. The modern Jewish understanding of days as running from sunset to sunset began in the intertestamental period.
20. Henri Blocher offers a penetrating insight: "Now what is the meaning of the Sabbath that was given to Israel? . . . It protects mankind from total absorption by the task of subduing the earth, it anticipates the distortion which makes work the sum and purpose of human life, and it informs mankind that he will not fulfill his humanity in his relation to the world which he is transforming but only when he raises his eyes above, in the blessed, holy hour of communion with the Creator. . . . The essence of mankind is not work!" (*In the Beginning*, 57).

the *Sabbath* rest, is unique, with no "evening and morning" to conclude. This is a rest that, while repeated each week, is also unending.[21] The significance is not immediately obvious from the text, but subsequent Scriptures lend their aid. Multiple passages tell us that the Sabbath rest was and is something grander than a simple cessation of work.[22] God's work on earth did not stop at the end of day 6. When Jesus was challenged by the Pharisees for working miracles on the Sabbath, he responded that "my Father is working until now, and I am working" (John 5:17). Though the ordering of creation was complete and declared very good at the end of day 6, God did not then sit idle. He continued, and continues, to work in people's hearts, in the rise and fall of civilizations, and—if we think about it—even in the continued molding of the earth. Do we think that colliding tectonic plates raising the Himalayas, or the eruption of Kilauea building up the island of Hawaii, do not represent the work of God? The psalmist answers,

> [He] looks on the earth and it trembles,
>   who touches the mountains and they smoke! (Ps. 104:32).

Psalm 95 addresses Sabbath rest in still another way. It begins as a joyful march into the presence of the God who created and possesses all of creation. It moves on to call for worship, bowing the knee to the Great Shepherd, and warning not to harden hearts as Israel did in the desert leading to forty years of wandering. The psalm ends with the sobering reminder that Israel's rebellion meant that they did not enter *God's rest*. In this context, the *rest* was, at least metaphorically, the land of Canaan—the *promised land*. No one thought that work would forever cease once the boundary into Canaan was crossed, but that land, "flowing with milk and honey," represented something more profound.[23]

---

21. For a review of early theologians who viewed the seventh day as unending, see Collins, "Reading Genesis 1–2 with the Grain," 87. Augustine wrote: "But the seventh day is without an evening, and it has no setting, for thou hast sanctified it with an everlasting duration" (*Confessions* 13.36.51). Some theologians disagree, arguing that the writer of Genesis 1 assumes an ending to the seventh day (e.g., John Walton's response to Collins's essay in *Reading Genesis 1–2*, 101).

22. Concerning God's ceasing of work on day 7, Aristobulus (second century B.C.) states, "This does not, as some suppose, substantiate the view that God no longer does anything, but rather means that once he had 'ceased' the arrangement of his works, that they were thus arranged for all time. . . . For, once he arranged all things, he thus holds them all together and presides over their movements" (quoted in Collins, "Reading Genesis 1–2 with the Grain," 87).

23. Some passages in Isaiah suggest there is even work in the new creation. In describing the new heavens and new earth (65:17–25), God says, "...my chosen shall long enjoy the work of their hands. They shall not labor in vain" (vv. 22–23).

Hebrews 3–4 picks up on the theme from Psalm 95, repeatedly referring to the same rest, and explicitly telling us that Joshua did not bring Israel fully into that rest. There remains even now a Sabbath rest for the people of God (Heb. 4:9–11). Here we get a glimpse of why the seventh day of creation does not close. The joy of the completed creation and the milk and honey of the promised land are analogies for the ultimate Sabbath rest that God has prepared for his people. It is the new creation, but not just as a future abode. It is a condition of the heart, even now, that so fully trusts in the sovereignty and grace of God that there is no longer room for fear, for crippling doubt, for depression, for loneliness, or for empty longing. Though days may be filled with labor, though storms may rage around us, though momentary suffering may befall us, we can know joy and boundless belonging in the arms of God.

I (Gregg) am reminded of a Sunday morning when tornadoes had been sighted inside the borders of my small town. An announcement was made that one was headed our way. Wisely, the preacher encouraged the congregation to move into interior rooms. Though there were likely some frightened individuals, the atmosphere was not characterized by fear. Worship continued with songs of praise, as if the sky outside were calm and blue. A sense of God's sovereignty filled the spaces, not with a naïve sense that nothing could touch us, but with the knowledge that God would choose to protect or choose to take us home, and each was good. A few of us even slipped outside on the pretense of reporting what we saw, but really just to take in the magnificent display of God's power. It was a momentary walk into the promise of Sabbath rest, now and still to come. The Sabbath rest of day 7.

CHALLENGES AND RESPONSES

Objection 1: The analogical view is based on circular reasoning.

Some have charged that an analogical view is based on circular (thus, false) reasoning in which (1) God's creation days are patterned after a human workweek (Gen. 1), and (2) humans' days are patterned after God's (Exod. 20:11).[24] This objection may not be obvious to readers without more explanation. The objection is driven largely by a concern with any figurative understanding of the creation days. From this perspective, Genesis 1 is a simple historical narration; God's actual days of creation are the pattern after which humans should structure their work and rest. It represents a unidirectional flow of

---

24. For example, Coppes, "Of C. John Collins and the Analogical View," 341.

understanding. An analogical view is said to represent an unfounded, bidirectional flow of understanding, where humans' *actual* workdays are used as a pattern for describing God's *figurative* creation days, and God's *figurative* creation days are described as a basis for establishing human's *actual* workdays. A depends on B, which depends on A—circular reasoning.

A genuinely circular argument would indeed be problematic, for if A is the basis for establishing B, and B is the basis for establishing A, then the whole argument is effectively floating without a logical foundation. But an unjustified assumption is made in the present context that conflates *bidirectional analogy* with *circular reasoning*. That statement likely leaves some readers scratching their heads, so allow us to explain with another example from Scripture.

Consider the ubiquitous references to God as father, husband, or master. We initially have no understanding of what these terms mean without reference to earthly fathers, husbands, and masters, so our earthly experience informs us, by way of analogy, about God's relationship to his people. The earthly helps us understand the heavenly. At the same time, as we grow in knowledge of how God behaves in the role of father or husband or master, we learn how to conduct ourselves in ways that reflect that perfection in our earthly relations—to become better parents, spouses, rulers, and servants. The heavenly informs us, by way of analogy, of the earthly.

This is not circular reasoning. It is more accurately described as a *positive-feedback cycle*. We can illustrate this, not surprisingly, with another analogy—this time from nature. When a small notch is carved into the top of an earthen dam, a trickle of water begins to flow. A small flow has limited erosional power, so the channel grows larger slowly. As the channel deepens, the water flows faster and more energetically, resulting in faster erosion and enlargement of the channel, allowing water to flow and erode still faster. Faster flow contributes to enlarging the channel, and enlarging the channel contributes to faster flow. It is a bidirectional, positive-feedback cycle. In a comparable fashion, my experience as an earthly father enhances my understanding of God as father, and examples of God acting in the role of father in Scripture improves my understanding of what it means to be a *good* earthly father. The flow of information and understanding goes both directions.

It should not be so surprising, then, to find the same principle at work in Genesis 1. The creation story taps the human experience of work and rest, patterning the story after a human workweek to illustrate the character of God and his relationship to his creation. At the same time, the story serves to instruct, not just on how many days we should work before resting, but on how we should understand and value work, creativity, rest, and worship.

Objection 2: Days cannot be sequential and nonsequential.

Recall that the title of this book is not, *Seven Competing Views of Genesis One*, but *The Manifold Beauty of Genesis One*. Each layer of understanding is presented as complementing the others. All could be true at once.[25] To some, it may seem nonsensical to argue that the days of creation could be structured both as a series of sequential days (Layer 2) *and* as a nonsequential set of parallel days (Layer 1). It must be one or the other.

If the Bible was truly one-dimensional, with a single truth to be drawn out of every passage, the reaction would be a reasonable one. But few Christians believe this. God, who is the source and embodiment of creativity, inspired his written work to reflect his nature. In the Introduction, we described the unique properties of the mineral fluorite. The same sample, under different wavelengths of light, appears as distinctly different colors. It is one rock. It is two (or more) colors depending on the light that is reflected or emanated. In Genesis 1, we see one message in the sequential ordering of days, and we see another in the parallel structure of days.

As another illustration of how two seemingly competing views can both be true, consider the famous drawing by William Ely Hill, titled *My Wife and My Mother-in-Law* (see fig. 1). It appears to be a single portrait, yet, depending on the perspective of the viewer, two different women are represented. Both cannot be seen at once (at least by normal viewers). Depending on what aspects of the illustration your eye is drawn to, it is either an old woman, worn with age and gazing left, or a young aristocratic woman facing away from the viewer. Only one woman appears in each perspective. One could argue the intended portrait must be one or the other, but the artist declares—it is both.

---

25. If not in their totality, at least in their primary theses.

Figure 1. My Wife and My Mother-in-Law, by William Ely Hill

DISCUSSION QUESTIONS

1. What does it mean for us to pattern our days after God's? Is there more here than just making sure one day out of seven is spent in rest and worship?

2. Do you view work as good? Why or why not? How does sin affect work? What should retirement for the Christian look like?

3. What does godly creativity look like? Can we take pride in our own creativity?

4. What does this layer communicate about the meaning of Sabbath rest?

5. How do the authors address the charge of circular reasoning? What do they mean by a bidirectional analogy?

6. What are your thoughts on Genesis 1 being understood as *both* a sequence of days (Layer 2) and a set of parallel days (Layer 1)?

LAYER 3

Polemic

(*musar*, "correction")

> *For thus says Yahweh,*
> *who created the heavens*
> *(he is God!),*
> *who formed the earth and made it*
> *(he established it; he did not create it empty,*
> *he formed it to be inhabited!):*
> *"I am Yahweh, and there is no other."*
> *(Isa. 45:18)*

*W*e encounter debates and debate tactics with regularity. Politicians debate myriad topics, such as the best way to help the poor, the best tax system, and how to address illegal immigration. Sports commentators debate anything from who is going to win the next game to what player is the GOAT (Greatest of All Time). Theologians debate women in ministry, the mode and recipients of baptism, charismatic gifts, divine sovereignty and human freedom, and the age of the earth. As observers of these debates, we not only evaluate the subject matter at hand but also intuitively understand the importance of the *art* of debate.

To be a good debater takes practiced rhetorical skills. One needs to start with a thorough knowledge of the subject material, weaving the findings and statistics from the most credible studies into an overall narrative that creates a sound, logical argument. This alone, however, is rarely enough to win a debate. For maximum effectiveness, one must also challenge the interlocutor's position—questioning specific details, tearing down general logic, warning about the consequences of accepting such a position, even attacking an opponent's character or motives. These negative tactics constitute a *polemic*—a strong verbal or written attack against an opponent's position.

Understanding the polemical nature of Genesis 1 requires more background than our first two layers. We will start with examples of the pervasive use of polemics in both the New and Old Testaments, aimed against perverted theology and false gods, followed by a closer look at the pagan religions repeatedly challenged.

NEW TESTAMENT POLEMICS

We don't have to look hard to find polemics at work in the New Testament. We see it in the words of Jesus, most often applied to the pride and false piety of the Jewish religious leadership. Matthew 23 is a blistering polemic against the Pharisees who demanded observance of a litany of religious laws as evidence of personal righteousness. To a crowd of gathered listeners, Jesus declares the legalism of the Pharisees to be devoid of true godliness and warns of the consequences of their teaching and practice. At the forefront of his condemnation are outward appearances of righteousness—wearing broad tassels and phylacteries, tithing on the smallest of income (mint and dill), ceremonial cleaning of dishes, and proclaiming innocence of the murder of the prophets—while secretly delighting in the respectful greetings in the market and seats of honor at banquets; ignoring justice, mercy, and faithfulness; being filled with greed, self-indulgence, and a murderous spirit.

The apostle Paul takes up a theological polemic in his famed address at the Areopagus, a site in Athens that occasioned intellectual and religious debates (Acts 17:16–34). Paul declares the true God over and against the many idols represented there. Positively, Paul identifies the true Creator and Lord with what the Athenians were calling "the unknown god." Negatively (i.e., polemically), this God is *not* like a god of "gold or silver or stone, an image formed by the art and imagination of man" (Acts 17:29). The rivalry of gods—and implicit clash of worldviews—was not missed by the philosophers in the audience, who recognized Paul as a "preacher of foreign divinities" (17:18). Elsewhere, Paul adds to the polemical nature of his argument, drawing attention to actions of real spiritual entities and forces at work behind these false gods: "For we do not wrestle against flesh and blood, but against the rulers, against the authorities, against the cosmic powers over this present darkness, against the spiritual forces of evil in the heavenly places" (Eph. 6:12).

The theological polemics in the New Testament go deeper. Note particularly the presentations of Jesus as the true king (Matt. 27:11, 29, 37;

Acts 17:7), set against earthy kings who boasted to be more. Caesar claimed semidivinity, and that he was charged by the gods to maintain religious order and promote the Roman pantheon. Calling Jesus *king*, whether physically or spiritually, was a direct challenge to the reigning worldview. Moreover, New Testament scholars have shown that the Greek word for "gospel" (*euangelion*), often translated as "good news," carried a specific connotation at the time for the empire, normally associated with an event such as the birth or accession of a king or emperor. Linking the "gospel" with Jesus—combined with calling him "king" and "Lord"—represented a polemic aimed at the religious foundations of the age.[1]

OLD TESTAMENT POLEMICS

The polemical edge in the New Testament follows a well-established history in the Old Testament. The ancient Near Eastern (ANE) world of the Old Testament exhibits some differences in forms, perspectives, and deities from the Greco-Roman world of the New Testament, but the basic theological message is similar: Israel's God, Yahweh, is superior to all others, whether real or imagined. In his focus on the Old Testament perspective, John Currid defines "polemical theology" as "the use by biblical writers of the thought forms and stories that were common in ancient Near Eastern culture, while filling them with radically new meaning. The biblical authors take well-known expression and motifs from the ancient Near Eastern milieu and apply them to the person and work of Yahweh, and not to the others gods of the ancient world."[2]

The Hebrews did not migrate from some far distant land into an alien culture. They were raised up and set apart from *within* the people and lands of the ANE (see fig. 2). As Currid notes, Israel shared many experiences with their immediate neighbors (Egyptian, Mesopotamian, Canaanite): language, literary genres, history, geography, and even some philosophical and theological concepts. The frequent warnings in the Scriptures against intermarriage and the allure of idolatry testify to the continuing nearness and familiarity of the customs and beliefs of the surrounding nations. The writers of the Old Testament take direct aim at the false gods and errant worldviews that surrounded and too often reinvaded Israel. Polemics abound.

---

1. Wright, "Paul's Gospel and Caesar's Empire"; Wright, *What Saint Paul Really Said*, esp. chaps. 3–6.
2. Currid, *Against the Gods*, 25. Some of the discussion that follows is drawn from Turner's review of Currid's book in *The Journal of Baptist Studies*, 83–86.

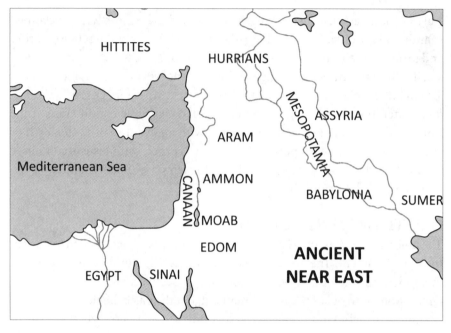

Figure 2. Map of the ancient Near East
(Not all identified people groups or nations were present at the same time.)

Yahweh versus the Egyptian pantheon

We find a particularly dramatic polemic in the exodus narrative. The Hebrew people had lived in Egypt and marinated in Egyptian culture for four hundred years. Moses, by virtue of his adoption, was educated in the history and religion of Egypt. As God prepared to launch Israel as an independent nation, set apart as a holy people, he wished to leave no uncertainty regarding the differences between himself and the Egyptian pantheon. A single plague would have been sufficient to demonstrate God's surpassing power. So why the grand theater of *ten* plagues? The plagues were not random acts of judgment. Each one directly challenged the supposed rule of an Egyptian god over a subset of the human experience (see table 4). The final plague makes the polemic against the Egyptian deities explicit: "For I will pass through the land of Egypt that night, and I will strike all the firstborn in the land of Egypt, both man and beast; and on all the gods of Egypt I will execute judgments: I am Yahweh" (Exod. 12:12). The polemic continues in the Song of Moses after God's destruction of the Egyptian army, in which he proclaims,

Who is like you, O Yahweh, among the gods?

  Who is like you, majestic in holiness,

    awesome in glorious deeds, doing wonders? (Exod. 15:11)[3]

TABLE 4. PLAGUES OF EXODUS AND POSSIBLE GODS IDENTIFIED AS TARGETS[4]	
Plague	**Egyptian god**
water to blood	Hapi, god of Nile
frogs	Hekt, goddess of fertility, water, renewal (head of a frog)
gnats/lice	Geb, god of earth—lice/gnats formed from the ground
flies	Khepri, god of creation, rebirth (head of a fly)
cattle	Hathor, goddess of love, protection (head of a cow)
boils	Isis, goddess of medicine, peace
hail	Nut, goddess of sky
locust	Seth, god of storms, chaos—locusts from the sky
darkness	Ra, god of sun
death	Pharaoh

Yahweh versus gods of the surrounding nations

From the immersive existence in Egyptian culture, Israel marched into lands dominated by the pagan religions of the Canaanites and surrounding nations. The Old Testament writers frequently identify specific gods of Israel's neighbors as worthy of distain.[5] Molech, Asherah, and Chemosh get numerous mentions for the detestable practices associated with their worship, but the most common targets of God's wrath are the gods said to control the sun, rain, and fertility—gods such as Baal, Marduk, and Dagon.

---

3. For a brief summary of the polemics in the exodus narrative, see Turner, "Exodus," 42–44.
4. Copan and Jacoby, *Origins*, 37–38.
5. Shirley, "How Many Pagan/False Gods Does the Bible Mention?"

The attention is understandable, for the life-giving forces of nature, the growth of crops and herds and families, were attributed to someone other than Yahweh, and gave rise to the contemptable practices of temple prostitution and child sacrifice.

From this flows the polemical descriptions of Gideon tearing down the idol of Baal (Judg. 6:11–32), and of the idol of Dagon falling shattered before the captured ark of the covenant in a Philistine temple (1 Sam. 5:1–5). Elijah's taunt of the prophets of Baal and Asherah on Mount Carmel called out the deafness of the pagan deities (1 Kings 18:19–40), and a Syrian king suffered an ignominious defeat by a much smaller Israeli force for saying, "Yahweh is a god of the hills but he is not a god of the valleys" (1 Kings 20:28).

Through Isaiah, God mocks the impotence of Babylon's gods, Bel (Marduk), the head of the pantheon, and his son Nebo (or Nabu), the god of writing and wisdom (Isa. 46). It is Yahweh who sustains and rescues, not the mute idols that must be fashioned and transported and erected by human beings. Perhaps the most stinging polemic comes in Isaiah 44, where Yahweh scoffs at the man who takes a tree, burns one end for warmth in a fire, and fashions the other end into an idol, bowing down in worship to a block of wood (vv. 9–20).

DRAWING OUT THE DISTINCTIONS
The objective of these polemics is to make clear the distinctions between Yahweh and all would-be competitors.[6] The differences are vast.

Monotheism versus polytheism
Heaven may be populated by supernatural beings such as angels and cherubim, but there is no committee of equals ruling or vying for power. Yahweh alone is God.[7] "Know therefore today, and lay it to your heart, that Yahweh is God in heaven above and on the earth beneath; there is no other" (Deut. 4:39).

Consistency versus caprice
Ancient Near Eastern morality was largely an outgrowth of what was perceived to bring about the favor of gods. Different gods had different

---

6. Longman, "What Genesis 1–2 Teaches," 103–19.
7. The Old Testament sometimes uses *elohim* (God, gods) for other supernatural beings, both those united to Yahweh and those opposed to him. But none of these so-called gods share the same attributes as Yahweh. This is what biblical monotheism means: Yahweh is incomparable to all in heaven, on earth, and under the earth.

expectations and might not behave the same way today as tomorrow. Not so with the God of Israel. Ethics and morality flow out of the self-consistency and immutability of God's character. Obedience is an act of love rather than manipulation for capricious favor.[8]

> He has told you, O man, what is good;
>   and what does Yahweh require of you;
> but to do justice, and to love kindness,
>   and to walk humbly with your God?
>   (Mic. 6:8)

Transcendence versus continuity

The nations surrounding Israel viewed humanity, nature, and the gods as all part of the same system—what some theologians refer to as *continuity*.[9] Gods were more powerful than humans but were ultimately made of the same cosmic materials and subject to similar flaws of character. Yahweh is the antithesis. While he freely acts on his material creation, he is entirely other. He is *transcendent*. Solomon captured elements of all the above in his prayer and dedication of the temple: "O Yahweh, God of Israel, there is no God like you, in heaven above or on earth beneath, keeping covenant and showing steadfast love to your servants who walk before you with all their heart. . . . But will God indeed dwell on the earth? Behold, heaven and the highest heaven cannot contain you; how much less this house that I have built!" (1 Kings 8:22–23, 27).

ORIGIN STORIES

After four centuries of living among and under the Egyptians, the benefit for Israel of a radical demonstration of the impotence of the pagan gods is obvious. A major realignment in perception was needed. The Hebrews had not governed or protected themselves for generations, and were about to set out as an independent nation destined for a land that would not like to see them arrive. Israel needed to know that the gods they were leaving behind and the

---

8. Theologians employ the term *ethical monotheism*, referring to the oneness of God and his moral consistency (Waltke with Yu, *Old Testament Theology*, 172–73).
9. Oswalt, *Bible among the Myths*, 48. For general implications and specific characteristics of *continuity*, see pp. 49–62. For an overview of its counterpart, *transcendence*, see pp. 63–84; cf. Currid, *Against the Gods*, 40–41.

gods they would face in Canaan had no power over them. Yahweh, the only true God, would sustain them.

One might think creation was quite different—there was nothing yet to correct. In Genesis 1, everything was fresh and declared to be good. So why would it contain a theological polemic? The answer is quite simple. While Genesis 1 may be looking back to the beginning, it was written for Israel, at a much later time, when there were many competing origin accounts. Every ANE nation had a story (or several) to explain how things came to be as they are. All attributed existence and outcomes to a suite of gods or to some mystical eternal state. Except for the Hebrews. Their story was not just a variant among the ANE creation myths. The God of the Hebrews was, and is, like no other.

Many of the same themes from above are found in Genesis 1, plus a few more. As we start to explore the text, it will be helpful to first summarize what is known about ANE origin stories. Thanks to the work of archaeologists over the past two hundred years, the relevant ANE texts include stories from Mesopotamians (Sumerians, Assyrians, and Babylonians), Egyptians (with several competing versions), Canaanites, Hittites, Hurrians, and early Greeks. We cannot possibly do a full comparison and contrast between Genesis 1 and ANE myths. Entire books are devoted to the subject.[10] For the sake of space and reader patience, we will focus on two representative examples: the Babylonian account called *Enuma Elish*, and a composite of Egyptian accounts (see comparisons with Gen. 1 in table 5). After summarizing these accounts and the major points of contact with Genesis 1, the polemical points will be cataloged.

Babylonian Story: Enuma Elish

Enuma Elish tells of the original gods Apsu and Tiamat arising from swirling primordial waters, mating to produce various gods, and subsequently engaging in familial battles and assassinations. One offspring, Marduk (god of order), rises to the head of the pantheon by killing Tiamat (goddess of chaos). From her split corpse, Marduk creates the heavens and the earth.

---

10. For good starting resources on ANE parallels to Gen. 1 and the polemical theology involved, see Currid, *Against the Gods*, 33–46; Miller and Soden, *In the Beginning*, 77–144; cf. Oswalt, *Bible among the Myths*, 99–104. The seminal work goes back to Hasel, "Polemic Nature of the Genesis Cosmology." See also Hasel, "Significance of the Cosmology," 1–20. For a lengthier scholarly treatment on ANE parallels, see Walton, *Genesis 1 as Ancient Cosmology*.

The Tigris and Euphrates Rivers flow from her eyes. Humans are formed, as slaves of the gods, from the blood of Quingu, a god found guilty of instigating Tiamat to war. The creation elements summarized here represent a relatively small portion of the text. Most of the text is devoted to the origin and exploits of the gods (theogony).

Egyptian stories

Like Enuma Elish, the Egyptian accounts focus most of their attention on the history of the gods rather than creation. Egypt produced three rival cosmogonies but, despite inherent contradictions, apparently did not see the need to discard any of them. Some common elements nevertheless exist. In contrast to Enuma Elish, the Egyptian myths have one creator god (either the sun god Ra, Ptah, or Khum) and do not emphasize gods fighting each other—though Ra does take control of the eight preexisting gods. In the accounts involving Ra as creator god, he self-generates on a primeval mound that appears from the chaotic primordial waters (personified as the god Nun) and then creates other gods, described variously via acts of masturbation, spitting, or the contemplation and naming of his body parts.[11] In the other accounts, either Ptah or Khum create as a potter on his potter's wheel. Humans, created from the tears of Ra (by some accounts), lived with the gods until the gods tired of earth and left for the heavens. The Pharaohs were tasked with ruling as image-bearers of the departed gods. The specific things created (e.g., gods, humans, various kinds of animals), and the amount of detail given to these creative acts, vary depending on the individual story.[12]

---

11. In one Egyptian account, Ptah speaks things into existence. Oswalt, *Bible among the Gods*, 69n8.
12. Shetter, "Genesis 1–2 in Light of Ancient Egyptian Creation Myths."

	Egyptian	Genesis 1	Mesopotamian
TABLE 5. SUMMARY OF SIMILARITIES AND CONTRASTS BETWEEN ANE ORIGIN STORIES[13]			
View of reality	Static	Dynamic	Dynamic
Gods and Beginning (see Gen. 1:1)	Some preexistent gods, who embodied principal elements (earth, primeval waters, sky, outer limits)	One eternal God creates cosmic matter by divine spirit and thus exists independent of his creation	Some preexistent gods, subject to impersonal cosmic principles; divine spirit and cosmic matter coexistent and coeternal
	Theogony One self-created (sun) god brings order by subduing preexisting gods, then creates other gods from own body (by naming, sneezing, spitting, or masturbating)	No Theogony (because one eternal God)	Theogony Preexisting gods create other gods by sexual procreation
Pre-creation (see Gen. 1:2)	Original chaos, primordial waters, darkness, primeval hillocks	Original nonfunctional matter: formless and empty (*tohu wabohu*); darkness; deep (*tehom*) = primordial waters	Original chaos; Tiamat enveloped in darkness
	God of wind/breath on waters	Spirit of God over waters	
Means of Creation			Theomachy (Enuma Elish)
	Various, including mere verbal fiat	Verbal fiat	(e.g., Marduk destroys/restores constellation with his word)
	Image of creator gods crafting cosmos on potter's wheel or as a metalworker	(Potter imagery behind "formed" in Gen. 2:7; cf. Isa. 29:16; 45:9; 64:8)	Creation is done by crafting

---

13. Adapted from various sources: Currid, *Against the Gods*, 37–39; Currid, *Ancient Egypt and the Old Testament*, 33–49; Miller and Soden, *In the Beginning*, 125–26; Walton, *Genesis 1 as Ancient Cosmology*, 139–84. See also the chart in Walton, *Genesis*, 29–31.

TABLE 5. SUMMARY OF SIMILARITIES AND CONTRASTS BETWEEN ANE ORIGIN STORIES			
	Egyptian	**Genesis 1**	**Mesopotamian**
View of reality	Static	Dynamic	Dynamic
(see day 1)	Overcomes chaos by creating light (light before sun rises in its place)	Overcomes darkness and emptiness by creating light (before sun); separates day and night	Light emanating from the gods (light, day, and night exist before luminaries)
(see day 2)	Separates sky and earth	Separates sky and earth	Separates sky and earth
(see day 3)	(cf. primeval hillocks)	Separates dry land and water	
	Vegetation	Vegetation	
(see day 4)	Luminaries (sun rises on first day)	Luminaries (for signs, seasons, etc.)	Luminaries (for signs, seasons, etc.)
(see day 5)	Fish and birds	Fish and birds	
(see day 6)	Land animals	Land animals	
	Humanity in deity's image from divine breath or tears	Humanity in God's image from dust and divine breath (Gen. 2)	Humanity as gods' slaves (only kings in deity's image) from clay or blood of deity
(see day 7)	(e.g., Ptah rested after completing work of creation)	God rests and sanctifies day 7	The gods rest and celebrate; gods typically rest in temples they build

POLEMICS OF GENESIS 1

Old Testament scholars are in general agreement about the presence of polemical elements in Genesis 1. Where disagreement exists, it is typically on the more nuanced questions of degree and enumeration: *How intentional* is the polemical edge, and *how many* pagan practices or beliefs are challenged? Some would argue that the list of unequivocal polemical statements in Genesis 1 is shorter than we propose below, but even a subset still communicates a powerful challenge to the gods of the surrounding nations.

No backstory for God

Perhaps the most striking difference between Yahweh and would-be competitors is the absence of a divine backstory. The primary focus of the ANE stories is not creation of the earth or humans, but an accounting of the existence, creation, and history of the gods. As such, the ANE myths are more theogony than creation stories, as most of the attention is on the origin and history of the gods.[14] Genesis 1 stands in stark contrast. Yahweh needs no origin or backstory. He is self-existent and eternal, independent of time and the material creation. At the beginning of creation, God already is.

A real beginning

People have an innate sense that material things come *from* something. As the gods were part of the material world (continuity), they also needed to come from something that preceded them. That something was typically a timeless primordial sea or mist. With no ultimate beginning, there was likewise no sense of historical progression. There was only what some refer to as the "eternal now." Not so, says Genesis 1. While God is self-existent and eternal, the cosmos had a real beginning and has a real trajectory of history.

One God, not many

There is only one God.[15] At the inception of the material universe, there was no competition between deities vying for supremacy.[16] No consulting or consorting, no fighting or frustration, no accidents or afterthoughts. God acts of his own volition, speaking order and the material world into existence.

---

14. Regarding the many ANE origin stories, John Walton summarizes, "It is questionable whether any of them can be labeled as creation accounts. . . . Instead, these reports are often embedded in other types of literature" ("Creation," 156). Elsewhere Walton states, "Mesopotamian literature has no extant literature that systematically recounts the details of creation," after which he also states that Egyptian literature is similar (*Ancient Israelite Literature in Its Cultural Context*, 19).
15. This is the consistent biblical and orthodox Christian teaching, no matter how one addresses the spirit in Gen. 1:2 and the divine plural ("us") in Gen. 1:26.
16. The Bible does include heavenly conflict in the rebellion of Satan, but Satan is a created being, never described as a potential coequal with Yahweh.

Creatures, not deities

The polytheism of the ANE manifested in the deification and worship of material objects, including the sun and moon. The Old Testament prohibitions against the worship of the heavenly host attest to this (e.g., Deut. 4:19; 17:3; 2 Kings 21:3; 23:5; Job 31:26–28; Jer. 8:2). Genesis 1 polemicizes against this in several ways. First, the sun and moon are given important but limited creaturely functions at the command of God—to serve as clocks and luminaries (Gen. 1:14–18; cf. Pss. 104:19; 136:7–9). Second, their creation is relegated to day 4, indicating that light itself could and did exist independently of these heavenly bodies. Third, even their normal labels—"sun" (*shemesh*) and "moon" (*yareakh*), which reflect ANE names of deities—are dismissed in place of "greater light" and "lesser light" (Gen. 1:16).[17] These textual features combine to downplay the special status conferred to sun and moon outside of Israel.

Creation was not an accident

Contrary to the ANE stories, Genesis tells of a *purposeful* creation. The cosmos did not form organically from the body of a god or by accidents of conflict, but by the deliberate attention of a master craftsman. The intentionality is illustrated beautifully by drawing attention to three "problems" that require solutions. Darkness, formlessness, and emptiness (Gen. 1:2) are resolved by the creation of light (day 1), a series of separations to give form and function (days 1–3), and a sequence of deliberate fillings (days 4–6). The activities of days 1 and 4 show interest in light, not just as a "physical" substance, but particularly for the measure of time: "Let there be lights . . . to separate the day from the night . . . for signs and for seasons, and for days and years" (v. 14). There is purpose even in the sequence of days, serving not as the "eternal now," but working toward an objective, culminating with its double climax: the creation of humanity (day 6) and the divine Sabbath (day 7).

---

17. There are many names for ANE sun gods and moon gods, but some are similar to the Hebrew terms. Shemesh was a Canaanite sun god, noted by several eponyms in Joshua: Beth-Shemesh (15:10; 21:16); En-Shemesh (15:7; 18:17); and Ir-Shemesh (19:41). Interestingly, Jer. 43:13 (NKJV) uses Beth-Shemesh for the Egyptian sun god Ra. The Mesopotamian counterpart is Shamash. Moon gods include Yarikh and Erakh (cf. Hebrew *yareakh*).

No personification of primeval chaos

Ancient Near Eastern origin stories commonly start with a disordered condition—chaos embodied in a primordial sea, often personified by a god that must be subdued or defeated to allow ordered forms to emanate. The Old Testament elsewhere takes advantage of the ANE mythic tradition to show Yahweh's superiority and sovereignty over various chaos monsters: Leviathan, Rahab, Nahar, Yam, and Tannin.[18]

Genesis 1 appears at first to draw on the familiar theme of primordial chaos in the dark and formless deep of verse 2, but it goes in a markedly different direction, serving as yet another polemic against the prevailing worldview. The formless deep is not timeless or self-existent, nor does Genesis 1 countenance a personification of chaos, either as a god or as the monsters mentioned above. The "deep" is not a rival deity in need of resistance, subjection, or defeat (like Tiamat in Enuma Elish). While lacking order and purpose, it is nonetheless under God's sovereignty, ripe with potential for his divine creativity.[19] The great sea creatures (*tanninim*) in verse 21 are not only mere creatures, but ones pleasing to their creator—declared to be part of his good creation and called on to give praise to their creator:

> Praise Yahweh from the earth,
>> you great sea creatures and all deeps.
>>> (Ps. 148:7)[20]

Consistency in creation reflects its maker

We discussed earlier the ANE concept of continuity that blurs the distinction between the material and the divine. By virtue of the continuity between nature and the gods, and their capricious character, there was no sense of inherent consistency to be found in nature. At the whim or accidental action

---

18. Leviathan (Job 3:8; 41:1; Ps. 74:14; Isa. 27:1); Rahab (Job 9:13; 26:12; Ps. 89:10; Isa. 51:9); Nahar (river; e.g., Hab. 3:8; cf. Nah. 1:4); Yam (sea; e.g., Ps. 74:13; Hab. 3:8, 15; cf. Nah. 1:4); and Tannin (dragon, sea monster; e.g., Ps. 74:13; Isa. 27:1; 51:9; cf. Ezek. 29:3; 32:2). While Leviathan is a personified chaos monster in several texts, it is merely a creature in Ps. 104:26. Of course, "sea" and "river" are usually non-personified in the OT.
19. In fact, the deep is never personified as a personal deity in its thirty-five OT references. For "deep" in creation-oriented texts, see Gen. 1:2; 7:11; Ps. 104:6; Prov. 8:27–28; Isa. 51:10; cf. Gen. 49:25; Deut. 33:13; Job 28:14; 38:16, 30; Pss. 77:16; 78:15.
20. There is some disagreement among OT scholars over the degree to which the primordial waters of Gen. 1:2 are intended to parallel ANE origin stories. Larger parallels are seen by Richter, *Epic of Eden*, 143–44; Walton, *Lost World of Genesis One*, 47–53. Lesser parallels are seen by Collins, *Reading Genesis Well*, 166; Dumbrell, *Covenant and Creation*, 120–26.

of a god, an animal or a woman might give birth to any number of aberrations.[21] For example, Enuma Elish mentions multiple creatures that are either hybrids (animal-human or animal-god) or deities that appear in animal form: monster-serpents, dragons, scorpion-men, fish-men, and monster-vipers.[22] Another Akkadian text, *Šumma Izbu*, records omens manifested by aberrant births, believed to predict future blessings or calamities. Some of the births described are also impossible hybrids, as exemplified in table 6.[23]

TABLE 6. HYBRID BIRTHS AS OMENS OF COMING EVENTS		
Parent	**Offspring**	**Examples**
Human	Demon	If a woman gives birth, and (the child) is a female demon with a male face, the king and his family will disappear. (II.67)
Human	Animal	If a woman gives birth and [the child] has a dog's head, that city will go mad; there will be carnage in the land. (II.3)
Animal	Human	If a mare bears twins and they have a human head . . . the prince's army will revolt against him. (XX.13)
Animal	Animal	If a ewe gives birth to a lion and it has the body of a ram, and the head of a lion—omen of Sargon who ruled the world. (V.87)
Animal	Hybrid	If an anomaly's womb is full of faces . . . one head of a monkey, one head of a lion one head of a human, one head of a pig—the land will go mad; . . . the prince . . . attack of a usurper. (XVII.76)

Once again, Genesis 1 presents a vastly different picture of both the creation and the Creator. Nature is not continuous with the gods, nor is its behavior an outgrowth of their whims. God is transcendent, causing but not continuous with

---

21. This section draws on the fuller argument in Turner, "Kind-ness of God."
22. "Enuma Elish" in *Babylonian Creation Myths*, trans. W. G. Lambert (Eisenbrauns, 2013), reproduced at the ETANA archive, http://www.etana.org/node/581. Creatures include monster serpents, dragons, scorpion-men, fish-men, and bull-men (found in tablet and line numbers: 1.134–143, II.20–29).
23. The largest collection of physiognomic omen texts is the Akkadian series *Šumma izbu*, found in the library of Assurbanipal. The twenty-four tablets of more than two thousand omens are given in full in Leichty, *Omen Series Šumma Izbu*. Tablet and number references in table 6 are from this source.

his creation. There is order to the creation in its production and in its operation. The order is reflected in the intentional structure of days (see Layer 1), and in the repeated statements of creatures made and reproducing "after their kind."

The precise meaning of "kind" (*min*) is often debated. It does not seem to correspond in a technical sense to modern biological taxonomy, especially given some variance in its different contexts of creation (Gen. 1), the flood (Gen. 6–7), and kosher food laws (Lev. 11; Deut. 14).[24] Nevertheless, the term most naturally speaks to distinctions recognizable and reproducible (and thus entails reproduction itself).

At one level, kind (*min*) is simply a term for differentiating between categories of organisms. Its usage in Genesis 1, however, has a deeper significance. It carries the implicit assurance that the material creation has been infused with order. In human experience, fig seeds will grow into fig trees, doves' eggs will hatch dove chicks, and sheep will give birth to lambs. Israel has no reason to fear the imagined aberrant and impossible births of their neighbors. The behavior of the natural world is not an outgrowth of capricious and bickering gods, but reflects the order of its Author.

That order extends in a special way to the pinnacle of creation—humans. While humans are called to reproduce as all other life, there is no added "after their kinds." They are a kind unto themselves, distinct from all other life. Additional order is expressed in the explicit creation of separate sexes, designed to express the image of God both individually and in the union of the two.

Human worth and exceptionalism

Humans alone, of all creation, are said to be made "in the image of God." Being an image-bearer includes a royal status, conferred on one class of creatures, resulting in a unique relationship with God and special calling within God's creation (Gen. 1:26–30). Though some Egyptian traditions speak of humanity in the image of a deity (mostly for the Pharaohs), the dominant ANE view is that human beings were created, often as an afterthought, to be slaves to the gods.

> . . . (Ea) created mankind,
> on whom he imposed the service of the gods, and set the gods free.
> (Enuma Elish VI.33–34)[25]

---

24. Thirty of the thirty-one occurrences of *min* appear in these contexts (10 in Gen. 1; 3 in Gen. 6:20; 4 in Gen. 7:14; 9 in Lev. 11; 4 in Deut. 14). The final reference is in Ezek. 47:10 concerning fish in a vision of the eschatological temple.
25. "Enuma Elish" in *Babylonian Creation Myths*, trans. W. G. Lambert (Eisenbrauns, 2013),

Humans were useful in doing work that the gods did not want to do and to feed the gods through their sacrifices.[26] In this dominant stream, the "image of god" was limited to special (male) roles, especially kings and sometimes priests. In contrast, Genesis 1 universalizes and democratizes this special status to all human beings. In further contrast to ANE myths, Genesis explicitly identifies women as co-image-bearers with men (Gen. 1:27).

The unity of humanity signaled in the image of God is also highlighted by the lack of creation according to "kinds" for humans. This emphasizes a sharp contrast between humans and the animals (and plants); moreover, vegetation and animals were created explicitly for the benefit and blessing of humans (Gen. 1:28–29). This distinction of humans from other life forms is less clear in ANE accounts. Instead, humans are similar to plants and animals as births of the gods, and humans join the other creatures purely to serve the interest of the gods. The ANE worldview gives greater attention to distinctions *between* human beings—distinctions of class—rather than humans versus nonhumans.

God feeds humans—humans do not feed God

In ANE thought, humans did the work the gods did not wish to do. Sacrifices were offered to feed the gods. In one well-known example, the Mesopotamian flood story of Gilgamesh ends with the hero offering up sacrifices to the gods, who "smelled the sweet savor and collected like flies over a [sheep] sacrifice."[27] In Genesis 1, it is God who provides food for humans. The purpose of sacrifices come later, not to feed God, but as a result of sin. At the end of the biblical flood story, the aroma of the sacrifice offered by Noah draws no buzzing horde of hungry gods, but a pleased response of God to the thankful worship of his people (Gen. 8:20–21).

Divine assessment of creation

The God of Genesis does something no other god does: he offers an evaluation of the parts and the whole of his own creative work. Seven times God

---

reproduced at the ETANA archive, http://www.etana.org/node/581.

26. Similar arguments can be made from comparisons of the biblical and ANE flood stories. C. John Collins notes that ANE gods try to wipe out men because they are noisy and annoying; Yahweh wipes out men for their corruption. ANE gods smell sacrifice and gather like flies in their hunger; Yahweh smells and honors the sacrifice but has no need of it for sustenance. Collins, *Reading Genesis Well*, 190.

27. Epic of Gilgamesh, tablet XI (trans. Maureen Gallery Kovacs [Stanford, CA: Stanford University Press, 1989]), reproduced at Ancient Texts, http://www.ancienttexts.org/library/mesopotamian/gilgamesh/tab11.htm).

"saw" that his work was "good," six times for specific creative acts (1:4, 10, 12, 18, 21, 25), and a seventh for "everything that he had made" (v. 31).[28] The word "good" (*tob*) carries aesthetic, functional, and moral connotations. God's creation is a work of physical beauty (see 2:9; 3:5), all its parts work together to function as designed, and no incipient evil is hidden within. This evaluation yields a divine blessing for the animate creatures' fruitful activity (1:22, 28) and the Creator's own rest (2:3).

Worship, not appeasement or manipulation

All of the above—God's complete sovereignty, purposefulness, evaluation, and blessing—call for the response of worshipful obedience. Worship is not an act of appeasement, designed to manipulate a desirable response from mercurial gods. Worship is the appropriate response to a God who has given us stewardship over a world that reflects his own character.

What Is Not Challenged

Given the strength of the polemics against the pagan worldviews, it is interesting to see what was not challenged. If one were to try to draw a picture of the cosmos from the information in the Bible, the result would look remarkably similar to non-Israelite ANE descriptions. All perceived a three-tier universe (heavens, earth, sea/underworld), with boundaries that set the regions apart.[29] Genesis 1 draws on the familiar ANE cosmology with descriptions that include a domed firmament holding up the waters above (vv. 6–8).[30] The absence of any challenges to the physical structure of the cosmos ensures that the full weight of the polemic is directed at errant theology—mistaken beliefs of the identity and character of God. Superficial *physical* similarities actually accentuate the *theological* divide, strategically written to exalt Yahweh (and Israel) over the other gods (and nations).

---

28. Good (*tob*) is used seven times by leaving it out of day 2 and repeating twice in days 3 and 6; see Layer 1 for more in-depth discussion.

29. Greenwood, *Scripture and Cosmology*, 25–27, 38–40; Walton, *Genesis 1 as Ancient Cosmology*, 88–89.

30. There is debate whether the *raqia'* of day 2 refers to a solid surface ("dome, firmament") or the open space of the atmosphere ("expanse"). For a helpful discussion, see Walton, *Genesis 1 as Ancient Cosmology*, 155–61. Also, there is a difference between how ancient people *depicted* the cosmos and what they truly *believed* about the structure of the cosmos. These issues do not need to be settled here. Our point is that the Israelites largely agreed with their neighbors when it came to describing the cosmos.

Pertinence for Our Time?

With all the emphasis in this layer on the cultures of the ANE, one might reasonably wonder whether the polemical aspects of Genesis 1 still carry force in modern times. The answer is an emphatic *yes*. Despite our advanced technological innovations and scientific discoveries, the battles are remarkably the same. We commonly hear origin stories today, taught as truth, of our universe birthed from the timeless, primordial waters of the multiverse. Morality is not an outgrowth of a self-existent and consistent God, but from the organic adaptations of incipient cultures to environmental pressures. Nature cannot be trusted to reliably produce order, for a woman may find herself mistakenly in a male body, in need of chemical and surgical correction. A steady stream of publications attack human exceptionalism, where an act of apparent empathy in a chimp is argued to wipe out the differences between us.[31] The earth and its creatures are not here as a blessing to humans (who are to serve as caretakers and stewards), but are elevated to be served and receive our worship. By some evaluations, the earth would be better off with humans drastically reduced or even eradicated.[32] Even within our Bible-believing churches, there are forces at work arguing creation is not good, nor does it reflect the order and character of God—even questioning whether a sheep can always be counted on to give birth to sheep.[33]

Modern society has come full circle. Apart from God, we cannot help but fall into the same traps. The polemics of Genesis 1 are as pertinent today as they were when they were first written. As one of us (Ken) has stated elsewhere, "The gods of our day may look vastly different than those in ancient Israel's day, but does not polemical theology in the Bible provide us a platform to engage in worldview debates today? In true evangelical fashion, we have biblical grounds to show that the triune God is superior to all would-be contenders to his throne."[34]

---

31. For example, Hogenboom, "Humans Are Nowhere Near as Special as We Like to Think"; Kenneally, "So You Think Humans Are Unique?"; Dean, "Not So Unique?"
32. An example at the extreme end of this view is the Voluntary Human Extinction Movement, http://vhemt.org.
33. Examples provided in Davidson, *Friend of Science, Friend of Faith*, 253–55.
34. Turner, review of *Against the Gods*, 86.

CHALLENGES AND RESPONSES

Objection 1: How can Genesis 1 be a polemic if it came before all other stories?

This question was raised and partly addressed in the section above on origin stories, where we noted that while Genesis 1 refers back to the first of all stories, it was not written down until many generations later, after the exodus of Israel from Egypt. We revisit the question here because some assume that God revealed the creation story to Moses exactly as Adam and Eve heard it in the garden. As such, it would predate all other stories. How could it then be a polemic against competing stories that had not yet been invented?

The first response is that such an assumption is just that—an assumption. The Bible makes no claim for or against this belief. Given that there are many ways of truthfully telling the same story, it is reasonable and logical to allow that the version communicated to the nation of Israel highlighted aspects necessary to counter the twisted origin stories of their neighbors. A second option—one we would consider less likely but still possible—is that God foreknew the challenges Israel would one day face, and communicated the story accordingly. A polemic could thus have been wrapped into the story from the start, with application at the time Israel was ready to advance into Canaan.

Objection 2: A negative theme (polemic) does not seem like the primary message.

Those who find the word *polemic* too strong for Genesis 1 usually still acknowledge the contrasting worldviews. It becomes a matter of degree rather than outright rejection of the idea. If asked whether we think the primary message of Genesis 1 is a polemic, we would say no. Rather, Genesis 1 is primarily a positive exaltation of Yahweh. Yet we are in agreement with the majority of scholars who see a real polemic at work—one layer of its manifold message. Given the known ANE accounts of creation (known to us and known to Israel), and the nature of both similarities and differences, it is hard to read Genesis 1 as if it were written without these other accounts in mind.

DISCUSSION QUESTIONS

1. What is a polemic? Does the Bible engage in polemics?

2. What was the point of *ten* plagues in Egypt?

3. What pagan concepts about the gods are challenged in the Genesis account? What concepts are left unchallenged?

4. What is meant by the theological distinctions of consistency versus caprice, or transcendence versus continuity?

5. Discussions of creatures reproducing "after their kind" is usually about how close it matches modern taxonomy. What significance does kind (*min*) carry according to this layer?

6. How is a polemic against views thousands of years old still relevant today?

LAYER 4

Covenant

בְּרִית

(*berit*, "covenant")

If you can break my covenant with the day
and my covenant with the night . . .
(Jer. 33:20)

*C*ovenants play a critical role in the biblical narrative. Most Christians have at least a vague sense of this from the primary division of our Bibles. Though typically identified as Old and New *Testaments*, their identity is more truly expressed in the lesser-used label *Covenants* (Heb. 8).[1] A testament, or testimony, is a record of something experienced or witnessed. While the Bible does indeed provide a testimony of the works of God, it is more than that. The Bible, from beginning to end, is a record of God's *covenantal* relationships—relationships, as we shall see, that extend not just to his people but also to animals, the earth, and even the cycle of seasons and days.

The concept of covenant is described by some theologians as central to biblical theology, even as the backbone of Scripture—not in the sense of being the primary focus, but in its role as a framework from which the central themes of sin and redemption emanate.[2] The prophet Isaiah went so far as to say the coming Messiah will *be a covenant*—the personification of God's promises and relationship to his people (Isa. 42:6; 49:8).

To lay the groundwork for this layer, we will need to first ensure we have an adequate big-picture understanding of biblical covenants. We will start with

---

1. Richter, *Epic of Eden*, 69–70.
2. Schreiner, *Covenant and God's Purpose for the World*, 12; Gentry and Wellum, *Kingdom through Covenant*, 31–50; Richter, *Epic of Eden*, 69–70; Williamson, *Sealed with an Oath*, 17–43; Eichrodt, *Theology of the Old Testament* (each of the ten major divisions has "covenant" in the title). Of note, Daniel Block's just published tome, *Covenant*, is subtitled *The Framework of God's Grand Plan*.

the Mosaic covenant at Mount Sinai and work backward. Once arriving at the creation story, we will find that a covenantal perspective is best understood in the context of both Genesis 1 and Genesis 2 (and even spilling over into Gen. 3).

The Hebrew word for covenant is *berit*. In its most basic form, a covenant is a formal agreement between two parties, with specified obligations, to establish a relationship by law that did not exist by nature.[3] The relational character is what makes a covenant unique from a contract, which may be established between parties simply to cover a one-time transaction. Sandra Richter notes that "a covenant was a way of making kin out of non-kin," illustrated most clearly in a marriage, adoption, or a "blood brother" bond of friendship.[4] This general sense is readily gleaned from the 284 times *berit* appears in the Old Testament, where it is applied to a wide range of parties and purposes. Covenants are found between individuals (1 Sam. 18:3; Mal. 2:14), nations (Josh. 9), and, most importantly, between God and his people (Exod. 19).[5]

Covenants are more than earthly agreements, as they appear to carry *spiritual* weight, even if established only between humans or only for political or personal ends. A good example is found in the expanded story of Israel's covenant of peace with the Gibeonites as the Hebrew nation advanced into Canaan (Josh. 9). Though the Gibeonites lied about the location of their lands, Israel's covenant promising mutual aid and protection was considered inviolable—not just culturally but by God as well. We see this affirmed several generations later when King Saul, in misguided zeal, tried to wipe out the Gibeonite people. God brought about a famine as a direct consequence of breaking the covenant (2 Sam. 21:1). Covenants made on earth are registered in the heavenly court.

We gain a greater appreciation for the nuances of covenants from archaeological discoveries that began in the early 1900s.[6] Ancient Hittite and Assyrian libraries dating to the second and first millennium B.C. reveal insights into the culture and legal language of societies that were contemporary with Israel in time and place. Treaties of the ancient Near East (ANE) included *parity* treaties,

---

3. Wording courtesy of Michael LeFebvre, personal communication. Various definitions on the theme are found in Mendenhall and Herion, "Covenant," 1:1179; Dumbrell, *Covenant and Creation*, 1–2; Block, *Covenant*, 1.

4. Richter, *Epic of Eden*, 73.

5. Referenced verses are just a few of many examples.

6. The treatment of biblical covenants in relation to ANE treaties draws from Beckman, *Hittite Diplomatic Texts*, 2–3; Kitchen, *Ancient Orient and Old Testament*, 90–102; Kline, *Treaty of the Great King*; Levenson, *Sinai and Zion*, 26–36; Richter, *Epic of Eden*, 72–77; Walton, *Ancient Israelite Literature in Its Cultural Context*, 46–53.

which were contracts of mutual agreements between equals, and *suzerain-vassal* treaties, which were imposed by a superior king or nation (the suzerain) on a lesser king or nation (the vassal). A suzerain-vassal treaty could also include a *royal land-grant* treaty, where a suzerain granted land and local governance to a vassal, conditional upon continued service and homage to the suzerain.

Hittite treaties and Mount Sinai (the Mosaic covenant)

The parallels between ANE treaties and biblical covenants run deep, particularly when comparing Hittite treaties to the Mosaic covenant at Mount Sinai.[7] A typical Hittite suzerain-vassal treaty followed a general pattern:

1. Title/identity: the name of the suzerain
2. Historical prologue: lauding the accomplishments of the suzerain and what had been done for the vassal
3. Stipulations: expectations of the vassal
4. Placement/reading: treaty to be housed in a vassal temple and read with regulated frequency
5. Witnesses: often a pantheon of gods
6. Curses/blessings: identification of the penalties for betrayal and the benefits of faithfulness

Establishment of a treaty was often accompanied by an animal sacrifice, with implicit or explicit reference to the analogous fate of the vassal if the terms of the treaty were violated. While a nation might have multiple parity treaties with other nations, there could be fealty to only one suzerain.

Now consider the covenant language weaved through the message Moses delivered to Israel at Mount Sinai. Exodus 20 summarizes Yahweh's law (repeated in Deut. 5):

1. Title/identity: "I am Yahweh your God" (Exod. 20:2a)
2. Historical prologue: "who brought you out of the land of Egypt, out of the house of slavery" (v. 2b)
3. Stipulations: the Ten Commandments (vv. 3–17)

---

7. There is debate among OT scholars regarding the relative influence of Hittite versus Neo-Assyrian treaties on the structure of the Sinai covenant (and more so regarding treaty-parallels with the book of Deuteronomy). We lean toward the Hittite treaties based on timing, geographical proximity to Israel, and emphasis on what the suzerain has done that is often lacking in Assyrian treaties. Richter, *Epic of Eden*, 81–89.

As Moses expounds on the law, we find:

4. Placement/reading: the tablets were to be placed in the tabernacle in the ark of the covenant (Exod. 25:21); the law was to be read to the people on a schedule (Deut. 31:10–12)
5. Witnesses: "heaven and earth" are called on as witnesses against Israel if they failed to obey (Deut. 4:26)
6. Curses/blessings: a list of curses for failure to obey (Lev. 26:14–46; Deut. 27:11–26; 28:15–68); a list of blessings for obedience (Lev. 26:1–13; Deut. 28:1–14)

To these observations we can add the record of animal sacrifices to confirm the covenant (Exod. 24:1–8), promises of a land grant of Canaan conditional on faithfulness to Yahweh (Exod. 6:4), and the forbidding of covenants with any other gods (Exod. 23:32)—no other suzerain-vassal treaties!

There are some differences, of course, between God's covenant and the familiar political treaties. The stipulations of Yahweh's covenant focus on the nature of the vassal's character and worship rather than what the vassal was expected to supply to the suzerain in tribute and military conscripts. The list of witnesses is also profoundly different. No pantheon of gods was necessary. In their place, all of creation is called on to bear witness to the covenant (e.g., Deut. 4:26). There is likewise significance in the differing order of curses and blessings. Hittite treaties started with warnings of the dire consequences of unfaithfulness before addressing the blessings (Assyrian treaties included *only* curses). The Bible reverses the order, opening with the benefits of faithfulness.

When noting similarities between the Bible and the customs or stories of contemporary civilizations, some Christians have an instinctively suspicious reaction. There is an understandable fear that the authority of Scripture is being diminished by claims of "borrowing" ideas from influential pagan neighbors. This is not what is being suggested. Rather, the comparisons reveal widespread cultural norms, familiar to societies across the region, which God *intentionally drew on* to help his people apprehend his message. Israel's intimate knowledge of suzerain-vassal and land-grant treaties provided a cultural foundation for understanding the significance and meaning of the covenantal relationship between Yahweh and his people. Life experience served to ground their theology. Knowledge of these cultural norms can likewise contribute to our own understanding and appreciation of the biblical message.

We started with the Mosaic covenant at Mount Sinai for two reasons. First, it is here that we see the clearest cultural link with known ANE treaties, which helps us recognize similar treaty elements elsewhere in Scripture. Second, it is at Mount Sinai that the Hebrew people established themselves as an independent nation. For the first time, laws and societal structures were codified in order to effectively govern the fledgling nation and to establish them as a people "set apart" (Lev. 20:22–26).

It was also at this time, according to Jewish tradition, that the Genesis account was written. The purpose of Genesis was not a comprehensive history (an impossible task), but a selective record highlighting the shared roots of human experience and the pathway leading to the nation of Israel. In this context, the importance placed on the covenantal nature of God's relationship with his people is particularly clear.[8]

Theologians delving into the covenant theme of the Bible typically draw special attention to pivotal moments in Old Testament history associated with Adam, Abraham, Noah, Moses, David, and ultimately Jesus. Much could be said about the nature of covenants moving forward in time from Mount Sinai, but for the purposes of this book, we will focus our gaze backward toward Eden and the creation.

The Abrahamic covenant

The covenant at Mount Sinai was not invented from scratch. It was a national outworking of the earlier covenants with the Hebrew patriarchs. As the people of Israel suffered under their bondage in Egypt, "God heard their groaning, and God remembered his covenant with Abraham, with Isaac, and with Jacob" (Exod. 2:24).

With the knowledge we have gained so far of ANE treaties and the parallels with God's covenant with Israel at Mount Sinai, the details of the covenant with Abraham look familiar. The parallel elements include the suzerain's identity, "I am Yahweh" (Gen. 15:7a), and the historical prologue, "who brought you out from Ur of the Chaldeans to give you this land to possess" (v. 7b). In Genesis 17 we find stipulations: "walk before me, and be blameless" (v. 1), and "every male among you shall be circumcised" (v. 10). Blessings are also clearly articulated, with promises that Abraham will live to an old age (15:15), and that he will become father to a multitude of nations (17:3–6).

---

8. The argument is not wholly dependent on Mosaic authorship, as the same motivation and reasoning would have applied to later compilers of Israel's history.

The blessings include a *land grant,* promising that his descendants will come back to possess the land of Canaan (15:18–21; 17:8). The occasion was also confirmed with animal sacrifices (15:7–17).

Typical treaty elements missing include storing a document in a temple (one did not yet exist), and calling on witnesses. Curses are not explicitly stated, but are inferred from the conditional nature of blessings (Gen. 22:18; 26:5) and the cutting of the sacrifices. The act of cutting animals in two was understood to represent what would happen to the party who violated the covenant.[9] In treaties between unequal parties, one might expect only the vassal to be subject to such a curse, yet when Abraham cut the animals, God's presence—the *suzerain*—passed alone between the animals (Gen. 15:17). The unprecedented action is seen by many as an indicator that God himself would one day take on the curse (to be cut) to ransom his people from their repeated failures to keep the covenant.[10]

Of additional interest for this layer, the covenant promises to make Abraham "into a great nation" and that in him "all the families of the earth shall be blessed" (Gen. 12:1–3) came well before the covenant was formalized, before God changed Abraham's name from Abram (Gen. 17:5). The word for covenant (*berit*) was not brought to bear on the promises until years later in the land of Canaan (Gen. 15:18; 17:2).

The Noahic covenant

The covenant with Noah follows after the flood (Gen. 9). We will again draw attention to some of the significant similarities and differences with ANE treaties. The *identity* and *historical prologue* can be found in the story leading up to and through the flood. It is Yahweh who saw the earth was filled with wickedness (6:5) and determined to blot out life, choosing to preserve only Noah, his family, and the animals on the ark (6:18–19). *Stipulations* include being fruitful and multiplying (9:1, 7), not eating blood (9:4), and a prohibition against murder (9:5–6). For *blessings,* Yahweh provided animals as well as plants as food (9:3), and promised not to destroy the earth again (8:21–22; 9:11). The only *curse* itemized is the penalty for murder:

---

9. The standard Hebrew verb for initiating a covenant is *karat,* literally, "to cut." A later prophecy against the leaders of Israel says, "The men who transgressed my covenant and did not keep the terms of the covenant that they made before me, I will make them like the calf that they cut in two and passed between its parts" (Jer. 34:18).

10. Longman, *Genesis,* 202–6. Some see the smoking pot passing between the animals more as a sign of acceptance of the sacrifices rather than a christological reference (e.g., Walton, *Genesis,* 423).

Whoever sheds the blood of man,
> by man shall his blood be shed.
>> (9:6)

After Noah and his family left the ark, the covenant was confirmed by animal sacrifices (8:20).

As with Abraham, there was not yet a temple in which to store a written document, and no witnesses were called. The most striking difference in this covenant, however, is with whom the covenant is established. To Noah, God says, "I establish my covenant with you and your offspring after you, and with every living creature that is with you, the birds, the livestock, and every beast of the earth with you. . . . I have set my bow in the cloud, and it shall be a sign of the covenant between me and the earth" (Gen. 9:9–10, 13). A suzerain-vassal covenant is drawn between Yahweh and the *earth*. Moreover, the animals are recipients of a land grant. The whole earth is given to them to fill and swarm (v. 7). Though no criterion is provided in Genesis for their continued possession of the earth, Psalm 148 provides a plausible answer—to return praise to their Creator:

Praise Yahweh from the earth,
> you great sea creatures and all deeps,
fire and hail, snow and mist,
> stormy wind fulfilling his word!
Mountains and all hills,
> fruit trees and all cedars!
Beasts and all livestock,
> creeping things and flying birds! (Ps. 148:7–10)

Even the inanimate material of the earth appears to be wrapped into the covenant, as Genesis 8:21–22 declares that the ground shall not again be cursed—there is a promise of an earthly and cosmic stability: "While the earth remains, seedtime and harvest, cold and heat, summer and winter, day and night, shall not cease."[11]

Introduction of this covenant back in Genesis 6:18 is of particular interest, as it is the first occurrence of the Hebrew word *berit*, leading some theologians

---

11. Some have suggested that this verse marks an ending to the curse against the ground that was made when Adam and Eve sinned. Garvey, *God's Good Earth*, 28–29.

to believe it is the first covenant.[12] Others, however, have noted that the unique grammatical construction here suggests a continuation of something begun earlier. Robert Gonzales notes, "Rather than employing the standard terminology for *inaugurating* a covenant, the author uses the *Hiphil* form of the verb קום [*qûm*], which commonly denotes *the fulfillment of a prior obligation or commitment*."[13] Based on this reading, the covenant with Noah was not the establishment of something new, but a reaffirmation of earlier promises—an earlier covenant. The only available option is back at the creation.

CREATION COVENANT

In choosing a subtitle for this section, we debated calling this a "creation" covenant or "Edenic" covenant, recognizing a tendency for some to read into the titles an emphasis on either Genesis 1 or 2, respectively. Neither is our intention, as we would instead argue that a single overarching covenant is found in the continuum of Genesis 1 and 2.[14]

Suzerain-vassal

While the word for covenant (*berit*) does not appear in the creation story, the elements of covenant language are present. We find the suzerain identified in the opening words of Scripture, "In the beginning, God . . ." (Gen. 1:1a), followed by what he has done: "made the heavens and the earth," along with the subsequent days of creation (1:3–2:3). Stipulations include commands to multiply to fill the earth and exercise dominion over living things (1:28), together with a solitary prohibition: "of the tree of the knowledge of good and evil you shall not eat" (2:17a). Blessings include the provision of food—the fruit of trees and "every plant yielding seed"—and dominion over the other creatures (1:26, 28). The punishment for disobedience, for breaking the covenant, is death (2:17b).

As with the Noahic and Abrahamic covenants, there was no temple building in which to place a document and no witnesses are called on.[15] The principal difference between the descriptions in Genesis 1–2 and the covenants

---

12. This will be addressed in the "Challenges and Responses" section.
13. Gonzales, "Covenantal Context of the Fall," 5 (emphasis original). See also Dumbrell, *Covenant and Creation*, 15–19; Gentry and Wellum, *Kingdom through Covenant*, 187–95.
14. For an approach that discusses Gen. 1 and Gen. 2 separately with respect to covenant, see Block, *Covenant*, chap. 1 ("The Cosmic Covenant") and chap. 2 ("The Adamic Covenant"). However, Block also recognizes unity across the individual biblical covenants.
15. Layer 5 ("Temple") makes the argument that all of Eden was a temple.

with Noah, Abraham, or at Mount Sinai is the absence of an animal sacrifice.[16] In the creation story, the absence may simply reflect the fact that where there is no sin, there is no need or place for sacrifice.

The strongest parallels are found with the Noahic covenant. Both Adam and Noah were promised food to eat, with specified consumptive prohibitions (fruit of a particular tree for Adam, blood for Noah), and both were given commands to have dominion over the earth and to multiply and fill it. Inclusion of the earth in the Noahic covenant is also found in the creation covenant, implied in the language of Genesis 1 and later made explicit by a prophetic encouragement to Israel. In order to emphasize the certainty of God's covenant with David, Jeremiah called on the covenant God made with the creation itself, saying, "Thus says Yahweh, 'If you can break my covenant with the day and my covenant with the night, so that day and night will not come at their appointed time, then also my covenant with David my servant may be broken'" (Jer. 33:20–21). In Genesis 1, the repeated blessings, provisions, and commands directed to the nonhuman creation are covenantal expressions. The luminaries of the sky are given roles of ruling over day and night (v. 17). Fish and birds receive blessings and are told to fill the earth (v. 22). Birds and beasts are provided with food (v. 30).

Royal land grant

We find still more covenant language in the placement of Adam in the garden, in this case as a *royal land grant*.[17] All the earth belonged to the suzerain, Yahweh, but a particular domain, Eden, was gifted to Adam (and subsequently to Eve). A measure of autonomy was granted to Adam and Eve, who served as steward-rulers and caretakers. The authority granted is reflected in Adam's naming of the animals. In the ANE, naming was the purview of kings. We find this illustrated in Scripture during the exile when Nebuchadnezzar assigned Babylonian names to Daniel and his three Hebrew compatriots. On a smaller scale, we see this in practice even today, with parents serving in the sovereign role of giving names to their children. In Eden, Yahweh did not simply tell Adam what to call each type of animal, but brought them to Adam to name.

---

16. Animals were killed to make clothing for Adam and Eve after they sinned (Gen. 3:21), though not concurrent with the establishment of a covenant.
17. Richter, *Epic of Eden*, 103–4.

Authority was not independent of the suzerain. As stewards, Adam and Eve were to serve as representatives of the ultimate ruler, Yahweh. This expectation is wrapped into the description of being made, not as gods or demigods, but *in the image of God* (Gen. 1:26–27). This was a familiar phrase in the ANE, commonly applied to idols or kings as representatives of the gods on earth.[18] Such representation did not permit unbridled license to pillage the earth, but a responsibility to work and care for it. A wise ruler tended the land with posterity in mind, acting as caretaker and gardener of the creation. Some ANE manuscripts even refer to kings as divine gardeners.[19] When Adam and Eve broke the suzerain-vassal covenant, it served to break the land-grant covenant as well. Access to and authority over Eden was revoked. Adam and Eve were sent out of the garden, and deadly cherubim were stationed to prevent reentry.

Recognition of land-grant language in the creation story emphasizes the important role land plays in communicating God's message to his people. Yahweh's covenants with Abraham and the patriarchs, with Moses and the nation of Israel, and with David and his progeny were always linked with land—the *promised land* (e.g., Gen. 17:1–8; Exod. 6:4; 1 Chron. 16:14–18). The consequences for breaking the covenant were not just removal of blessings and protections but also of being cast out of the land—*exile.*

The significance of exile (loss of land grant)

We miss the weightiness of exile when we think of it only in terms of loss of property or national sovereignty. In the Old Testament, exile carried the additional connotation of being cut off from the presence of God—an act equated with death.[20] In preparing his people to enter the land of Canaan, Yahweh warned that if they persisted in disobedience, they would be dispersed into the surrounding nations and would eventually be destroyed and perish (Deut. 4:26; 6:15; 11:17; 28:20, 63). We see the same essence in the warning given to Adam when he is told, concerning the tree of the knowledge of good and evil, "in the day that you eat of it you shall surely die" (Gen. 2:17). Notably, Israel and Adam did disobey, yet Israel was not completely destroyed and Adam did not physically die in the day he ate the fruit. What did happen to both was

---

18. Middleton, *Liberating Image*, 93–146.
19. Dumbrell, *Covenant and Creation*, 38; LeFebvre, "Adam Reigns in Eden," 30–32; Widengren, *King and the Tree of Life*, 5–41; Wyatt, "Royal Garden," 24; Wyatt, "When Adam Delved," 118.
20. Turner, "Deuteronomy's Theology of Exile."

exile. Being cast out meant being sent away from God's presence—a representation of spiritual as well as physical death.

The link between land and God's presence may seem strange: God's position and rule is not limited by geography. Psalm 139:7–12 assures us that there is nowhere in heaven or on earth that one can go to hide from God's spirit, and all the earth belongs to him (Exod. 19:5; Ps. 47:2–7). God is not a territorial deity, yet he chose to manifest himself to his covenant people in ways that related to their earthly experience. The gift of land—in the sense of the royal land grant—came with assurances that the great Suzerain would come to the aid of the vassal when threatened. It was a promise of provision and protection—of life. Even more wondrous, this Suzerain had such love for his vassal that he chose to live among them, not only as Lord but also as father and husband (Deut. 32:6; Isa. 54:5). He *walked* in the garden in Eden (Gen. 3:8); he promised Israel he would make his *dwelling* in the land and walk among them (Lev. 26:11–12); and he *filled* the new temple in Jerusalem with his glory (2 Chron. 7:1).[21]

Exile was the undoing of all the above. Retraction of the land grant was loss of provision and protection—exposing the disobedient vassal to the malignant whims of surrounding forces. It was the separation of an unfaithful wife from the emotional and material support of a loving husband. It was the assurance of death.

Though Adam and Israel knew both disobedience and exile, it was not the end of their stories. In the midst of exile, God interceded to provide, touch hearts, and give new life to his covenants. Though he cast them from the garden, God did not abandon his people, granting Eve children (Gen. 4:1–2, 25), placing a mark on Cain to protect him (4:15), and reestablishing his covenant through Noah (6:18; 8:20–9:17). Many generations later, during Israel's exile following the Babylonian conquest, God looked after his people through servants such as Daniel and Esther, until he renewed the land grant through the work of Ezra, Nehemiah, and others. It is no accident that we see the theme of a land grant revisited in Revelation 21, where the final restoration is represented with the imagery of land—the new Jerusalem—established from heaven on the earth.

GOD'S COVENANT WITH NATURE
We drew attention to Jeremiah 33 earlier, which contains a messianic address to Israel challenging their doubts about God's ability to fulfill his promise that

---

21. "The ultimate indicative is not the land which Yahweh gives, but the relationship which that land affords." Millar, *Now Choose Life*, 56.

David would always have a son on the throne. In this context, God twice refers to his covenant with day and with night. The first was quoted above (vv. 20–21). A few verses later we read, "Thus says Yahweh, 'If I have not established my covenant with day and night and the fixed order of heaven and earth, then I will reject the offspring of Jacob and David my servant and will not choose one of his offspring to rule over the offspring of Abraham, Isaac, and Jacob'" (vv. 25–26).

God's covenant promise to David for a ruling lineage was absolute. Though the privilege of sitting on the throne by any individual was conditional (Jer. 22), the throne of David was established forever, independent of the actions of David's descendants (2 Sam. 7:16). To emphasize the certainty of this promise, God called on another, equally unbreakable covenant: a covenant established with all of creation—a covenant that established a "fixed order of heaven and earth." Implicit in this passage is a declaration that the structure and order imprinted on the cosmos at its inception has never been interrupted. We see this affirmed in what later Scriptures proclaim about the earth and cosmos.

> The heavens declare the glory of God,
>> and the sky above proclaims his handiwork.
> Day to day pours out speech,
>> and night to night reveals knowledge.
>> (Ps. 19:1)

Note that the psalmist does not say that the heavens declare the corruption of sin or the workmanship of Satan. They declare the glory of God. They proclaim the handiwork of the Creator. The apostle Paul makes an even more explicit statement in Romans 1:20: "For [God's] invisible attributes, namely, his eternal power and divine nature, have been clearly perceived, ever *since the creation of the world*, in the things that have been made." Paul does not say that God's character *used to be* evident in nature before it was corrupted. Nature has been manifesting God's character from the time of creation to this very day. God's creation covenant with nature is still in effect.

We affirm this biblical understanding when we stand in awe of a stunning landscape, or marvel at the beauty of one of God's creatures. We see it manifest in the incredible fine-tuning of the universe, with myriad physical constants precisely configured to allow planets to form, stars to shine, and life to exist.[22] And we appreciate its truth when we realize that the material world

---

22. Ross, *Fingerprint of God*, 119–38; Lewis and Barnes, *Fortunate Universe*.

is fashioned with apparent intentionality, even the placement of our moon and our position in our galaxy to allow us to explore stars and distant galaxies that we will never physically visit.[23]

All this may understandably raise some misgivings. Wasn't the once-good creation corrupted by sin? The curse following the disobedience of Adam and Eve included a pronouncement against the earth:

> Cursed is the *ground* because of you;[24]
>   in pain you shall eat of it all the days of your life;
> thorns and thistles it shall bring forth for you.
> (Gen. 3:17–18)

This seems to be a statement that the functioning of nature changed when humans introduced sin into the world, consistent with our experience with things that *don't* seem so wondrous: earthquakes, storms, pests, and diseases. Romans 8:20–21 is commonly cited as evidence of this twisting: "the creation was subjected to futility" and groans as in childbirth for the day when it will be "set free from its bondage to corruption."

It is a surprise to many modern Christians to learn that this understanding is a theological latecomer. Jon Garvey devotes a chapter of his book *God's Good Earth* to quotes from Jewish and Christian theologians over the last two thousand years, pointing out that a common or entrenched sense of nature corrupted by human sin did not develop until the Renaissance, *fourteen centuries* after Christ. Garvey's assessment is that the belief came about, ironically, through the cultural influence of humanism and the Enlightenment, with a shift toward placing greater value on scientific reasoning.[25]

It is worth pausing here to state that these observations are not intended as an argument against a literal reading of Genesis. The question of what physically happened to nature when the ground was cursed is equally germane within a literal six-day framework. To Garvey's point, theologians holding a literal understanding in past centuries did not ascribe to the same understanding of a fallen creation as is common today.

Returning to the question at hand, how does one reconcile the seemingly conflicting verses in Genesis, Psalms, and Romans? We'll address the curse

---

23. Guillermo and Richards, *Privileged Planet*.
24. The Hebrew word for ground is *adamah*, the same root word as Adam.
25. Garvey, *God's God Earth*, 71–90.

of Genesis 3 first before revisiting Romans. C. John Collins offers valuable insights here, drawing attention to additional Scriptures that shed light on the apparent conundrum.[26] As the people of Israel wandered in the wilderness, God promised blessings for obedience and curses for disobedience, establishing the conditions of the Mosaic covenant. The consequences of disobedience can be found in Deuteronomy 28, where God says, "Cursed shall be your basket and your kneading bowl. Cursed shall be the fruit of your womb and the fruit of your ground, the increase of your herds and the young of your flock" (vv. 17–18). These words include curses directed at animals and material objects: sheep, goats, crops, bowls, and baskets.

We know that Israel did disobey and did experience these curses, yet few would argue that sheep started giving birth to lambs with fangs, that wheat began growing with thorns, or that bowls and baskets miraculously morphed into deformed shapes. Sheep continued to give birth to fangless lambs, wheat continued to grow without thorns, and bowls and baskets retained their precurse functional shapes. Nature did not change. Rather, people's *experience with nature* was transformed from something positive to something negative. Lions eating wild goats in the wilderness posed no threat to Israel. Lions eating their flocks meant loss of wool and meat. Tares growing in a meadow caused no harm. Tares infesting a wheat field meant diminished baskets and bowls at the harvest.

The wording of Deuteronomy 28, as in Genesis 3, appears at first to say that the objects themselves are cursed, but knowing how these curses were fulfilled in Israel's history informs us that it is not the physical objects that became twisted, but the way in which Israel began to interact with them. Nature did not break God's covenant; humans did. As a result, humanity's experience with nature changed. Where nature does feel the direct consequence of sin is from the impact of fallen humans. This flows naturally back to Romans 8. Sin in humans produces behaviors that negatively affect the earth.[27] The creation is degraded when we fail to act as good stewards, extracting resources without restoration, discharging pollutants beyond nature's capacity to filter them, or engaging in inhumane treatment of fellow creatures.

Creation groans from the want of humans to fulfill their godly calling and where it suffers from human sin, yet it does not cease to revel in the natural goodness imparted to it by God. If this seems like a logical contradiction,

---

26. Collins, *Reading Genesis Well*, 235–38.
27. Dumbrell, *Covenant and Creation*, 47–58; Richter, *Epic of Eden*, 114–15; Collins, *Reading Genesis Well*, 235–38.

consider believers who at once bemoan their own imperfection (Ps. 51) while also rejoicing that they are "fearfully and wonderfully made" (Ps. 139:14). In this light, contemplate Psalm 104, described by most Old Testament scholars as a psalm of creation. It is bursting with a sense of joy from the creation itself, as springs gush forth to give drink to every beast (vv. 10–11), birds trill and nest among the trees (vv. 12, 17), plants spring up for food and for wine to gladden the heart (vv. 14–15), and mountains rise for goats and badgers (v. 18). Remarkably, it is in this same context that the earth shakes and the mountains smoke at God's touch (v. 32), Leviathan, the mysterious monster of the sea *plays* in the seas (vv. 25–26), and young lions, receiving their prey from the hand of God, are satisfied with *good* (vv. 21, 28)—the same Hebrew word for good (*tob*) used in Genesis 1.[28] The psalm comes to a close rejoicing in God *and* acknowledging sin, longing for sinners to be no more (vv. 34–35).

This is puzzling to modern ears. How can a creation psalm, unconstrained in its joy of God's goodness and provision, include earthquakes, volcanic eruptions, and animals eating other animals? How could God feed one animal to another and call it good?[29] Such reactions reflect an unfortunate tendency to conflate our own understanding with God's. If *we* think that a tiger eating a fawn is bad, then *God* must think so too. And if *we* think volcanic eruptions are bad, *God* must concur. Yet God has made it abundantly clear that his ways are *not* our ways, nor are our thoughts his (Isa. 55:8–9). If God declares that a lion eating prey is good, who am I to insist that it is not?[30]

In the same vein, it is common to hear that things like volcanic eruptions, tornados, and floods must be the result of sin—nature twisted by human disobedience. Yet each is considered bad only in the context of human interaction with them. Volcanic eruptions blanket the landscape with fresh, nutrient-rich minerals that support new life, and seasonal floods introduce fresh nutrients and create flat land for forests and crops. These are *good* things. What is broken is humans' unprotected interaction with nature. Eruptions and floods are only problems when our intersection with them creates hardship. Nature continues to declare the character and glory of its Creator.[31]

---

28. Some English translations expand the expression at the end of Ps. 104:28 to read as satisfied "with good *things*" (e.g., ESV, NIV), but the more literal translation is satisfied or filled "with good" (e.g., NASB, KJV).

29. The question of carnivory is discussed in more detail in Objection 3.

30. Voltaire is attributed with the quip, "In the beginning, God created man in his own image, and we have been trying to return the favor ever since."

31. A more in-depth discussion of the goodness of God's creation and the implications of calling evil what God has declared good can be found in Davidson, *Friend of Science,*

We'll finish this section cycling back to the exile of Adam and Eve from the garden. If nature was not corrupted by sin, what was so bad about being tossed out? What were the physical implications of living outside the garden? To address this question, recall that annulment of a land grant meant loss of the suzerain's provision and protection. Prior to sin, Adam and Eve were providentially shielded from negative interactions with the normal functions of nature. After sin, those protections were at least partially lifted.[32]

By way of analogy, consider the experience of going to a tiger exhibit at a zoo or to a giant aquarium with sharks swimming about. Our normal reaction is *not* revulsion at the corruption on display, but a sense of awe and wonder. There is an appreciation of the power and artistry found in nature, without fear of a negative encounter. The reason for our lack of fear is simple enough; there is a wall of high-strength glass between human and predator. Removal of the barrier changes nothing about nature—but our experience is dramatically altered.

In the garden, humans knew only the awe and wonder, with God's providence shielding them from negative encounters. In exile, those protections were suddenly in question.[33]

THE CARE AND STUDY OF NATURE

The realization that God's covenant with creation is still in effect can have a transformative effect on our perception of the world in which we live. Modern Christians, particularly in the West, have been basted in the tainted theological marinade of a material world hopelessly infused with the corruption of sin. The church has stumbled into hearty agreement with materialists who have preached a pitiless universe, red in tooth and claw, with organisms selfishly competing for survival at the expense and oppression of all who do not share the same genes. The power and elegance of nature is not to be admired, but distained for its waste and carnage. In centuries past, Christians aspired to excel in the study of nature. Now the church steers far too many gifted young people away from the study of nature (science), as if its gates are tended by the devil's minions. Stewardship of the earthly garden has been largely left to others.

Friend of Faith, 253–55; Garvey, *God's Good Earth,* 58–59.

32. Other provisions lost included access to the tree of life, and, critically, God's dwelling presence.

33. There are similar parallels in the exile experienced by a wife sent away for breaking the marriage covenant (Isa. 50:1; Jer. 3:8). The world into which a divorced woman was sent did not change, but the experience with the world was dramatically altered, exposing her to much greater risks.

Genesis 1–2 calls us to a very different view, reiterated and reinforced in Psalm 104, Jeremiah 33, Romans 1, and Job 38–39.[34] Nature rejoices and returns praise to her covenant-Creator. Christians should be eager to enter the sciences, not simply to challenge perceived paradigms, but to share in God's delight in his material works and to learn how to redeem our image-bearing role of stewards and caretakers of creation.

CHALLENGES AND RESPONSES

Objection 1: *The word for covenant is not used.*

Before directly addressing this objection, we will first remind readers that appreciation of the multi-layered character of the creation story is not an all or nothing proposition. One need not ascribe to all seven of our proposed layers, or to all elements of a defense for an individual layer. In this case, if there is reluctance to accepting a formal covenant with Adam or the creation, you may nonetheless appreciate the rich use of covenantal language and its implications moving through history.

The principal objection to a covenant understanding of the creation story is that the word for covenant, *berit*, is not used in Genesis 1–2. There are other examples in Scripture, however, where a covenant was clearly established without using *berit*. The Davidic covenant, in which God promised David his kingly line would never end, was pronounced without using *berit* (2 Sam. 7). It is not until later in Scripture that we find a prophet referring back to the promise as a covenant (2 Chron. 13:5; Jer. 33:21).[35]

A similar pattern may be argued for a covenant at creation, with a prophet later referring back to the events as a *berit*. In Hosea 6, God chastises the people of Israel for their rebellion, saying in verse 7, "Like Adam they transgressed the covenant." This appears to be a clear reference to a covenant at creation, broken by Adam. Not all agree on this point, however, with some theologians arguing that the Hebrew could also be translated as "at Adam" (NJB, NRSV, NIV), referring to a town upstream from where Israel crossed the Jordan into Canaan

---

34. Try reading Job 38–39 out loud and asking whether God is pleased with his natural creation or dejected at its corruption.

35. Several points made within this layer could be added to this response, including the rich use of covenantal language in the creation account, the repeated cultural mandates given at creation (Gen. 1:28–30) and after the flood (Gen. 9:1–3), and the grammatical construction where *berit* is first used (Gen. 6:18) that can be understood as confirming a previous covenant rather than establishing something new.

(Josh. 3:16), or as a more general "like men" (JPS, KJV).[36] The reasoning behind the disagreement is worth an extra paragraph of discussion.

The justification for an alternate translation of Hosea 6:7 is often the perceived absence of a covenant with Adam in Genesis. If there was no covenant, then it would not make sense for Hosea to make a covenantal reference to Adam. Yet there is no scriptural reference to a covenant established at the town of Adam either, which was not even at the location of the river crossing but where water heaped up "very far away" (Josh. 3:16). As for the second alternative, a statement that Israel broke the covenant "like men" is a weak rebuke, effectively saying Israel just did what people are prone to do. How else were the Israelites to break a covenant other than like other people? The context of Hosea suggests a much stronger reprimand. Israel broke the covenant, just as bad as the first sin—the sin of their father Adam.[37]

Objection 2: Biblical covenants always . . .

Many objections to a creation covenant are based on an aspect of a biblical covenant that is deemed essential and missing from Genesis 1–2. At one level, we would argue that these assessments work in the wrong direction, defining covenants with a too-small subset of the biblical data before applying the subsequent metric to the creation story. Rather, the strong parallel in language found in the creation story with the Noahic covenant, Jeremiah's declaration of a covenant established with the creation (day and night and the fixed order of heaven and earth), and Hosea's apparent reference to a covenant broken by Adam, all argue that Genesis 1–2 should be factored into what defines a covenant.[38]

Nevertheless, it is still important to consider some of the specific claims made of missing elements that are argued to disqualify creation as a covenantal event. We will consider claims that covenants are always redemptive, always solve a problem of uncertainty, or always include the taking of oaths. Individuals mentioned below are singled out only as examples of those holding the respective views.

---

36. Murray, "Adamic Administration," 49; Hoekema, *Created in God's Image*, 121; Andersen and Freedman, *Hosea*, 438–39.
37. Habig, "Hosea 6:7 Revisited"; Collins, *Adam and Eve in the Old Testament*; Vasholz, note on Hosea 6:7 in *ESV Study Bible*, 1631.
38. As an analogy from nature, if you were only permitted to consider the characteristics of North American creatures to define a mammal, the Australian platypus and spiny anteater might not be recognized as genuine mammals. But when the larger data set is considered to determine what defines a mammal, including apparent outliers, the platypus and spiny anteater are readily recognized as mammals.

Covenants are always redemptive.

According to John Murray, a biblical covenant applied to God's interaction with humans is always "in reference to a provision that is redemptive or closely related to redemptive design."[39] Murray is not suggesting that *all* covenants are redemptive, but that when God initiates with humans, they by design redeem people from their sin-derived predicament. The first observation we would make is that the covenants at creation and after the flood were not limited to humans. The covenantal language includes various aspects of the natural creation—days, seasons, and animals. Second, a redemptive requirement artificially separates God-human covenants from all other biblical covenants that also illustrate relationships within the kingdom of God. Nonredemptive covenants are frequent in Scripture between individuals and nations.[40] Third, one could assert that God's creation covenant was, in fact, redemptive. There was no moral disorder (no sin) to redeem, but there was natural disorder (*tohu wabohu*; Gen. 1:2) that God wished to redeem for humanity.

Covenants always address uncertainty.

John Stek has argued that biblical covenants were "*ad hoc* emergency measures" that functioned to guarantee, in situations fraught with uncertainties, that specified actions would be carried out. Since there were no "situations fraught with uncertainties" before the fall, then God's relationship with Adam should not be viewed in terms of covenant.[41] We do not take issue here with covenants addressing some uncertainty, but rather disagree that uncertainty was somehow absent in Eden. Adam and Eve's continued obedience was quite uncertain (at least from a human perspective), starting from the moment they were instructed not to eat from one particular tree.

Covenants always includes oaths.

Paul Williamson identifies divine sanctions and oath-taking to be common to all God-human covenants, with the taking of solemn oaths as a critical defining element. Since the creation account contains no explicit reference to oath-taking, Williamson argues it is not properly conceived as a covenant.[42]

---

39. Murray, "Adamic Administration," 49.
40. Examples of nonredemptive covenants may be found between David and Jonathan (1 Sam. 18:3; 23:18); husband and wife (Mal. 2:14); Isaac and Abimelech (Gen. 26); Israel and Tyre (1 Kings 5:12).
41. Stek, "Covenant Overload in Reformed Theology," 39.
42. Williamson, *Sealed with an Oath*, 39, 43, 50.

Our response here has similarities to the one above, where we do not challenge the conceptual link between oath and covenant, but disagree that it is absent from the creation account. An oath is essentially an elevated promise, one typically associated with a declaration that binds the oath-taker to be faithful to the promise. While covenants by their nature include such promises, they are not always itemized or made explicit in the biblical text. As an example, the covenant made between David and Jonathan in 1 Samuel 18:3 and reiterated in 23:18 includes no stated promise or oath. The promise is implicit and obvious from the context of the story—as far as it is in the power of each man, neither will allow harm to come the other. The creation story likewise contains statements of implicit promise. When God looked on his creation and declared it to be good, it was not just a comment on its fleeting beauty. It was a promise of durability, of assurance that the natural order set in place was God ordained and God blessed. It was not fragile, perched on the knife-edge of a single human decision. If one wonders if this assumes too much, Jeremiah 33:19–26 serves as a reminder that the order found in nature is not an accident or twisted remnant of antiquity, but is the manifestation of God's covenant promise—his "covenant with day and with night and the fixed order of heaven and earth."

Objection 3: How can animal death be reconciled with an unbroken covenant with nature?

This objection is unique in that it does not necessarily challenge the concept of a covenant at creation, but questions whether a covenant with nature remains unbroken. We will thus note that it is possible, in principle, to concur with our arguments for a covenantal view of Genesis 1–3 without necessarily agreeing that the covenant God made with nature remains in place. In other words, the entire layer should not be tossed out over disagreement on this point. At the same time, the answer to this question has significant ramifications for how we view God's creation today.

Fully addressing the question requires delving into closely related subjects such as the relationship between animal death and sin, the nature of present-day carnivores at the time of creation, and what happened to these creatures following sin. There is considerable rancor within the church on these subjects, leaving us with some uncertainty on the best way to handle the objection in terms of the overarching purpose of this book. We have no wish to ignore relevant and important questions, yet we also do not wish to let a side debate distract readers from the overall beauty of the covenant layer. With this in mind, we have elected to offer a very brief, two-part response below, with additional observations and suggestions for further reading moved to appendix 1.

Nature according to Scripture

As discussed earlier in this layer, church history and the weight of Scripture do not support a natural world that manifests or proclaims the corruption of sin. Extended passages (e.g., Jer. 33; Job 38–40; Pss. 8; 19; 104) are unfettered in expressions of God's pleasure in his present creation. Carnivores are not spoken of as unfortunate relics of a broken world, but creatures in whom God delights—feeding the lions their prey and enjoying the sport of Leviathan in the seas. The heavens do not declare the ravages of sin, but the glory of God. The present order for heaven and earth is not a shattered remnant of a once good creation, but lies secure in the promise of the God who established it (Jer. 33:25–26). And Romans 1:20 tells us with no uncertainty that God's character is manifest in the creation today just as it was at the beginning. Such recognition should make us wary of allowing human sentiments, such as reaction to a tiger eating a fawn, to overshadow an otherwise clear biblical message.[43]

Nature according to nature

A popular understanding of the fall holds that sin reversed the work of creation. All nature now works backward toward a return to the *tohu wabohu* (formless and void; Gen. 1:2) of the creation before day 1—an undoing of the order and purpose for which the earth was once endowed. One problem with this view is that nature itself does not support it. We don't need to call on science per se to explore this. A common understanding of how nature works will suffice.

When observing nature at any level, from the vastness of a galaxy to the inner workings of a living cell, there is not a hodgepodge of dysfunctional interactions steadily eroding the ability of nature to function. Instead, we find great artistry and order. We observe an internal consistency that makes science and technology possible, giving rise to cures for diseases, computers that fit in our pockets, and rockets that can deliver a rover to a distant planet. When we use such knowledge for evil purposes, it is not nature exhibiting its corruption, but the fallenness of *human* nature. Nature does exactly what Romans 1:20 says it does—it reflects the character of its Author.

---

43. Examples of well known and respected church fathers who argued against nature being corrupted by sin include Augustine (especially in *The City of God, book 12*, chap. 4) and Thomas Aquinas (*Summa Theologica*, Part 1, question 96, article 1, Reply to Objection 2).

DISCUSSION QUESTIONS

1. What is your reaction to discovery that covenants in the Bible bear remarkable similarities to ANE treaties?

2. How are ANE suzerain-vassal and land-grant treaties reflected in biblical covenants between God and his people? Are these also found in Eden?

3. What reasons do the authors give for supporting a covenant understanding even though the word for covenant (*berit*) is not used in the story?

4. What is your reaction to the claim that nature was not twisted by sin? What defense do the authors provide? What did it mean to be kicked out of the garden if nature was not corrupted?

5. How is our attitude about nature (appreciation, study, stewardship) influenced by thinking of it as corrupted by sin or as still reflecting the glory of God?

LAYER 5

Temple

הֵיכָל

(*hekhal*, "temple")

He built his sanctuary like the high heavens,
like the earth, which he has founded forever.
(Ps. 78:69)

A t first glance, viewing creation as a temple may seem counterintuitive. A temple is a building, made by human hands. Temples serve as places for the faithful to gather to worship or to offer prayers, gifts, and sacrifices. Across many religions, temples represent houses in which the presence of spirits or the gods are manifest. If one wishes to encounter a particular god, the first choice of destination is the temple to attract the attention of the resident deity.

The temple for Israel's God had a similar purpose and function. It was a house in which God said he would make his presence dwell among his people. That presence was sometimes literal, with the glory of God filling the tabernacle (a mobile temple) or the temple in Jerusalem, but it was also understood that the omnipresent God cannot be contained in one place or one building (1 Kings 8:27; Jer. 23:24; Ps. 139:8). Even descriptions of God's "real" temple or dwelling in the heavens were understood to ultimately be insufficient, for "heaven and the highest heaven cannot contain you" (1 Kings 8:27).

How does any of this relate to the creation? Asked another way, what warrant do we have for even looking for a link between the temple and creation? One clue is found in connecting the beginning with the end. While theologians differ in the degree to which heaven is considered a restoration of Eden, all recognize the existence of theological parallels. Looking forward to the last days, the prophetic visions of Ezekiel, Haggai, and John each make rich use of temple imagery to describe the expansion of God's kingdom and his presence into all the earth (Ezek. 40–48; Hag. 2; Rev. 21–22).

A second clue comes from wording within the creation story that likely evoked a strong temple connection in the minds of the original audience. On day 7, God *rested* (Gen. 2:1–3). Western readers think of rest as simply ceasing from labor or reflecting on one's work, but rest in the biblical sense carries the additional meaning of an abiding presence. Divine rest is linked elsewhere in Scripture to Yahweh's temple presence (2 Sam. 7:6; 1 Chron. 28:2; Isa. 11:2–10). Studies of ancient Near Eastern (ANE) texts have affirmed an apparently universal cultural conception of a temple as a house of rest for a god. John Walton comments on what "everyone knew in the ancient world. . . . Deity rests in a temple, and only in a temple."[1]

These observations serve as a sufficient prompt to consider a temple-creation theme, but we have much work to do to fully explain the perspective. In this layer, the case will be made for the temple as a microcosm of the whole of creation, not with cryptic alignments in phrases or descriptions, but as a divine illustration of God's intention and interaction with the world. In a nutshell, it describes God's plan to bridge the gap between heaven and earth, establishing a temple presence among his image-bearers who were given a priestly task of expanding that presence from Eden to the whole earth (Gen. 1:28). Sin delayed but did not overturn the original objective. God's desire to walk among his people and expand his kingdom continued through his presence in the tabernacle in the wilderness (Exod. 40:34–35) and later temple in Jerusalem (1 Kings 8:11). It was powerfully manifest in the incarnation, with Jesus declaring himself to be the temple of God (John 2:19). The mission continues today with the outpouring of God's Spirit on the church (Eph. 2:18–22) and within individual believers, each serving as a temple of the Holy Spirit (1 Cor. 6:19). And a final day will come when the temple of God will descend to encompass all of heaven and earth (Rev. 21). Of that day we are told, "Behold, the dwelling place [*skene*, "tent, tabernacle"] of God is with man. He will dwell with them, and they will be his people, and God himself will be with them as their God." In that city, "its temple is the Lord God the Almighty and the Lamb" (Rev. 21:3, 22).

Our first stop in the development of a temple layer will take a deeper look at how the nations contemporary with Israel thought of temples and connections with creation, and how those understandings intersect with biblical understanding. From there we will look internally in the Bible at the many ways Scripture links temple language with Eden and the creation. Finally, we will see how all the pieces weave an unbroken thread from creation to the final restoration.

---

1. Walton, *Lost World of Genesis One*, 72.

TEMPLES IN THE ANCIENT NEAR EAST

As we investigate views of the ANE, we will remind readers that our intention is not to suggest that Israel borrowed and adapted stories from its neighbors. The objective is simply to see through the eyes of the original audience. Israel did not rise up in a cultural vacuum. They were acquainted with the stories and practices of their neighbors, sometimes far *too* familiar. All that Israel heard from Moses and the prophets was naturally understood against the backdrop of the ANE worldview—affirming what was true and challenging what was false. It is thus reasonable to expect that some insights into the meaning of Scripture could come from a greater awareness of ANE beliefs.[2]

Temples and cosmology

In the ANE mindset, temples were not invented by humans—the first temples were made by the gods themselves. Many of the ANE origin stories associate the first appearance of land or cities with the establishment of temples as earthly abodes for the gods (see appendix 2 for excerpts).

- In the Babylonian Enuma Elish, the god Marduk establishes his temple and the city of Babylon immediately after his creation of the heavenly bodies, night and day, weather, and agriculture. Marduk later declares his temple shall represent his kingship, a house of festivals, an "abode of my pleasure," and a stopping (resting) place for the gods on earth.[3]
- An Akkadian prayer dedicating the foundation brick of a temple tells of the gods (Anu, Enlil, and Ea) who, when they had the idea of heaven and earth, "found a wise means of providing support of the gods: they prepared, in the land, a pleasant dwelling, and the gods were installed in this dwelling: Their principal temple."[4]
- A Sumerian hymn speaks of the house (temple) of the Anuna gods, saying ". . . reposeful dwelling of the great gods! House, which was planned together with the plans of heaven and earth . . . which underpins the Land and supports the shrines!"[5]

---

2. Overviews of the relevant ANE texts may be found in Beale, *Temple and the Church's Mission*, esp. 50–59, 87–92; Walton, *Genesis 1 as Ancient Cosmology*, 17–22; Walton, "Reading Genesis 1 as Ancient Cosmology."
3. Foster, *Before the Muses*, 488. See also Walton, *Lost World of Genesis One*, 79.
4. Clifford, *Creation Accounts in the Ancient Near East*, 61.
5. Temple Hymn of Keš 4.80.2, D.58A–F, Electronic Text Corpus of Sumerian Literature, https://etcsl.orinst.ox.ac.uk/cgi-bin/etcsl.cgi?text=t.4.80.2#, quoted in Walton, *Lost World*

- An Egyptian text tells of the chief god, Ptah, coming to rest after giving birth to the gods and founding their territories and their cultic shrines.[6]

These texts tell us is that there was a widespread ANE understanding that linked temples with creation and divine rest. We will hold additional comment on parallels and differences with biblical understanding until fleshing out the next section.

The cosmic mountain

There is a natural tendency, even today with our knowledge of living on a sphere, to think of God's dwelling as being "up." For the ancients, with awareness only of the earth below and the heavens above, this sentiment was intuitively obvious. Mortals walked on the land and went down into the earth at death. The heavens were above and reserved for the gods.

In this respect, it made sense to think of a mountain or high point as a place where the heavens and earth could meet.[7] While any high mountain might serve the purpose, there was a common sense that a god would establish a primary temple residence at one location, giving rise to the concept of the *cosmic mountain*.[8] Vertically, the mountain was the intersection of heaven and earth. Horizontally, the mountain was the center of the world. A temple built on the slopes of such a mountain was often surrounded by lush gardens watered by springs of life-giving waters. The temple gardens carried an aura of holiness in which all was perfect, ideal, and unblemished—immune from the ravages of time.

Biblical and ANE parallels

We saw in Layer 3 ("Polemic") that there are many aspects of ANE belief that are corrected by the Genesis account. In contrast here, the Bible embraces and even expands on ANE imagery of the cosmic mountain, including links between temple and creation. Moses first encountered Yahweh at Horeb, "the

---

of Genesis One, 74–75. Another part of the text (lines 13–16) describes the temple as "embracing the heavens" and "lifting its 'head among the mountains.'"

6. From the Egyptian cosmology "Memphite Theology" (Hallo and Younger, *Context of Scripture*, 1:15).

7. This is also true of the ancient ziggurat: a massive, stepped, and multileveled tower (sometimes surmounted by a temple) used for religious purposes. The ziggurat is likely behind the biblical story of the tower of Babel (Gen. 11).

8. This section and following draws from Levenson, *Sinai and Zion*, 111–37; Clifford, *Cosmic Mountain*; Clifford, "Temple and the Holy Mountain," 85–98. See also Clements, "Sacred Mountains, Temples, and the Presence of God."

mountain of God," where he stood on "holy ground" (Exod. 3:1–5). When leaving Egypt, the Hebrews were not just told to go into the desert to pray or to make haste to the promised land. Rather, they were directed to Mount Sinai (another name for Horeb). While God manifested his power and presence on the journey, it was on the mountain that Moses met with Yahweh to receive the law. On that holy ground, Moses was divinely sustained without food or water for forty days and forty nights (Exod. 34:28).

Moses received instruction on the mountain for the design of the tabernacle (*mishkan*), which literally means "dwelling place."[9] God described it as a sanctuary or holy place (*miqdash*)—a mobile temple, so that he might dwell in their midst (Exod. 25:9, 40). God's continued presence with Israel in the circuitous journey to Palestine highlights a significant difference between Yahweh and the ANE gods, as the presence of Yahweh is not dictated by geography. His dwelling is where he chooses.[10] Once settled in the promised land, the permanent temple was placed in Jerusalem on Mount Zion. Psalm 68 speaks of the transfer of God's abode from Sinai (vv. 7–8) to Zion, "the mount that God desired for his abode, yes, where Yahweh will dwell forever. . . . Sinai is now in the sanctuary" (vv. 16–17). Zion became "my holy mountain" (Isa. 66:20; Obad. 16; Ps. 2:6) and "the mountain of Yahweh of hosts, the holy mountain" (Zech. 8:3). The Psalms intended for recitation as the faithful journeyed to Jerusalem are called "Songs of Ascent"—going *up* to Zion (Pss. 120–134). Zion and its temple, the representational dwelling of Yahweh, were together considered the center of the world (e.g., Ezek. 5:5; 38:12; 48:1–35).

Though he is unfettered by a particular landscape, God made it clear that not just any high mountain would serve the purpose of connecting heaven and earth. Building altars or temples on the "high places" was forbidden. There was only one high place and one temple where God's presence was represented. Failure to abide by this command was a generational stumbling block for Israel.[11]

---

9. The Hebrew word for "tabernacle" is *mishkan* (from *shakan*, "to dwell"; cf. Greek *skenoo*, "dwell, spread a tent," and *skene*, "tent, tabernacle"). For helpful overviews of the tabernacle, see Alexander, *From Paradise to the Promised Land*, 192–203; and Averbeck, "Tabernacle."

10. Another significant difference between Yahweh and all others is how the presence of deity is manifest. In ANE temples (and many modern ones), the presence of a god is manifest through its image erected inside. Yahweh declared, under no uncertain terms, that his temple would have no such image (Exod. 20:4–6; Lev. 26:1; Deut. 4:15–16).

11. For example, 1 Kings 3:2–3; 12:31; 15:14; 22:43; 2 Kings 12:3; 14:4; 15:4; 16:4; 17:9, 32; 18:4; 21:3; Hos. 4:13.

One might think of these concepts as unique to the timeframe of the Old Testament, but we find them reiterated in prophecies and visions looking far forward in time to the new heavens and new earth. Isaiah wrote of a final time of peace, when the wolf and the lion will cause no harm "in all my holy mountain," and when God's people will be drawn from distant lands "to my holy mountain Jerusalem" (Isa. 65:17–25; 66:20–22). Micah spoke of the latter days when "the mountain of the house of Yahweh shall be established as the highest of the mountains" and peoples from many nations shall to be drawn to it (Mic. 4:1–2). During the exile, Ezekiel received a vision in which God "brought me to the land of Israel, and set me down on a very high mountain," where he saw a city and a new temple (Ezek. 40; cf. 17:22–24). From that temple, life-giving water flowed, turning the seas into fresh water (Ezek. 47).

Ezekiel's visions are further developed in the final vision of the apostle John (Rev. 21–22). The new heavens and the new earth are embodied in the descent of the holy city, the new Jerusalem, seen from and encompassing a high mountain. In seeming contrast to Ezekiel, the temple John saw in the city was not a building, but God himself, "for its temple is the Lord God the Almighty and the Lamb" (Rev. 21:22), dwelling in and filling the earth. From this holy mountain, John saw a river, similar to Ezekiel, of life-giving water flowing, nourishing a garden with trees yielding fruit in every month of the year.[12]

We find still more parallels in the description of Eden. We are conditioned today to think of Eden and the garden as a lowland tropical forest, but Ezekiel referred to Eden as the "garden of God . . . on the holy mountain of God," a land with gold and precious gem stones (Ezek. 28:13–15). In Genesis 2 we read that "a river flowed out of Eden to water the garden" to lands where there was gold and precious gem stones. The garden produced "every tree that is pleasant to the sight and good for food. The tree of life was in the midst of the garden, and the tree of the knowledge of good and evil" (vv. 8–12). Only the latter tree was forbidden, meaning the tree of life was freely available, providing timeless divine provision (vv. 15–17).

Something fascinating is going on here. The association of a central temple with God's rest, a mountain, timeless divine provision, springs of life-giving water, and an eternal garden are all elements found in various ANE *creation* stories. It is as if—imagine this—the nations of the earth retained a

---

12. Though beyond the scope of our study, we could further explore the importance of mountains in the NT, particularly in Matthew (e.g., Sermon on the Mount [Matt. 5–7], the Mount of Transfiguration [Matt. 17], and Calvary/Golgotha [Matt. 27:33]).

sense of the true story. Sin and idolatry twisted those stories in innumerable ways, yet not entirely erasing truth.[13]

The discussion above should be a sufficient prompt to ask if there are other creation-temple parallels found within the Bible. Theologians have noted several, which we have divided into parallels of *function* in God's initial creation and the later temples, and parallels of *symbolism* in the configuration or design of each. We will revisit themes previously addressed in links between the Bible and ANE understanding, but with the focus shifted internally to biblical connections between creation and the temple.[14]

For those familiar with the groundbreaking work of John Walton on ancient temples and creation, an additional note is warranted to avoid confusion when we speak about functional parallels. Walton has argued that the focus of all origin stories originating in the ANE, including the biblical story, was on bringing function and order, with little, if any, importance placed on the creation of material objects.[15] On this point, we concur on the greater importance of bringing order and purpose to the cosmos, but also find ample evidence in the biblical story for God's interest in material things.[16] In the first layer ("Song") we noted the parallel structure of days, divided between giving form to the formless (function) and filling the empty (material things). In the section following, discussion of function is not intended to weigh in on the relative importance of functional versus material creation. Rather, it is intended to draw attention to similarities in how the temple and the creation are put to use.

CREATION-TEMPLE FUNCTIONAL PARALLELS

A unique place of God's presence

God repeatedly tells us in Scripture that he desires to be present among his people. While this is easy to say, it is harder to describe what it means. How does a God who is omnipresent manifest his presence in a particular place or with a particular people? To gain a glimpse of an answer, consider a human analogy. Suppose you ask a friend whether they have ever visited the city of Chicago. Your friend answers, "Yes, I drove through the city last year on a road trip from

---

13. Alternatively, God may have simply employed broadly shared cultural views to illustrate eternal truths.
14. This section draws from many sources including Averbeck, "Tabernacle"; Postell, *Adam as Israel*, 108–14; Wenham, "Sanctuary Symbolism," 399.
15. Walton, *Lost World of Genesis One*, 23–37; Walton, *Genesis 1 as Ancient Cosmology*, 122–38.
16. Weeks, "Bible and the 'Universal' Ancient World"; Postell, *Adam as Israel*, 58–59. Cf. Beall's response to Walton's essay in *Reading Genesis 1–2*, 173–74.

Cleveland to Kansas City." More than likely, you will counter that such a transitory passage does not count as a *visit*. Yes, your friend was physically present in Chicago for an interval of time, but the sights and culture were not engaged.

While there are obvious limitations to the analogy, it at least points us toward the difference between God's universal existence versus the personal insertion of his presence—a presence that stops and engages with the community. The Bible commonly describes God's desire or promise to be among his people in terms of dwelling, walking, or resting. Consider the verses in box 2, noting that *sanctuary* is commonly used as a reference to the tabernacle or temple.

BOX 2: VERSES HIGHLIGHTING GOD'S TEMPLE PRESENCE AS DWELLING, RESTING, WALKING, OR ABIDING AMONG HIS PEOPLE, IN A SANCTUARY OR TEMPLE, OR ON THE MOUNTAIN OF GOD

And let them make me a sanctuary, that I may **dwell** in their midst. (Exod. 25:8)

I . . . will set my sanctuary in their midst forevermore. My **dwelling** place shall be with them, and I will be their God, and they shall be my people. (Ezek. 37:26–27)

I will make my **dwelling** among you, and my soul shall not abhor you. And I will **walk** among you and will be your God, and you shall be my people. (Lev. 26:11–12)

Because Yahweh your God **walks** in the midst of your camp, to deliver you and to give up your enemies before you, therefore your camp must be holy. (Deut. 23:14)

You have led in your steadfast love the people whom you have redeemed; you have guided them by your strength to your holy **abode**. . . . You will bring them in and plant them on your own mountain, the place, O Yahweh, which you have made for your **abode**, the sanctuary, O Yahweh, which your hands have established. Yahweh will **reign** forever and ever. (Exod. 15:13, 17–18)

Isaiah speaking of the Messiah: "the spirit of Yahweh shall **rest** upon him" . . . there will be no harm "in all my holy mountain," and "of him shall the nations inquire, and his **resting place** shall be glorious." (Isa. 11:2, 9, 10)

David's intention for the temple: "I had it in my heart to build a **house of rest** for the ark of the covenant of Yahweh and for the footstool of our God." (1 Chron. 28:2)

God's response to David: "I have not lived in a house since the day I brought up the people of Israel from Egypt to this day, but I have been **moving about** in a tent for my **dwelling**." (2 Sam. 7:6)

Solomon's temple dedication: "And now arise, O Yahweh God, and go to your **resting place**, you and the ark of your might." (2 Chron. 6:41)

It is evident from these verses that the Hebrew concept of rest (both *shabat* and *nuakh*) is more active than implied by its typical use in English. It is not just a time of passive reflection or a cessation of labor. This rest connotes taking up residence—inhabiting, walking, and moving about the dwelling place. It is the same word used when God's spirit *rested* on individuals prompting them to prophesy (Num. 11:25–26; 2 Kings 2:15).

In this light, consider the work of God at creation and his subsequent interaction with Adam and Eve. Initially, the earth was dark, without form, and "the Spirit of God was hovering over the face of the waters" (Gen. 1:2). We often read this verse without stopping to contemplate its meaning. It is a beautiful word picture with layers of meaning in a single phrase. The context of the Hebrew word for hover (*rakhaf*) is one of quiet or gentle observation. God did not have to arm for battle against a raging demon of chaos. All was already under his control. Instead, the hovering may be viewed as the contemplative brooding of a mother bird who looks about for the best place for the nest (Deut. 32:10–11). The latter image is particularly fitting, as there is a sense, figuratively speaking, of seeking but not finding a place of rest. Not a rest from fatigue, but of *dwelling*. Ordering and filling were first required to create a place in which to rest.

When the nest was ready, God took Adam and placed him in the garden in Eden. The significance of word choice is typically lost in English translations. A literal translation of Genesis 2:15 is "Yahweh took the man [Adam] and *rested* him in the garden." We later read that God made his presence dwell among them, even describing a scene in which God walked in the garden in the cool of the day (Gen. 3:8). In other words, God did not rest *from* his creation, he took up rest *in* his creation.

The creation-temple parallel carries over into the New Testament even with the transition from a physical building to the indwelling of the Holy Spirit, complete with the imagery of God *walking* among us:

> For we are the temple of the living God; as God said,
> "I will make my *dwelling* among them and *walk* among them,
>   and I will be their God,
>   and they shall be my people."
>   (2 Cor. 6:16)

The place of God's throne

The concept of rest as described above is consistent with the ANE understanding of what a god did with a temple. The *nature* of the indwelling God of Israel, however, is unique. While the pagan gods of Israel's neighbors were to be feared and revered, they could also be manipulated. Providing the gods with sacrificial food or combining the right cultic rituals could elicit a desired action or response—assuming the targeted god was not distracted or otherwise engaged. The God of Israel is the antithesis. Sacrifice and ritual were of considerable importance, but not to attract or appease the capricious appetite of a god (e.g., Isa. 66). Yahweh is sovereign.

Expanding on the temple as a place of God's rest, we also see the temple as an extension of God's cosmic rule. The temple is frequently referred to as the location of God's throne, though there is a clear sense that it cannot be fully contained within an earthly building. The throne is alternately described as being in a heavenly temple (Ps. 11:4; Rev. 7:15; 16:17), or as extending in various ways into the earthly temple. In one of his early visions, Isaiah "saw the Lord sitting upon a throne, high and lifted up; and the train of his robe filled the temple" (Isa. 6:1). Other Scriptures refer to the temple as the location of God's royal footstool.

> "Let us go to his dwelling place;
>   let us worship at his footstool!"
> Arise, O Yahweh, and go to your resting place,
>   you and the ark of your might. . . .
> For Yahweh has chosen Zion;
>   he has desired it for his dwelling place:
> "This is my resting place forever;
>   here I will dwell, for I have desired it."
>   (Ps. 132:7–8, 13–14)

> The glory of Lebanon shall come to you,
>   the cypress, the plane, and the pine,
> to beautify the place of my sanctuary,
>   and I will make the place of my feet glorious.
>   (Isa. 60:13)

The footstool metaphor is yet another connection between the temple and the creation, as other verses make use of the same descriptive language with heaven as God's throne and the *earth* as the royal stool for his feet:

> Heaven is my throne,
>   and the earth is my footstool;

> what is the house that you would build for me,
>> and what is the place of my rest?
>>> (Isa. 66:1)

But I say to you, Do not take an oath at all, either by heaven, for it is the throne of God, or by the earth, for it is his footstool, or by Jerusalem, for it is the city of the great King. (Matt. 5:34–35)

Priestly inhabitants

The service of the Levitical priests was to serve and guard the house of God from what is unclean or profane (Num. 3:7–8; 8:25–26; 18:5–6; 1 Chron. 23:32; Ezek. 44:14). The Hebrew words for serve and guard (*'abad* and *shamar*) are the same as used to describe the expectation of Adam when placed in the garden, translated in English Bibles as variations of "work and keep."[17] The role of Adam (and by extension, Eve) thus carries a priestly function. Allowing the serpent a place in the garden—something unholy and profane—represented a failure to fulfill their priestly duty, ultimately leading to their ejection and replacement by cherubim.

As with humanity in general, God did not completely reject Adam and Eve for their sin. He made provisions for their redemption and continued service. The clothing God gave to Adam and Eve (*kotnot*, "tunics") employs the same terminology used for priestly garments (Exod. 29:5, 8; 40:14; Lev. 8:13; 16:4), provided to set them apart and to cover their nakedness (Exod. 20:26).

Moreover, a day was foretold when the promised Messiah would combine the roles of king and high priest in the context of the temple. Zechariah 6:9–15 speaks of placing a crown on the head of the high priest, and looks forward to the coming of the chosen one of God. "It is he who shall build the temple of Yahweh and shall bear royal honor, and shall sit and rule on his throne. And there shall be a priest on his throne, and the counsel of peace shall be between them" (v. 13).

Rivers and the source of life

We already mentioned the parallel between the rivers of Eden and the rivers of the temple visons of Ezekiel and John (and with ANE temple stories). Expanding

---

17. Scholars debate whether the verbs (*'abad*, "work, serve"; *shamar*, "keep, guard") in the garden focuses more on the agricultural ("work and keep") or religious ("serve and guard"). In the context of Gen. 1–2, the focus may be argued to be both secular and sacred.

on the observation, flowing water frequently represents the source of life, which ultimately flows from God's temple presence. Zechariah also wrote of a future day when the surrounding lands will become a plain, "but Jerusalem shall remain aloft on its site" (Zech. 14:10; mountain motif). Its people will live in peace, and "living waters shall flow out from Jerusalem, half of them to the eastern sea and the other half to the western sea. It shall continue in summer as in winter" (v. 8).

The link between the rivers of Eden and the temple as sources of God's provision is more explicit than we find in most English Bibles. Consider Psalm 36:8–9:

> They feast on the abundance of your house,
>   and you give them drink from the river of your delights.
> For with you is the fountain of life.

A literal translation of "river of your delights" is "river of your Edens."

CREATION-TEMPLE SYMBOLIC PARALLELS

There are many literary or symbolic parallels between the description of the creation and the temple, further suggesting that the temple represented a microcosm of God's intention for the whole of creation.

Shared metaphysical foundations

The same triad of terms—wisdom, understanding, and knowledge—is used in Proverbs to describe building a house (temple) and creating the heavens and the earth.[18]

> By wisdom a house is built,
>   and by understanding it is established;
> by knowledge the rooms are filled
>   with all precious and pleasant riches.
>   (Prov. 24:3–4)

> Yahweh by wisdom founded the earth;
>   by understanding he established the heavens;
> by his knowledge the deeps broke open,
>   and the clouds drop down the dew. (Prov. 3:19–20)

---

18. Middleton, *New Heavens and a New Earth*, 46–49; Van Leeuwen, "Cosmos, Temple, House," 67–90.

Position and orientation

Instructions for erecting the tabernacle each time Israel stopped included its orientation, with its gate facing east (Num. 3:38). Later descriptions of the temple on Mount Zion in Jerusalem did not include explicit references to its orientation, but Ezekiel's visions of the final temple include repeated references to its placement on a high mountain facing toward the east (Ezek. 40:2, 6; 43:12; 46:1). Eden is likewise described as situated on the mountain of God with an east-facing entrance indicated by the placement of the guardian cherubim (Gen. 3:24).

Cherubim

Cherubim, or cherubs, are not sweet chubby babies with wings as depicted in Renaissance paintings. While we don't have a certain description today, Ezekiel 10 gives us an indication they were far more awe-inspiring than flying infants. They were represented in carvings that stood over the ark in the holy of holies and embroidered on the tabernacle curtains and veil (Exod. 25:18–22; 26:1, 31).[19] They stood guard over the ark—over the footstool of God—protecting it from the profane.[20] Cherubim were assigned a similar role at the creation after the failure of the human guardians. When Adam and Eve entertained the profane inside the garden (the snake) and disobeyed God's singular command not eat from one tree, their priestly role in protecting the garden was given to cherubim with a flaming sword (Gen. 3:24).

Tree of life and lampstand

The seven-branched lampstand (menorah; Exod. 25:32–36) represents a tree with almond blossoms, possibly drawing on the garden's fruit trees and, especially, the tree of life. The tabernacle and temple also portrayed images of plant life, reflections of Eden (Exod. 28:33–34; 1 Kings 6).

Tree of knowledge of good and evil and the ark of the covenant

The ark of the covenant contained a copy of the law, which made clear the boundaries of good and evil. The tree of the knowledge of good and evil in the garden was a source of related knowledge. There was death in the disobedient treatment of each (Gen. 3:15–17; 2 Sam. 6:6–7).

---

19. See also Exod. 36:8; 37:7–9; Num. 7:89; 1 Kings 6:23–28.
20. Ezekiel's vision of the throne in heaven was "over the heads of the cherubim" (Ezek. 10:1), and several verses make reference to God who sits "enthroned above/on the cherubim" (1 Sam. 4:4; 2 Sam. 6:2; 1 Chron. 13:6).

Gold and gemstones

Gold and precious stones were an integral part of the design of the temple and the priestly garments (Exod. 25:7–31). Genesis 2:11–12 also makes specific mention of lands with gold and precious gemstones associated with Eden. In Ezekiel 28, we find remarkable ties between Eden and the temple, with mention of gemstones, Eden, the garden of God, the mountain of God, a cherub, and the role of guardian.

> Moreover, the word of Yahweh came to me: "Son of man, raise a lamentation over the king of Tyre, and say to him, Thus says the Lord Yahweh:
> 'You were the signet of perfection,
>> full of wisdom and perfect in beauty.
> You were in Eden, the garden of God;
>> every precious stone was your covering,
> sardius, topaz, and diamond,
>> beryl, onyx, and jasper,
> sapphire, emerald, and carbuncle;
>> and crafted in gold were your settings
>> and your engravings.
> On the day that you were created
>> they were prepared.
> You were an anointed guardian cherub.
>> I placed you; you were on the holy mountain of God;
>> in the midst of the stones of fire you walked.'"
>   (vv. 11–14)

Layered design

The tabernacle and temple were not just structures containing holy or dedicated furnishings. The design included layers of access which some theologians argue parallel Eden, the garden, and the creation (see fig. 3; table 7).

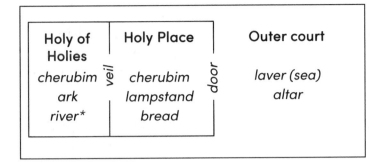

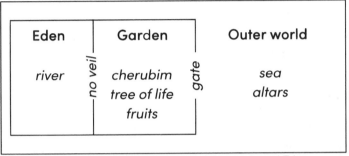

Figure 3. Schematic comparison of the temple and Eden
(* river in temple is only in visions, e.g. Ezek. 47)

TABLE 7. THREE-TIERED LAYOUT OF THE TABERNACLE OR TEMPLE AND DESCRIPTION OF CREATION	
Tabernacle/Temple	**Creation**
Holy of holies: The most sacred space was guarded by the cherubim on the ark. The heavenly throne of God was above the cherubim, linking heaven and earth (Ezek. 10:1). In Ezekiel a river flows out of the temple (Ezek. 47:1). In Revelation, the river originates at the throne of God (Rev. 22:1).	*Eden*: Eden was also called the mountain of God (Ezek. 28:11–14), from which a river flowed to water the garden (Gen. 2:10).
Holy place: The space contained the lampstand, incense, and holy bread with cherubim embroidered into the curtains. Carvings of fruits and flowers decorated the posts and curtained walls (1 Kings 6).	*Garden*: The garden contained the tree of life and many fruits ultimately protected by cherubim.
Outer court: The outer area contained the altar of uncut stone and the washbasin, referred to as the sea (1 Kings 7:23) and supported by carved bulls facing in the four cardinal directions (1 Kings 7:25).	*Outer world*: The sea and land are still under God's sovereignty, but necessitating altars for sacrifice.

Tabernacle instruction in seven speeches

In Exodus 25–31, God delivers the instructions for the tabernacle divided into seven speeches.[21] The subjects covered in each section do not obviously align with the subjects or mission of each creation day, but it represents an additional parallel.[22]

FROM CREATION TO NEW HEAVENS AND EARTH

No passage or book of Scripture stands by itself in a theological vacuum. Each is to be understood in the context of the Bible as a whole. To understand the beginning of the Bible it is helpful to consider its end. Many parallels exist between Eden and the final restoration, but there are important differences as well. The creation was good, but it was not the final plan.

As part of the initial creation, Eden was limited in size, it depended on the sun for light and heat, it experienced nightly darkness, there were distant seas, an unholy creature had access to the garden, and Adam and Eve were naked. In contrast, we read in Revelation 21–22 that the new heavens and earth—the new Jerusalem, God's holy mountain—will fill the earth. The expanse of the city is vertical as well as horizontal. John describes it as extending just as high upward as outward, linking heaven and earth far beyond the dream of the tallest earthly mountain.[23] The sun is no longer needed because of the radiance of God's glory; there is no night, nor is there a sea in the modern sense, as streams flowing from the city make all the surrounding waters fresh. The residents are not naked, but clothed in fine raiment. And nothing unholy can ever again enter.

The new heavens and earth is thus not a return to Eden, as commonly preached, but what Eden was intended to one day become. With glimpses of the end, we have a better view of the intentions at the beginning. The mission of humans in Eden was not just to live a carefree life, sipping on piña coladas in a tropical paradise. The human residents were given the title of "image-bearers"—made in the image and likeness of God. That title came with expectations. As said before, to be an image-bearer in the ANE was to serve as a representative of the divine, acting as caretaker, gardener, steward-ruler, and sometimes as priest. All these roles can be seen in the biblical mandate, but attributed to all humans rather than to a single magistrate. As children were

---

21. Note introductory formula, "Yahweh said to Moses," in Exod. 25:1; 30:11, 17, 22, 34; 31:1, 12.
22. Kearney, "Creation and Liturgy," 375.
23. A height of twelve thousand stadia is more than one thousand miles. Mount Everest is less than six miles in height and the earth's atmosphere (troposphere) is only about eight miles thick.

born, adding to the number of image-bearers, the work of the garden was to expand, spreading the garden and the mountain of God to all the earth. John Walton notes,

> If people were going to fill the earth [according to Genesis 1], we must conclude that they were not intended to stay in the garden in a static situation. Yet moving out of the garden would appear a hardship since the land outside the garden was not as hospitable as that inside the garden (otherwise the garden would not be distinguishable). Perhaps, then, we should surmise that people were gradually supposed to extend the garden as they went about subduing and ruling. Extending the garden would extend the food supply as well as extend sacred space (since that is what the garden represented).[24]

Fulfilling that mandate required continued obedience to God, an obedience they failed to uphold. Sin did not catch God by surprise, forcing some unforeseen plan B. God knows the end from the beginning. But sin nonetheless altered the course of human experience, starting with the eviction of Adam and Eve from the garden and loss of access to the tree of life. While their resources and ease of life drastically changed, their role as image-bearers, amazingly, did not.

Being cast from Eden meant that humans no longer lived in a place where God's presence intrinsically dwelled. Instead, God chose a people that he would come to meet, bringing them first to a holy mountain, dwelling among them in a mobile tabernacle, and establishing them in the land of promise, where his presence was represented in the temple in Jerusalem. From there, the mission was similar to the original. The prophets spoke of God's plan to expand the sacred precinct of the temple to encompass Jerusalem (Isa. 4:4–6; 54:2–3, 11–12; Jer. 3:16–17; Zech. 1:16–2:11), then all of Israel (Ezek. 37:25–28), and then the whole earth (Dan. 2:34–35, 44–45).[25] This mission was often overlooked by the nation of Israel, who wrongly interpreted the command to be set apart as a holy nation as being the sole recipients of God's grace. The temple too often served as a symbol of their solitary election by God as an ethnic nation, rather than the mountain from which God's grace might extend to the world.[26]

---

24. Walton, *Genesis*, 136.
25. Beale and Kim, *God Dwells among Us*.
26. Beale, "Eden, the Temple, and the Church's Mission," 19.

The disobedience in Eden was the first of many failures of God's image-bearers to fulfill their temple mandate. Generational sin led to the removal of God's presence from the temple, ultimately symbolized in its destruction. But God never leaves his people without recourse. During the exile in Babylon, God spoke through Ezekiel saying that though he scattered Israel and Judah, "yet I have been a sanctuary to them for a while [or in a small measure] in the countries where they have gone" (Ezek. 11:16).[27]

The rebuilding of the temple after the exile was a mixture of hope and disappointment. After years of initial stagnation (Hag. 1:2–6; cf. Zech. 1:3–4), Haggai and Zechariah's preaching inspired the rebuilding project, along with the reminder that God was already in their midst by his Spirit (Hag. 2:4–5). God's presence was not conditioned upon the construction of a building, but the temple served as a critical symbol of the mission: "I have returned to Zion and will dwell in the midst of Jerusalem, and Jerusalem shall be called the faithful city, and the mountain of Yahweh of hosts, the holy mountain" (Zech. 8:3)

However, the ongoing spiritual failures and frustrations of the postexilic community,[28] matched by no indication that God filled the temple with his glory as he had at previous times, pushed the *real* temple restoration into the distant future. God spoke to Haggai of a coming day when the glory of the temple would exceed the glory of former times (Hag. 2:6–9), and Ezekiel looked forward to a day when the temple presence of God would be established with permanency: "My dwelling place shall be with them, and I will be their God, and they shall be my people. Then the nations will know that I am Yahweh who sanctifies Israel, when my sanctuary is in their midst forevermore" (Ezek. 37:27–28).

A defining moment—perhaps *the* defining moment—of what it meant for God to tabernacle among his people came with the arrival of the Messiah. Jesus declared himself to *be* the temple. God took on human form as a physical manifestation of his desire to walk and dwell among his people. The destruction of his body on the cross mirrored the destruction of the temple building—both were manifestations of human rejection of God's dwelling among them. Yet again, God did not leave us without aid. His sacrifice and resurrection initiated at least partial fulfillment of the prophecies of old, with God's indwelling Spirit now poured out on individual believers (Acts 2:15).

---

27. Jenson, "Temple," 771.
28. For example, Ezra 9; Neh. 13; Isa. 56–59; 65:1–16; Zech. 7; Mal. 1–2; 3:8–15.

The Great Commission was not an entirely new commandment, nor was it a change in God's ultimate plan. It was the renewal of the creation-temple mandate to spread God's temple presence to the ends of the earth. It is a mission that God himself will culminate with an end to sin, when the temple-dwelling of God's throne will encompass all the earth: "And I heard a loud voice from the throne saying, 'Behold, the dwelling place of God is with man. He will dwell with them, and they will be his people, and God himself will be with them as their God'" (Rev. 21:3).

CHALLENGES AND RESPONSES

Objection 1: This view is too dependent on recent archaeological discoveries.

The objection that views may be too dependent on archaeological discoveries was anticipated and addressed in the introduction to the book, but it is worth revisiting here. Concerns associated with this objection are expressed in at least three different ways, all related to the perceived independence of the Bible.

The first is a suspicion that any similarities found with ANE myths are designed to undermine belief in the uniqueness of the Bible as a divinely inspired text. Such concerns are fueled by secular scholars who argue that the biblical creation story is largely borrowed and adapted from the dominant cultures in which the Hebrew people were immersed. Bible-believing theologians, on the other hand, will note that if all humanity shared the same origin, it is entirely expected that the stories they carried with them into different regions would retain some commonalities. Generally speaking, the similarities that exist between the Bible and ANE myths are not in the "facts" of creation, per se, but in the use of common symbols. With respect to this layer, there are informative parallels in the symbolism of divine occupation of a mountain temple that reach all the way back to creation. It is not a symbolism borrowed from Israel's neighbors. It is a symbolism shared in common by both Israel and her neighbors that Scripture takes full advantage of to communicate what it means for God to rest among his people.

A second concern derives from the sense that the Bible should stand alone, without requiring *any* outside text or source to be understood. Absolute independence is not actually possible, for most of us depend on extra-biblical sources to understand things as simple as what a chariot looks like or how sheep behave. The Bible assumes the reader knows of such things without self-contained encyclopedic descriptions.

But what about theological principles? Should these not be ascertained through the study of Scripture alone? The answer is, *it depends*. It depends on the subject and the texts in question. The doctrine of perspicuity (clarity) holds that the central message of Scripture—our fallen nature, the need for a divine solution, and God's redemptive plan for salvation—is clearly presented within the pages of the Bible. But the nuances of biblical theology are not all equally clear, with theologians and lay readers wrestling with some texts across generations. The study of ancient cultures familiar to Israel should not *overturn* any clearly understood biblical doctrines, but we should not be surprised if we find that such study *enriches* our understanding.[29]

This brings us to a third concern over the timing and general availability of the ANE sources. Knowledge of the culture, cosmologies, and origin stories of ANE nations was largely unknown for the lion's share of Christian history. Are we suggesting that the richness of Scripture was impossible to apprehend for most of the last two thousand years, waiting for archaeologists to discover ancient libraries only within the last two hundred years?

Our answer to this is both no and yes. It is *no* in the sense that many of the layers expressed in this book are not dependent at all on archaeological discoveries. There is a richness to the text that is self-contained. But our answer is also *yes*, in the sense that God chooses to reveal himself in various ways to meet the needs of his people within the context of their own time and place. In our time, with all the secular challenges thrown at us attempting to undermine the Bible, God has given us glimpses into the cultures of the past that add additional layers of beauty—layers we believe make the biblical text outshine the modern challenges!

Objection 2: The words for "tabernacle" and "temple" do not appear in the creation story.

The objection that *tabernacle* and *temple* do not appear in the creation story is of the same nature as the objection against a covenant view of creation, arguing that the absence of a particular word in the story precludes interpreting the story in the light of that word. In this case, the Hebrew word for tabernacle (*skene*) does not appear in Scripture until late in Exodus (Exod. 25:9), and explicit reference to a temple (*hekhal*) is not made until many generations later during the period of the judges (1 Sam. 1:9). Daniel Block argues that finding a creation-temple theme in Genesis 1 requires an unwarranted,

---

29. Longman, "What Genesis 1–2 Teaches," 121–22.

backward reading of Scripture. [30] In other words, a temple understanding is not found in the creation story itself, but must be inferred after subsequent reading of the descriptions and function of the temple. Further issue is taken with a priestly role of Adam and Eve, the idea of God's throne being on earth, and arguing against some of the perceived alignments between the symbolism of the temple and creation. We will address the absence of expected words first, then expand to Block's particular concern of a "backward reading."

Our first response is to refer readers back to the parallel objection raised against a covenant view of creation (Objection 1 in Layer 4). Examples are provided there of biblical themes, such as establishing a covenant, that are clearly at play in the pages of Scripture without always explicitly identifying that theme by name. For the current layer, we argue that the same phenomenon is at work, with clear phrasing and descriptions that would have brought temple imagery to the minds of Hebrew readers. God's rest and his walking in the garden are exactly the words we would expect in an ANE text about what a god does in or with a temple, and these actions match the biblical descriptions of what it means for God to have a temple presence among his people. God dwelled, walked, rested, and ruled from his holy mountain, from his temple, and from his creation.

Our assessment of the backward-reading objection is that it stems from an expectation that the Bible was intended to be read as if Genesis were written long before the rest of the Pentateuch (the first five books). In this view, future revelation to Israel might draw on creation themes, but not the reverse. The weight of evidence, however, indicates that the Pentateuch was initially written by Moses with the intention of being a single body of work. The creation is to be understood in light of Mount Sinai as much as Mount Sinai is to be understood from the creation. It is not a unidirectional text.

---

30. Block, "Eden: A Temple?" Though we are disagreeing with Block's assessment on this subject, his essay is detailed and extensively footnoted, making it a good resource for multiple topics related to creation.

DISCUSSION QUESTIONS

1. In Layer 3 ("Polemic"), the focus was on challenges to mistaken pagan views of the gods and creation. In this layer, common ANE concepts of things like a *cosmic mountain* appear to be embraced. What is the basis for challenging one ANE view and employing another?

2. How does this layer add to our understanding of God's rest? What does biblical rest entail?

3. What parallels are drawn in this layer between creation and the tabernacle or temple?

4. What is the theological or practical significance of viewing the temple as a microcosm of the creation?

5. Is the new creation a return to Eden? How does the mandate of Adam and Eve relate to the mandate of Israel or to the church? Is the answer informed by comparisons between creation and the temple visions of Ezekiel and John?

LAYER 6

Calendar

(*luakh zemanim*, "timetable")

*Six days you shall labor, and do all your work, but the
seventh day is a Sabbath to Yahweh your God.
(Exod. 20:9–10)*

Since the days of Einstein, the concept of time has been one of considerable wonder and perplexity. But variable ideas of time—how cultures
track and mark its passage—go back long before the discovery of relativity. Different cultures, historically and today, have distinctly different ways
of communicating time. Does "three days" mean seventy-two hours or inclusion of parts of three periods of daylight? Is "tomorrow" a reference to the
following day or a general time in the near future? Does the reported age
at death represent the actual years lived or a symbolic representation of the
quality of the person's life? How is the start of a new year, a new century, or a
new millennium defined? Does time have an economic value? None of these
questions are answered the same by all cultures.[1] In international business
ventures, the surest way to fail is to assume your foreign counterparts will
understand the marking of time the same way as your own culture.[2]

A common thread throughout this book has been to read Genesis 1
through the historical and cultural lenses of ancient Israel—the original
audience—to better understand the richness of its message. We continue in
that vein here, now with a particular focus on how the passage of time was

---

1. An intriguing example is how age is assigned. In Korean society, a child is one at birth and
   everyone's age increases on January 1. A child born on December 31 thus turns two on her
   second day from the womb!
2. For an interesting summary of time in different cultures, see "Time in Different Cultures,"
   Exactly What Is . . . Time?, http://www.exactlywhatistime.com/other-aspects-of-time/
   time-in-different-cultures.

understood and marked. The underlying thesis of this layer is that dates and sequences of events were recorded in the Bible, and particularly in the Pentateuch, for liturgical purposes in ways that diverge from the journalistic expectations of modern readers. The term *liturgical* in this context does not refer to a chant or corporate reading, but as serving the purpose of guiding religious practice and worship.

This perspective derives significantly from the recent work of Michael LeFebvre, who has drawn attention to the theologically instructive role of the Hebrew calendar and the interweaving of historical and seasonal events with its festivals, new moons, and holy days. In this view, the creation story captures a sense of the entire annual cycle, serving as a "festival calendar narrative" to help Israel "remember God's work and God's rest through their own weekly labors and worship."[3]

Viewing Genesis 1 as a model for at least a weekly calendar is not new—it is as old as Moses:

> Remember the Sabbath day, to keep it holy. Six days you shall labor, and do all your work, but the seventh day is a Sabbath to Yahweh your God. On it you shall not do any work. . . . For in six days Yahweh made heaven and earth, the sea, and all that is in them, and rested on the seventh day. Therefore Yahweh blessed the Sabbath day and made it holy. (Exod. 20:8–11)

Whatever the historical and astronomical roots for the seven-day week, Moses's interest here is primarily *theological*.[4] As God, so Israel. The nation was to pattern its six-plus-one rhythm of work and rest after the description of God's workweek, culminating in the divine Sabbath on the seventh day. In fact, this liturgical connection is the only understanding of Genesis 1 that has achieved universal agreement in the church.[5] Unfortunately, what is obvious and most practical often gets muted when we get bogged down in debates over secondary issues.[6] In the multitude of books written in defense

---

3. LeFebvre, *Liturgy of Creation*, 114. For a quick overview of LeFebvre's thesis and methodology, see his "Cracking the Code of Cadence."

4. Moses and other biblical authors give different but equally theological rationales for the Sabbath elsewhere (e.g., Deut. 5:15). (Note: We use "Moses" here without denying the divine voice or the complicated discussion of the authorship, editing, and transmission of the text.)

5. Vogels, "Cultic and Civil Calendars of the Fourth Day," 168.

6. Secondary issues (in our estimation) include things like the exact meaning of day (*yom*), the nature of the firmament (*raqia'*), or the date of the creation events in earth history.

of different positions on Genesis 1, relatively few give serious attention to the importance of the weekly Sabbath.[7] LeFebvre's approach attempts to recapture the Sabbath focus of the creation by drawing attention to how the Pentateuch interweaves Israel's historical milestones within the framework of its festival calendar. Development of this layer will require some time outside of Genesis 1 to gain a big-picture understanding of what is at work in Scripture before applying what we learn to the creation story. Since it may not be intuitive where the next few sections are heading or how they will tie back to Genesis 1, a synopsis follows.

SYNOPSIS

The Pentateuch is a collection of books that are internally identified as law. The designation is important to understand, for the Pentateuch's stories and legal guidelines are interconnected, each to be read in light of the other. The connections are emphasized with the establishment of festivals that commemorate important historical events and celebrate God's continued providence in each year's harvests. When mapping the festivals to Israel's history, a remarkable alignment is found between historical dates and the agricultural cycle. The alignment suggests the historical dates are "dates of observance," with a liturgical purpose in mind, rather than journalistic time stamps.

Parallels are found in Genesis 1, where the annual agricultural cycle and festivals are represented in microcosm. In LeFebvre's words, "The creation week narrative contains the history of God's ordering of the world, mapped to Israel's observance schedule for stewarding that order with labor and worship."[8] God first prepares the land for fruitfulness, then fills it with life that include crops, orchards, fisheries, flocks, and herds, and finally blesses with harvests. It is a forward-looking story that notes the establishment of luminaries on day 4 for tracking the passage of days and of the coming festivals (Gen. 1:14), and finishes with the festival of Sabbath rest (Gen. 2:2–3).

THE IMPORTANCE OF GENRE: PENTATEUCH AS "LAW"

If we asked a Christian today to identify the genre of Genesis or Exodus, most would not hesitate to label it as "history" or "historical narrative."[9] This is a natural response and generally appropriate, for much of the contents of these

---

7. Alas, LeFebvre's observation is true even for some of our own work (e.g., Davidson, *Friend of Science, Friend of Faith*).
8. LeFebvre, *Liturgy of Creation*, 116.
9. Technically, "history" is not a literary genre, but it is still a common answer.

books are filled with stories from the past. Yet this is not the overarching label applied by the Bible itself.

Scripture identifies the first five books (Pentateuch) as a single "book"— the *Torah*. The Hebrew word *torah* is generally translated in English Bibles as "law" (or "the Law" when referring to the Pentateuch)."[10] This strikes Western readers as odd, as we are conditioned to think of law as statutes, precepts, and commandments. Yet a large percentage of the Pentateuch is filled with narratives and even poetry. How does all this fall under the heading, or genre, of *law*?

For the original audience, law (*torah*) was more than just legal codes. It was *instruction*, which could be communicated as much by stories as by edicts. Scholars sometimes use the phrase "narrative law,"[11] noting the purpose of the narratives was much more than just providing historical background, models of faith, or warnings against disobedience. The stories were not to be read as a *preamble* to the rules of Leviticus or Deuteronomy, but *alongside* them. The narratives anticipate the formalized code, and the legal statutes draw life from the stories.

Links between the narrative stories and the legal guidelines that followed are many. Rules setting Israel apart from the nations (e.g., Lev. 20:22–26) are modeled in the call of Abraham out from the land of his fathers (Gen. 12:1). The command to leave fields fallow every seven years and God's promise of subsequent provision (Lev. 25:1–7) is embodied in the provision of extra manna prior to each Sabbath during Israel's wilderness wanderings (Exod. 16:4–5, 22–26). Laws regarding God's claims on the firstborn of cattle and sons (Exod 13:1–2; Deut. 15:19–23) are inseparable from the near-sacrifice of Isaac on Mount Moriah (Gen. 22).[12] And all of these codes and stories ultimately become intertwined with the work and message of the Messiah.

The point is that we should consider the pentateuchal narratives as part of Israel's law and constitution, not mere stories about the past. The stories were selected and narrated with a theological purpose in mind. This does not deny the historical nature of the narratives (i.e., they are dealing with real people and events in a real past), but it acknowledges that the stories were included and shaped for reasons that go beyond the historical. This awareness

---

10. The Law (*torah*) is often used to identify the Pentateuch as a whole (e.g., Josh. 1:8; 1 Chron. 16:40; 22:12; Ezra 7:6; Ps. 1:2, 78:5; Mal. 4:4). New Testament references to the law are also generally references to the Pentateuch (e.g., Matt. 5:17; Acts 13:15; Rom. 3:21).
11. Bartor, "Narrative"; Carmichael, *Spirit of Biblical Law*, 10–24, 49–61; Peterson, *Genesis as Torah*, 3–8.
12. A different and expanded set of examples is given in LeFebvre, *Liturgy of Creation*, 96–98.

should caution us against imposing contemporary assumptions on how the term *historical* is defined and bounded.

From this vantage point, we will see how the Hebrew culture documented the passage of time, marking historical events and establishing festivals and holy days, with the same purpose of theological instruction in mind.

TIME, CALENDARS, AND THE PENTATEUCH

Festivals, new moons, and holy days play a prominent role in the Pentateuch, marking the passage of time and commemorating important historical events—all serving as reminders of God's provision, faithfulness, and sovereignty. If we look at the distribution of festivals and holy days, two observations stand out. The most obvious is the rich use of symbolism, particularly in the employment of the number seven, a number signifying wholeness, completion, or perfection. The Sabbath ended each seven-day week (Exod. 20:11). Seven festivals were named falling within the first seven months of each year (Lev. 23). The Festival of Weeks was celebrated seven weeks after the first harvest (Lev. 23:15). A Sabbath rest for the land was ordained every seventh year (Exod. 23:11). And the Year of Jubilee was to mark the end of seven sets of seven years (Lev. 25:8).

A second observation, less frequently noted, is how closely the festival calendar is tied to the annual agricultural cycle. The seven-month interval in which all the major festivals were celebrated aligned with the growing and harvest season (Lev. 23). The Hebrew year did not start on January 1, but on the new moon of the month following the spring equinox, when days began to grow longer than the nights (March for us). This was the end of the winter rainy season and the beginning of new life (Deut. 11:10–15). Months following were determined by the cycle of new moons rather than a fixed number of days on a calendar.

Table 8 maps the seven festivals to the agricultural rhythm of the land.[13] Agrarian societies of the ancient Near East (ANE) typically grew a variety of crops with different rates of maturation, diminishing the risk of loss due to a spell of bad weather, a blight, or raids. Harvests were thus spread out over the course of the spring and summer. The Hebrew festivals all fall between the first and final harvests.[14]

---

13. Reflecting on Gen. 1:14, LeFebvre concludes, "To follow the celestial calendar was to live on earth in keeping with the cadence of heaven." LeFebvre, *Liturgy of Creation*, 11–24 (quote on 24).

14. In the ANE religious worldview, agricultural blessings were the result of being in step with deity; dryness and rain signaled a "death and new life" principle. For Israel's neighbors, this yielded mythic stories of gods dying and being restored, or battles between gods of life and death. Sacrifices, rituals, and prayers were lifted to appease irritable gods, coaxing them

At one level, there is nothing particularly noteworthy about harvest festivals aligning with the timing of harvests (e.g., Firstfruits and Ingathering). More remarkable, however, is the alignment of Israel's commemorative history with the agricultural calendar.[15] Each year, festivals recalled the history of the exodus and experience in the wilderness. Passover, celebrating redemption of Israel from bondage, coincides with the start of new life during the first month of the year. The Festival of Weeks, celebrating the start of the wheat harvest, aligns with Israel's arrival at Mount Sinai—a time of covenant renewal and reminder to care for those in need. And the Festival of Booths (Ingathering), symbolizing God's provision while Israel lived in tents, falls at the end of the wheat harvest. Each year, "Israel 'participated' in the ancestral exodus from Egypt by remembering the exodus events in connection with the various phases of their harvests."[16] Harvests and history are weaved together in cultural and religious practice—story and statutes experienced in concert.

Before taking all this back to Genesis 1, we will go a bit deeper on the use of dates and chronologies in the Pentateuch. This will prove to be an important step, as it sheds additional light onto how the chronology of the creation story should be understood. We have noted how the festival commemorations of the exodus are aligned with the agricultural rhythm of the land, but there is evidence of even greater intentionality in communicating the historical narratives within a festival-calendar framework.

The festivals behind the stories: liturgical use of dates

Attentive readers may have caught an apparent error in the title of this section. Don't we mean, "The stories behind the festivals"? That would be the normal rendering for a section telling the stories that are represented by each festival. But there is evidence that a backward reading is also in line, reading the stories through the lens of the festival calendar. This requires some explanation.

---

to bless the fertility of the ground and the womb. Israel shared the sense of connection between the fruitfulness of the land and divine pleasure, but the understanding of God and its manifestation in their religious practice was vastly different.

15. LeFebvre, *Liturgy of Creation*, 11–12.
16. LeFebvre, *Liturgy of Creation*, 60. LeFebvre also quotes a Jewish saying, "In every generation a person is duty-bound to regard himself as if he personally has gone forth from Egypt, since it is said, *And you shall tell your son in that day saying, It is because of that which the Lord did for me when I came forth out of Egypt* (Exod. 13:8)."

TABLE 8. THE HEBREW CALENDAR AND FESTIVALS[17]			
Season	Date	Festival	Details
Spring	1/14	Passover	• Beginning of barley harvest (and lambing season); transition to eating from new crop/flock • Recalls sudden departure from Egypt (Exod. 12; Deut. 16:3)
	1/15	Firstfruits	
	1/15–21	Unleavened Bread	
	ca. 3/8	Weeks	• Beginning of wheat harvest (seven weeks after firstfruits of barley [a.k.a. Pentecost]) • Recalls hardship of slavery in Egypt (Deut. 16:10–12) and need to help less-fortunate neighbor (Lev. 23:22; cf. Ruth 2)
Summer			• Tending (and some harvesting) of orchard and vineyard crops (e.g., olives, fruits); firstfruits of each kept for Booths
Autumn	7/1	Trumpets	• After repentance and fasting, biggest feast, including summer firstfruits, wool, meat for sacrifices, and communal sharing • Trumpet blast of alarm to prep for Day of Atonement (only official fast day), recognizing need for forgiveness (Lev. 23:24, 27); then (Booths) give thanks to God, recalling protection during wilderness (Lev. 23:42–43)
	7/10	Atonement	
	7/15–22	Booths/Ingathering	
Winter (Rainy Season)			• Plant/prepare next year's crops as rain comes over about four months; work on other house projects

Most of the dating in the Old Testament is relative, meaning one event is recorded relative to the timing of another event of significance rather than by an independent chronometer (e.g., date on a calendar). The genealogies of Genesis 5 and 11 record births relative to the age of each ancestor. The

---

17. The table draws on charts and information in chap. 3 ("The Festivals of Israel") of LeFebvre, *Liturgy of Creation*, 38–54. The dates refer to the month/day of Israel's calendar, not ours (e.g., 1/14 refers to fourteenth day of the first month, not January 14). On the more practical realities (e.g., risk spreading and labor optimization), LeFebvre draws often on Hopkins, *Highlands of Canaan*.

ascension date of the kings of Judah and Israel are recorded relative to each other, with each king's start date listed as so many years into the reign of the other (e.g., 2 Kings 15:1). The words of the prophet Amos are dated relative to two contemporary kings and a famous natural disaster: "two years before the earthquake" (Amos 1:1). This method of dating is referred to as *event-sequencing*.[18]

There are twenty-one exceptions in the Pentateuch where day-and-month dates are given for events from Israel's history. Five are found in the story of the flood, and the rest are found in the exodus from Egypt and the subsequent wandering in the wilderness (table 9). It is somewhat odd that timeline dates are used at all, but it gets even more curious when we drill down into the details. Of the twenty-one exceptions, seventeen dates fall exactly on new moons and festival dates, and the remaining four all fall within the same two-week period between two harvest festivals.[19]

The correspondences are intriguing. To make sense out of the alignments between events and calendars, we will look first at those associated with the flood, then those tied to the exodus and wanderings.

Noah's flood

The flood story is unique in several ways, two of which are pertinent here.[20] First, it is the only story in the pre-Abraham narratives (Gen. 1–11) that contains timeline dates. Second, it uses a schematic (administrative) calendar rather than the normal civil (cultic) calendar. The typical civil calendar of the ANE was based on the observed cycle of the moon. Time between new moons is roughly 29.5 days, resulting in months varying between 29 and 30 days. Twelve lunar months takes only 354 days, requiring annual adjustments to round out the 365 days of a full year.[21] Conversely, a schematic calendar

---

18. Sacha Stern states, "Ethnographers have found that in many—if not all—'primitive' or nonmodern societies, the concept of time as a[n] entity in itself simply does not exist. Reality is explained in terms of events, changes, and processes, but in these worldviews, the notion of 'pure time' or an overarching 'time-dimension' is completely absent and unknown." Stern, *Time and Process in Ancient Judaism*, 12.

19. The list of twenty-one references does not include the five festival lists themselves (Exod. 23:10–17; 34:18–24; Lev. 23:4–43; Num. 28:18–29:40; Deut. 16:1–17).

20. One could also add the poetic structure of the flood narrative. See Anderson, "From Analysis to Synthesis," 37–38; Wenham, "Coherence of the Flood Narrative," 337–42.

21. Lunation actually varies 29.26–29.80 days; see Rochberg-Halton, "Calendars, Ancient Near East"; Cohen, *Cultic Calendars of the Ancient Near East*, 4. No instruction is found in the Bible on how Israel adjusted their lunar calendar to a 365-day year. For a more detailed discussion, see LeFebvre, *Liturgy of Creation*, 20–28.

arbitrarily assigns 30 days to every month, yielding a 360-day year. The latter calendar was typically used for recurring business dealings.[22]

The coming and going of the floodwaters are recorded as each requiring both five months and 150 days (Gen. 7–8), which means 30 days assigned to each month—a schematic calendar. This alone suggests there is more to these dates than mere timestamps, but we find additional evidence of symbolic intention when we consider the alignment of the dates within the context of the agricultural year (see table 9).

- The floodwaters begin in the second month (2/17) in the midst of the normally dry grain harvests, signaling divine judgment via unseasonal rains and the truncation of food production.
- The ark comes to rest safely on the mountains of Ararat from its watery wilderness (7/17) as if during the Festival of Booths (7/15–22), a commemoration of Israel's forty years living in tents (Lev. 23:39–43).
- The mountains become visible for Noah's first glance at the land (10/1) on a new moon between the end of one agricultural year and the start of the next, with anticipation of God giving new life.
- The floodwaters begin to recede on the new moon of New Year's Day (1/1), signifying renewal and corresponding to the beginning of a new growing season. The timing corresponds with Israel's arrival at Canaan after forty years of wandering. Passover was celebrated, the manna from heaven stopped, and they ate from the produce of the land (Josh. 5:10–12).
- Dry ground finally appears (2/27) at the normal time of harvest, signaling divine mercy and God's provision.

Exodus and wilderness wandering

The remaining sixteen timeline dates are in the story of Israel's rescue from bondage and wilderness experiences. Half of these dates are accounted for in the expected association of the exodus with the Festivals of Passover and Unleavened Bread (see table 10). Two are not linked directly with festival dates, but fall in the same week in the middle of the grain harvest.

---

22. LeFebvre, *Liturgy of Creation*, 99–103; Ben-Dov, "Calendars and Festivals." A schematic calendar may be loosely comparable to a modern organization's *fiscal* year—a "business year" that may be offset and treated differently from the calendar year.

These are the dates when manna was first provided, coupled with Israel's first mentioned Sabbath observance (Exod. 16) and the departure from Sinai (Num. 10:11). It is hard to miss the link between God's providence in providing manna as bread in the wilderness and grain for bread each harvest season.

The remaining five dates are all new moons, including the first erection of the tabernacle on New Year's Day, a census, and the deaths of Miriam, Aaron, and Moses. While it is possible God set his divine watch to line up each of these events on actual new moons, it is plausible that these are commemorative dates, or dates of *observance*, aligned to fit with the civil calendar and enhance recall. Erection of the tabernacle marks the start of the first year of Israel's wanderings. The deaths of the three siblings are likewise memorialized with symbolic intention. As the forty years of wilderness wandering comes to a close, Miriam dies one month into the final year, beginning the transition to the next generation. Aaron dies near its midpoint, and Moses dies one month prior to its end.

TABLE 9. THE HEBREW CALENDAR AND THE FLOOD		
Holy Day (Hebrew Dates)	**Theology/Symbolism**	**Event/Text**
two weeks between two grain harvest festivals (2/17–27)	time of harvests	flood begins (Gen. 7:11; on 2/17) [judgment for rain during harvest]
Booths (7/15–22)	ultimate safety and deliverance (to Land)	ark comes to rest on Ararat (Gen. 8:4)
new moon (10/1)	transition	mountaintops visible (Gen. 8:5; on 10/1) [in tenth month planting finishing; see if God gives new life]
New Year (1/1)	newness/hope	floodwaters recede (Gen. 8:13)
two weeks between two grain harvest festivals (2/17–27)	time of harvests	ground dry (Gen. 8:14; on 2/27) [cessation of rain signals mercy (contrast Gen. 7:11)]

TABLE 10. THE HEBREW CALENDAR AND THE EXODUS		
Holy Day (Hebrew Dates)	Theology/ Symbolism	Event/Text
New Year (1/1)	newness/hope	• exodus begins (Exod. 12:2) • tabernacle erected (Exod. 40:2, 17) • death of Miriam; transition to second generation (Num. 20:1)[23]
Passover/Unleavened Bread (1/14–21)	sudden redemption (from Egypt)	• 5× refer to original (Exod. 12:3, 6, 18; 13:3–4; Num. 33:3)[24] • 2× refer to first Passover at tabernacle (Num. 9:1–5, 11)[25]
new moon (2/1)	transition	• census (those traveling under God's care) (Num. 1:1, 18); first new moon following Passover, so year's "journey" under way
same week, between two grain harvest festivals (2/15–27)	time of harvests	• manna and Sabbath on 2/15–21 (Exod. 16); keep Sabbath even in harvest season • leaves Sinai on 2/20 (Num. 10:11)
Weeks (ca. 3/8)	covenant renewal (to Sinai)	• arrival at Sinai (Exod. 19:1); covenant renewal (e.g., 2 Chron. 15:10–12)
new moon (5/1)	transition	• death of Aaron (Num. 33:38) [midpoint of summer]
Booths (7/15–22)	providence through trials	• wilderness wandering in tents (Deut. 8:2–4; Lev. 23:43)
new moon (11/1)	transition	• death of Moses after final speeches (Deut. 1:3; cf. 32:48–50) [prep for New Year and Passover]

---

23. Exodus 2:2 and Num. 20.1 explicitly state only the month, with first day implied.
24. Exodus 12:3 refers to the 10th day for selecting the Passover lamb in preparation for killing and eating on the 14th.
25. Numbers 9:11 refers to an alternative Passover (on 2/14) due to some of them being unclean (see v. 6).

What to make of it all

The most plausible and parsimonious explanation is that these narratives, while truly historical, have dates recast to fit the later festival calendar (thus "calendar-law narratives"). That is, rather than providing journalistic chronology, the dates intentionally serve a liturgical purpose—the ancient Israelite read these stories and intuitively drew the connections between history and their present rhythm of work and worship. LeFebvre argues that "the Pentateuch uses dates for liturgical instruction, not to provide a journalistic chronology. Event sequencing, not dates, is the Pentateuch's method to indicate chronology."[26]

This type of reading, when applied consistently through all the dated events, brings together the flood narrative and the broader exodus journey (including first-year exodus, second-year tabernacle-centered events, and fortieth-year end-of-exodus generation) as parallel sanctuary stories. Both Noah's family and the people of Israel constructed "a mobile sanctuary that carries God's people through a barren wilderness to a land of bounty, where a mountaintop altar is (to be) constructed for worship. . . . Dates serve to link these two 'temple inauguration' histories to the annual worship festivals of later Israel."[27]

For those concerned that this view affirms errors in the Bible, it is helpful to recall that even today we celebrate commemorative holidays shifted from the historical dates—for practical or theological purposes. As examples, the actual date of a presidential birthday is typically shifted to a Monday to yield a three-day weekend, and the two most important Christian holidays, Christmas and Easter, are not fixed on the actual date of Christ's birth or resurrection. Easter is particularly noteworthy, as the date floats, assigned each year in the Western calendar to the Sunday following the full moon on or after March 21. The date is not technically the same day Christ arose, yet no one accuses calendar manufactures of affirming dating errors.

Dating discontinuities

Recognition of the liturgical intention of dates in the Old Testament has significant apologetic repercussions, "answering" some critical objections regarding the unity of the biblical text. Critical scholars have cited internal inconsistencies (e.g., chronological idiosyncrasies) and external inconsistencies (e.g., events described within implausible timeframes) as evidence that

---

26. LeFebvre, *Liturgy of Creation*, 60.
27. LeFebvre, *Liturgy of Creation*, 76–77 (n28 includes many sources that see Noah's ark as a floating "temple"). See also our Layer 5 ("Temple").

the text as we have it is a patchwork of disparate and often contradictory sources.[28] Internal inconsistencies include basic discrepancies like the timing of the journey from Egypt to Sinai as three days (Exod. 3:18; 5:3; 8:27) versus multiple months (Exod. 19:1; Num. 33:1–15). Subtler examples include the occasional use of a "schematic calendar" of 30-day months (e.g., Num. 20:29; Deut. 34:8; Esther 4:11; Dan. 6:7, 12), rather than the actual lunar-based months of alternating 29–30 days. Arguments have also been made for implausible timeframes allowed for things like floodwaters to dry up from the earth or in the construction of the tabernacle.[29]

Whether such discrepancies genuinely exist or not, the charge of *error* ultimately derives from inappropriately applying modern literary standards to an ancient text. Discordant timelines in the Old Testament are not errors, as ample evidence exists that dates were marked with literary-theological intention, serving the purpose of calendar-law narratives. This argument parallels our introductory "Model Approach," where we addressed apparent discrepancies in the number of ancestors in the genealogy of Christ. Shifts from simple numerical accounts in generations and in dates are intentional, effectively communicating the intended message.

CALENDAR-NARRATIVES AND GENESIS 1

We called attention in Layer 1 ("Song") to the fact that Genesis 1 is a unique genre found nowhere else in Scripture. It is neither classical Hebrew poetry nor typical historical narrative, but a blend of the two. At a broader level, however, Genesis 1 is part of the Pentateuch, self-identified by the Bible under the overarching theme or genre of *law* (torah). If Moses is the primary author, as commonly believed, it was part of the package of works initially recorded at the time Israel was being established as a nation. We made the case above that the narratives, including the flood, the patriarchs, and the exodus, were not just documenting events or people of significance in human history, but served a larger liturgical, theological purpose. Even the dates given for events appear to be assigned with liturgical rather than journalistic intention. Dates of historical events, of festivals, and holy days align with the Hebrew agricultural calendar.

---

28. For example, Jan van Goudoever (*Biblical Calendars*, 56) concludes, "From such conflicting indications it is clear that the 'calendar' in the Torah is not consistent. There are either different traditions, which are not harmonized, or some alterations were made by writers or redactors which disturbed a 'calendar' which was originally consistent" (cited in LeFebvre, *Liturgy of Creation*, 83).
29. For a more thorough discussion and many more examples of apparent timeline discrepancies, see LeFebvre, *Liturgy of Creation*, 82–93, including citations contained therein.

Genesis 1, as part of the narrative law (*torah*), is likewise more than a record of past events. It is a microcosm of each agricultural year of preparing the soil, planting, harvesting, and celebrating God's provision with feasts and holy days, repeated on a weekly cycle. The purpose is liturgical. Defense of this perspective will be threefold. First, we will zero in on verses related to time that signal a forward-looking understanding rather than a story of longing that looks only backward to a lost ecosystem. Second, we will briefly visit commonly noted internal timeline issues that point strongly away from a literalistic chronology. And third, we will build the case for Genesis 1 as a year-in-microcosm for the divine farmer and final focus on the Sabbath.

TIME, FESTIVALS, AND GENESIS 1:14

In Layer 4 ("Covenant"), we made the argument that nature itself was not corrupted by sin—it was the *interaction* between humans and the earth that was negatively altered. Nature continues to work as God designed. We revisit this theme here with a look at verses that indicate the creation story was written to the nation of Israel for *current* liturgical purpose, not as a story of a fragile utopian paradise now lost. For this subject, we will start in the middle of the creation week, when the sun, moon, and stars were placed in the firmament (day 4; Gen. 1:14–19). The luminaries were not just assigned their physical places, but served two specific and distinct purposes, to be "for signs and appointed times," and "for days and years."[30]

The Hebrew word for "appointed times" is *mo'adim*, variously translated in verse 14 as "seasons" (KJV, ESV, NASB), "fixed times" (NAB), "sacred times" (NIV), "sacred seasons" (CEB), or "festivals" (NJB, REB, HCSB). *Mo'adim* (or its singular, *mo'ed*) appears 160 times in the Pentateuch, always in the context of a gathering at a set time or place. Many times, it refers directly to festivals, new moons, or the Sabbath (e.g., Num. 10:10; Isa. 1:14; Hos. 2:11).[31] It is never used in the general sense of seasons of the year.[32] Leviticus 23, which describes each of the Hebrew festivals, starts with God telling Moses, "Speak to the people of Israel and say to them, these are the appointed feasts [*mo'adim*] of Yahweh that you shall proclaim as holy convocations; they are

---

30. The ESV translates the verse as "for signs and for seasons," with a footnote stating "seasons" can also be "appointed times."
31. New moons were more than just markers for the first day of each month, but had religious significance (e.g., 2 Kings 4:23; Ps. 81:3; Isa. 1:13; Ezek. 46:1; Hos. 2:11; Amos 8:5).
32. LeFebvre, *Liturgy of Creation*, 11, 15–16; Guillaume, *Land and Calendar*, 47; Vogels, "Cultic and Civil Calendars," 163–80 (esp. 165–66).

my appointed feasts [*mo'adim*]" (v. 2). The first of the *mo'adim* to be identified is the Sabbath (v. 3). Of the seven annual festivals then described, five are set relative to "fixed times" of the moon.[33]

The point of these observations is that there is an intentional grouping of words in Genesis 1:14 to differentiate the two purposes of the heavenly lights. To paraphrase the text: "let them be for signs and festivals on one hand, and let them be for days and years on the other hand." They were to serve both sacred time and ordinary time.[34] This text does not just describe an initial creation as it existed prior to sin. It is a forward-looking account that describes creation with Israel's future (and religious calendar) in mind.

In this light, the placement of verse 14 among the days is noteworthy, falling in the middle of the seven-day sequence and yielding a triangular 1-4-7 structure related to time. Day 1 introduces time by the separation of light and dark.[35] Day 4 brings in the sun, moon, and stars to set the cadence of religious and civil practice. Day 7 culminates by tying the two together with the Sabbath completing six calendar days of work with a religious day of rest and worship.

Timeline discontinuities

The placement of luminaries in the sky in the middle of the creation week, coupled with the resulting 1-4-7 structure, could be sufficient evidence on its own that the chronology of Genesis 1 was never intended to be read as a set of journalistic timestamps. We find such recognition in the writings of church fathers such as Origen (third century) and Augustine (early fifth century), long before challenges were raised by scientific observations. A short list of additional timeline discontinuities includes the following:

- Light before light sources (days 1–3)
- Light separated from dark twice (day 1 and again on day 4; vv. 3–5, 14–18)
- Discordant order of events in Genesis 1 (birds, land animals, humans) and Genesis 2 (man, beasts and birds, woman)[36]

---

33. A fixed day of a month refers to the number of days following the new moon. DiMattei, *Genesis 1 and the Creationism Debate*, 29–31.
34. Rudolph, "Festivals in Genesis 1:14"; Vogels, "Cultic and Civil Calendars," 168.
35. Guillaume, *Land and Calendar*, 47; Vogels, "Cultic and Civil Calendars," 176.
36. Some translations smooth over the apparent reversal in the order of creation in Gen. 2:19 by assuming "God formed" is intended to mean "God *had* formed" (e.g., ESV, NIV).

- Plant growth producing seeds and fruit in one day (verbs for growth
  and stages indicate normal processes of months for crops and years
  for orchards; Gen. 1:11–13)[37]

These discrepancies are too obvious for the writer to have missed if intending
the account to be understood as a simple timeline of creative acts.[38]

The thematic construction of the story further argues against a wooden
sequence, for the God who merely speaks and it is, who does not tire or grow
weary (Isa. 40:28; cf. John 5:17), is nonetheless represented "in overalls."[39] The
divine Farmer works during daylight hours, resting each night, and finishing
out six days with a day of rest—a rest described in Exodus 31:17 as including
a time of rejuvenation.[40] The figurative nature of "evenings and mornings" is
particularly apparent when we note the transition from day to night is only
meaningful from a fixed location on the earth. From an external perspective
(e.g., God's view of the earth), the planet is perpetually half day and half night.

These observations may be perceived as errors only if the text is arbitrarily
forced to conform to modern literary systematics unknown to the ANE. Dates
in the Old Testament, as with the genealogies in Matthew and Luke, record
genuine history, communicated in a culturally consistent fashion that is not
bound by the sensibilities of cultures thousands of years removed.[41]

The year in a week

Layer 1 ("Song") highlighted the rhyming words in Genesis 1:2, *tohu wabohu*,
usually translated as variations of "formless" and "empty." Commentators
have debated the exact meaning of this phrase. Some note that it could also
be translated as "desolate and barren," indicating a disordered wasteland.[42]
The lack of order may be seen in a negative sense as a chaotic condition in
need of conquering, consistent with the origin stories of other ANE cultures,

---

37. LeFebvre, *Liturgy of Creation*, 122–32, 149–63, 168, 173, 179–80, and esp. 196–220.
38. For additional examples and detailed descriptions, see Davidson, *Friend of Science, Friend of Faith*, 57–67.
39. LeFebvre, *Liturgy of Creation*, 119.
40. The verb *nafash* at the end of Exod. 31:17, typically translated as "refreshed," means "to inhale, breath, recover" (i.e., to "get one's breath back" after physical exertion).
41. LeFebvre draws a NT parallel with the chronological differences in the Gospels concerning Jesus's crucifixion—i.e., third hour, day after Passover (Matt, Mark, Luke) vs. sixth hour, before Passover (John)—which exist for theological reasons. LeFebvre, *Liturgy of Creation*, 1–8; see also Estes, *Temporal Mechanics of the Fourth Gospel*, esp. 146–47.
42. LeFebvre, *Liturgy of Creation*, 138.

or in a more neutral sense of something ripe with potential.[43] The variant translations and understandings are not necessarily in conflict. A desolate wasteland may be so because it is lacking purposeful form and is empty of life. The disordered initial state can, and perhaps *should*, be understood as both negative and full of potential. It is not initially in a good condition, lacking the order necessary to bring life; yet over this barren and lifeless state, the Spirit of God moves.

The anthropomorphism of the ensuing narrative concentrates the imagery of Genesis 1:2 on a farmer surveying the untended boundaries of his fields that have yet to be ordered (lacking the ability to support life) and lie barren (absent of life) (cf. Deut. 32:10; Isa. 34:11; 45:18; Jer. 4:23). These raw materials are the laborer's starting point to bring about order. Like a mother bird providing care (Deut. 32:11), the presence of God's hovering Spirit offers hope to overcome the present circumstances.[44]

As the divine Farmer sets to work, he divides his labor to address the disorder and barrenness. A three-plus-three structure of parallel days is similar to the framework described in Layer 1, but with a particular agricultural cadence in view that serves the predominant six-plus-one structure of work and worship.[45] The emphasis of days 1 through 3 are on *separating* and *gathering*, working to prepare the fields for planting and experiencing the firstfruits of harvest. Life on the land requires three things: light, water, and fertile soil. Each has its day, with light separated out from the darkness (day 1), waters separated below and above to provide life-giving rains (day 2), and waters below gathered into the sea to allow dry land to appear (day 3). The first triad of days comes to a climax with the realization of firstfruits—plants not only appear but also reach their first wave of fruitfulness. Plants yielding seed and trees bearing fruit (v. 12) speak of the first harvest.

Days 4 through 6 build on the ordering of days 1 through 3, eradicating the barrenness. They are days of continued fruitfulness, of harvest, and of

---

43. Collins, *Reading Genesis Well*, 166.
44. LeFebvre, *Liturgy of Creation*, 136–84. This perspective takes Gen. 1:1 as a title or introduction, not an initial creative act. Creation *ex nihilo* is implied but not explicitly stated in v. 1 (as it is in Heb. 11:3).
45. LeFebvre, *Liturgy of Creation*, 120. The overlaps seen here with other layers demonstrate our contention that the text profitably can be examined and understood from multiple viable perspectives without an either/or straightjacket. Interestingly, in his foreword to *The Liturgy of Creation*, the analogical-day advocate C. John Collins commends LeFebvre for improving the framework reading, "overcoming some of the of the difficulties that others have found with it" (p. x).

feasts. Day 4 introduces the timekeepers into the domain of light and dark created in day 1. The sun, moon, and stars serve to mark the harvest festivals and holy days, linking the rhythm of days and years to the coming history of God's people. Day 5 fills the domains of sea and sky from day 2 with fish and birds who feast on the fruits of God's preparatory work, and in turn provide food for creatures yet to come. Day 6 adds beasts to the dry land of day 3.[46]

The second triad of days comes to its own climax in two ways. The first is agricultural, completing the fruitfulness of the soil by adding flocks and herds to the crops from day 3. The text does not just say God brought forth animals, but specifically includes livestock (*behemah*). These are the domesticated animals that will be among the clean animals of Levitical law (Lev. 11). Identifying the type of animals suitable to eat and to sacrifice to God is further evidence that the creation story was addressing Israel's present as well as the earth's beginning.

The second and greater climax is in the creation of humans. All that has been made is given to these singular creatures to tend the fields and flocks of God's creation and to enjoy its bounty.[47] The harvest is complete, and God invites them to feast. The repeated phrase "it was good" (*tob*) is not merely a series of statements of satisfaction with a job well done, but "draws attention to an object's quality and fitness for its purpose."[48]

The week concludes not just with rest but also with a day that is "made holy"—the first Sabbath. Just as the work days of creation look forward in anticipation of Israel's fruitful occupation, the Sabbath likewise is anticipatory, encapsulating the need for and joy of celebrating the ultimate source of the land's bounty in festivals, new moons, and holy days.

Sabbath as festival

Chances are, few readers have heard a sermon that grouped the Sabbath in with the festivals of Israel. The Sabbath is typically treated as an independent

---

46. The framework view sees days 1–3 addressing the *formless* issue and days 4–6 addressing the *empty* issue. LeFebvre argues for both being addressed (as a disordered wasteland) in all six days. He characterizes the first triad of days as "Fruitfulness," and the second triad as "Feasting" (birds, fish, animals, and humans feasting on the fruitfulness of day 3). LeFebvre, *Liturgy of Creation*, 138–45.
47. LeFebvre, *Liturgy of Creation*, 174. Other clues of humans as climax include the increase in divine utterance (four vs. one or two); divine contemplation (i.e., gives reasons for creating); the addition of the definite article "*the* sixth day"; the poetic creedal statement of v. 27 (i.e., formal poetry makes this a rhetorical high point); the use of plural language for God, portraying God as a social being to make humanity in his likeness (LeFebvre, *Liturgy of Creation*, 175–77).
48. Wenham, *Genesis 1–15*, 18.

topic, thematically unrelated to the annual feasts. Yet we find them directly linked in Scripture. Leviticus 23, which describes each of the seven festivals, starts with the Sabbath (vv. 2–3), and the prophet Hosea warned Israel that God would ". . . put an end to all her mirth, her feasts, her new moons, her Sabbaths, and all her appointed feasts" (Hos. 2:11). As the end of the year-in-a-week, the first Sabbath represents its own microcosm of Israel's future festivals, to be read in concert with the rest of the Pentateuch.

This sense is captured in the wording of the fourth commandment, which does more than just admonish God's people to honor the Sabbath. It calls the faithful to remember the history of God's providence and redemption as part of the experience. The Ten Commandments appear twice in the Pentateuch, in Exodus 20 and Deuteronomy 5. In Exodus 20:11, the rhythm of work and rest is tied to the creation: "For in six days Yahweh made heaven and earth, the sea, and all that is in them, and rested on the seventh day. Therefore Yahweh blessed the Sabbath day and made it holy." In Deuteronomy 5:15, the link to the creation is replaced with remembering that "you were a slave in the land of Egypt, and Yahweh your God brought you out from there with a mighty hand and an outstretched arm. Therefore Yahweh your God commanded you to keep the Sabbath."

The juxtaposition of these parallel passages is informative. The link to creation in one version and to redemption (the exodus) in the other is consistent with the overarching understanding of the Pentateuch as narrative law, the earlier stories tying in with the later statutes. Creation is tied together with the exodus and, by implication, to the blessings of the promised land, recalled with each Sabbath, festival, and holy day. Israel was to read the creation story together with their experience living in Canaan, ensuring they understood the true source of the land's bounty: "Beware lest you say in your heart, 'My power and the might of my hand have gotten me this wealth.' You shall remember Yahweh your God, for it is he who gives you power to get wealth, that he may confirm his covenant that he swore to your fathers" (Deut. 8:17–18).

Sabbath and Sunday

Under the new covenant, the resurrection of the Messiah was so momentous that it resulted in a shift of Sabbath-day observance to Sunday (Luke 24:1; Acts 20:7; 1 Cor. 16:2)—the day of the resurrection and of Pentecost. Christians generally know of Pentecost as the visitation of the Holy Spirit on the gathered disciples fifty days after the resurrection. Fewer are aware that the reason so many Jews were drawn from far lands to hear the various languages spoken by the disciples is because it was the Festival of Weeks, occurring seven weeks after Passover. It was a festival of offerings, of rest from labors, and of seeking the welfare of the poor and sojourner (Lev. 23:15–22). The death and resurrection of Jesus and the outpouring of the Holy Spirit aligned with the sacrifice of the Passover Lamb, the offering up of Firstfruits, and the gift-giving of the Festival of Weeks. The beauty of the calendar narrative of Scripture is breathtaking.

CHALLENGES AND RESPONSES

Objection 1: *This view is new, so it can't be true.*
When a new understanding of the Bible is offered, there is wisdom in cautious consideration. While Scripture was written *to* a specific people at a specific time, it was also intended *for* believers at all times and places. To suggest all of humanity has missed an understanding of the Bible until today is tantamount to saying it is wrong. With this acknowledgment, we will make a few observations in support of the calendar-narrative perspective.

First, it is not a completely new view. LeFebvre makes the case that a calendar-narrative perspective was likely well understood by the original audience—a people immersed in the agricultural cycle and receiving the Pentateuch in the context of the exodus, Mount Sinai, and arrival at the promised land. It is an old perspective that got covered in a bit of dust with the passage of time and varied cultural experiences. In the history of the Christian church, it was not uncommon to drift away from the nuances of an older understanding, only to rediscover it at a later time. The medieval drift toward a works-based view of salvation with a later return to a faith-based message is but one of many examples. In this light, the calendar-narrative view may be argued to be a *recovered* understanding.

LeFebvre further argues that the core of his proposed view is not new at all. The fourth commandment (Exod. 20:8–11) has long been recognized as pointing to Genesis 1 as a "sabbath guidance calendar," making a calendar view perhaps the only universally accepted perspective. What is new in LeFebvre's work is the exegetical development of the calendar-narrative genre to more fully explain and interpret this understanding of the text.[49]

Finally, this perspective does not imply that all other views must be abandoned in favor of this one. We make exactly the opposite case. We offer this perspective more in the sense of the often-used analogy of the onion. If layers of an onion are pulled back and a new layer is discovered underneath, it does

---

49.   LeFebvre, *Liturgy of Creation*, 114, 119–21, 132–38, 144–45, 196.

not stop the old layers from being genuinely and truly *onion*. In our evaluation, the calendar view *enhances* rather than *replaces* traditional understandings of Genesis 1.

Objection 2: *This view is too complicated to be plausible.*

Is this view too complicated to be plausible? To respond bluntly, who are we to decide how "simple" things ought to be? The doctrine of the perspicuity of Scripture limits the "clear and obvious" to the Bible's fundamental message of salvation, the character of God, and basic ethics of Christian obedience. But the Bible itself (cf. 2 Pet. 3:16) and the history of theology recognize some things in Scripture to be quite difficult. Also, many of our struggles to understand Scripture and our feelings of its strangeness are due to trying to grasp an ancient text while influenced by our own, often very different, cultural context (e.g., Western, American, situated in a particular denominational tradition). It is easy to read into the text *our* understanding of a word (in an English translation) or a concept (e.g., time) without realizing *they* did not always think like *us*. Thus, what is strange and complicated to us may have been clear and obvious to the original audience. It will be of interest to see how Bible-honoring theologians engage with this perspective over the coming years.

DISCUSSION QUESTIONS

1. Why is this layer referred to as a calendar-narrative view?

2. Is it acceptable to consider an understanding of Scripture that is new? Why or why not?

3. The Bible itself identifies all five of the first books (Pentateuch) as the Law. How can poems and stories be lumped into "law"?

4. Does it create concern if celebrated or commemorated dates in the Bible are offset from the historical date of their occurrence? Why is it argued that this was likely done?

5. What significance is argued for the wording of Genesis 1:14?

6. How is the idea of the "year-in-a-week" communicated in Genesis 1?

7. How is the Sabbath a festival?

LAYER 7

Land

('*erets*, "land")

*For Yahweh your God is bringing you into a good land, a land of brooks of water,
of fountains and springs, flowing out in the valleys and hills, a land of wheat and barley,
of vines and fig trees and pomegranates, a land of olive trees and honey, a land in
which you will eat bread without scarcity, in which you will lack nothing, a land whose
stones are iron, and out of whose hills you can dig copper. And you shall eat and be full,
and you shall bless Yahweh your God for the good land he has given you.*
(Deut. 8:7–10)

When reading the stories of the Old Testament, a pattern of human behavior emerges that is not flattering. Faithfulness to God's calling and commandments is not the norm. The main characters repeatedly fail. We do not have to wait long in the history of humanity before the pattern appears. There is no prelude of early generations living righteous lives until one bad apple came along to spoil it for the rest. According to Genesis 1–3, sin and rebellion trace their history to the root of human existence.

While sin saddens and angers God, its beginnings and continued existence are not a surprise to him. He had a plan to address the shortcomings of his image-bearers, holding them accountable for the condition of their hearts, yet also recognizing their weakness. That plan did not develop piecemeal, figured out in haltering steps as God attempted various options from Adam to Abraham to Moses and finally to Jesus. God knew the plan from the start, and revealed it in a manner sufficient for each generation's need, always building toward a common future objective of drawing the people of God from all the nations into his rest (Heb. 4).

That rest is depicted consistently through Scripture in association with a land in which God's presence dwells—a land in which he walks and reigns (Layer 5, "Temple"). It is Eden. It is the promised land. It is Zion. It is the future new Jerusalem. Sin and exile from the land represents the loss of God's presence—ultimately leading to death. The centrality of land, repeated sin and exile, and the need for divine redemption are at the heart of this last layer.[1]

In several of the previous layers, we drew attention to the importance of reading the Pentateuch as a unified book rather than five loosely connected records. We will continue and expand on that emphasis in this layer, linking the creation story to Israel's experience at Sinai and beyond to their eternal hope. In brief, the story of creation is not the background leading up to Israel's story. It *is* Israel's story. The themes and history of Israel as a nation are all present in the microcosm of Eden. These themes include the theological importance of land, God's covenant relationship with Israel (with special attention to Sinai), the inevitability of human failure, and the certain hope of a divine restoration.[2]

We chose to present this perspective last for two reasons. First, the arguments used to support this layer overlap significantly with several of the others. We will periodically refer back to earlier discussions to avoid repetition and to highlight how this layer intersects with others. Second, the perspective has a rich eschatological component that will allow us to close the final layer with our attention fixed on the promised Messiah.

LAND AS EDEN

Seeing the creation story as Israel's story starts with a focus on the land. While most view the days of creation as describing the entire planet and cosmos, the days can also be understood more specifically as describing the preparation of the local landscape, Eden, for human habitation. It is land that represents both the material blessings of God and, more importantly, his presence among his people. From here the story of Adam and Eve's relationship with God, divine mandates, warnings, temptations, sin, exile, and future hope foreshadows the larger story of Israel, repeated corporately by the nation and individually by the patriarchs and kings. All that unfolds in Israel's history is found in condensed form in Eden and its loss.

---

1. Much in this layer is drawn from John Sailhamer and his former student Seth Postell. Sailhamer: "Creation, Genesis 1–11, and the Canon"; "Exegetical Notes: Genesis 1:1–2:4a"; *Making of the Pentateuch*; *Genesis Unbound*; "Mosaic Law and the Theology of the Pentateuch"; *Pentateuch as Narrative*. Postell: *Adam as Israel*.
2. These four themes are identified in Postell, *Adam as Israel*, 75–148, who references Sailhamer (and others) throughout, but we divert from Postell's order and content. See also Turner, "Deuteronomy's Theology of Exile," 203–15.

The links between Eden and Canaan are divided below following the biblical timeline from the formless waste of Genesis 1:2, to the days of creation and rest, to the geography of Eden, and finally to later descriptions of the land of Canaan.[3]

Uninhabitable wasteland

The land theme shares in common with Layer 2 ("Analogy") a focus on preparation of the land for human use. Picking up at the second verse of Genesis, we find the now-familiar expression that the earth was *tohu wabohu*, translated in most English Bibles as "formless and void." As mentioned earlier, these words can also be understood as variations of barren and empty of life—an uninhabitable wasteland. The alternate translations are not necessarily in conflict; the different English words have overlapping meaning. An uninhabitable wasteland can be argued to be without meaningful form and void of desirable life. The variant translation is useful, however, for drawing out an additional layer of understanding in which land (earth) represents the specific geography planned for human residence.

The only other places in Scripture where *tohu* and *bohu* are used together are in references to the land of Canaan after generational unfaithfulness has led to conquest and exile. Jeremiah speaks of the ruined land as follows:

> I looked on the earth [*'erets*], and behold, it was without form and void [*tohu wabohu*];
>> and to the heavens, and they had no light.
> I looked on the mountains, and behold, they were quaking,
>> and all the hills moved to and fro.
> I looked, and behold, there was no man,
>> and all the birds of the air had fled.
> I looked, and behold, the fruitful land was a desert,
>> and all its cities were laid in ruins
> before Yahweh, before his fierce anger.
>> (Jer. 4:23–26)

The words reflect an undoing or reversal of creation. Working backward, there are no humans (creation day 6), a desert indicates few animals or plants (days

---

3. For the most helpful and up-to-date summary of the connections between Eden and Canaan, see LeFebvre, "Adam Reigns in Eden," 35–42.

3 and 6), birds of the air have fled (days 2 and 5), stable land is absent (shaking hills) (day 3), light has fled (days 1 and 4), and we are back to being an uninhabited wasteland—formless and void (*tohu wabohu*). The waste is described in similar terms in the judgments observed in Deuteronomy 32 and Isaiah 34. These reversals are directed at the promised land, linking Canaan and Eden.[4]

Parallels are also found in the imagery of water as barrier between the waste and the coming good land. In Genesis 1:2, a watery abyss lays over the world. God's spirit (*ruakh*, "spirit, wind, breath") moved over these waters to bring function and order.[5] Following the deconstruction of creation by the flood, God brought a wind to free the land of the flood waters. And bringing Israel out of bondage and into the promised land, God parted the waters of the sea and the Jordan River, allowing traverses on dry ground (Exod. 14; 15:8; Josh. 3). Exodus 15:8 poetically speaks of the waters piled up at a "blast from [God's] nostrils."

The days of creation

From the perspective of Genesis 1:2, God surveys a local landscape that is barren and desolate, seeing that work needs to be done to transform it into a place suitable for human habitation. The necessary attention is divided into six parts, each accomplishing a different function designed to provide for a bountiful land. Day 1 brings light to give purpose to eyes and life to plants. Day 2 separates the waters, with the "waters above" establishing the cycle of lifegiving rains. Day 3 lifts out dry land that will become the home of crops and herds and humans. Day 4 provides the celestial bodies that will keep track of time and mark the festivals that will annually commemorate the care and providence of God (Layer 6, "Calendar"). Day 5 fills the seas and sky with fish and birds for God's own pleasure and to provide humans with food. The creative work culminates with day 6, filling the land with animals and cattle and making it finally ready for human habitation. With humans created and in place, it is all declared very good, leading to day 7, when God rests with his people (Layer 5, "Temple").[6]

---

4. If this sounds like it contradicts conclusions drawn in Layer 4 ("Covenant") regarding an unbroken covenant with nature, note that Jeremiah's vision is not about the condition of the world following Adam's sin. Rather, it addresses what Canaan *will* become if (when) Israel continues in sin. It is the experience of exile.
5. Hebrew includes a wordplay/alliteration of *tohu* (formlessness, wasteland) and *tehom* (deep).
6. Sailhamer asserts that Gen. 1:1 represents the creation of the entire cosmos, while the days of creation are literal days preparing Canaan (Sailhamer, "Genesis," 50–53; Sailhamer,

The Hebrew word for land is *'erets,* appearing over twenty times in Genesis 1. The meaning can range, depending on the context, from the soil beneath one's feet to broad regions where nations reside. While a case can be made for the land of the third day to be of global scale, the focus can also be argued to be directed at the formation of a particular land specifically prepared for God's image-bearers. It is the land of Eden and its environs.

The theological significance of land is immense. It serves as a principal method in the Bible of illustrating what it means for a people to walk with God. It is not just the notion of dry ground, but a particular place where God's presence is divinely manifest. *The land* was a place of bounty, of gardens, of fruitful labor, and of freedom from fear or negative encounters with nature. Most importantly, it was a place where God himself rested and reigned. To be exiled from this land, from Eden, was the loss of everything above. It represented death and a longing to return.

The concept of a promised land, in Genesis 12 and forward, is more than the gift of a place the Israelites could call home. It represents at least a partial restoration of Eden. God is still willing to dwell among his people and to provide the bounty of the earth if Israel will be faithful (Exod. 25:8; Zech. 8:3; Mal. 3:10).

Geography

There is no particular reason why we would need to know the location of Eden, yet Genesis describes it at some length, including its position relative to five rivers (one unnamed, dividing into the Pishon, Gihon, Tigris, Euphrates) and with respect to several geographical regions (Havilah, Cush, Assyria) (Gen. 2:10–14). Some of the map references have been lost, and river channels change over time, making it impossible for us today to know with certainty where Eden was located. The implication from the text, however, is that these names and regions were familiar to the original readers (see fig. 2).[7]

    Genesis Unbound, 38). We note his opinion here but do not see it as necessary for the general perspective. Our description for each day works equally well for a local (Canaan) or global understanding.

7.   We are only certain about the location of the Tigris and Euphrates. Gihon is the name of a spring in Jerusalem (1 Kings 1:33, 38, 45; 2 Chron. 32:30; 33:14), but its connection with Cush (i.e., Ethiopia, south of Egypt) may identify it with the Nile River. The unknown Pishon is in Havilah, elsewhere identified with the Arabian Peninsula (Gen. 25:18; 1 Sam. 15:7). Not all agree that Israel, by the time of the exodus, would have recognized the location of Eden (e.g., Longman, *Confronting Old Testament Controversies,* 36).

The general region and descriptions have much in common with Canaan. For example, Abraham is told he will be given land from the river of Egypt to the Euphrates (Gen. 15:18; cf. Deut. 1:7; 11:24; Josh. 1:4). The unnamed river of Genesis 2:10 could be the Jordan River, thought to be the river referred to in various psalms as the river of God (46:4; 65:9), or even as "the river of Edens" (36:8).[8]

The history of migration likewise links Eden with Canaan. Eden faced east, where the gate was guarded to prevent Adam and Eve's reentry. The sea was to the west; the world was to the east.[9] The spread of humanity after eviction from the garden in Genesis 3–11 (esp. 3:24; 4:16; 11:2) is presented as an eastward expansion toward Babylon. Barring discovery of an ancient map bearing all the biblical names, it is unlikely that the exact location of Eden will ever be rediscovered, though Eden and Canaan can at least be said to be in the same geographical region.[10]

Descriptions of the promised land

The name "Eden" ('eden) means "abundance" or "lushness." It was a place that was fully prepared for human habitation. Humans were called on to tend and cultivate the garden, but there was no need to first make it ready. The promised land is described in similar terms, often referred to as a "good land."[11] Its fruitfulness is captured by the common descriptor "a land flowing with milk and honey."[12] When Abraham and Lot parted ways in the land of Canaan, Lot looked out on the Jordan River to a valley "well watered everywhere like the garden of Yahweh" (Gen. 13:10). This was the same land that God promised to Israel, describing it as a land "in which you will lack nothing" (Deut. 8:9).

In his final speeches just outside the promised land, Moses was especially keen to portray the land as already nourished by Edenic resources (Deut. 8:7–10; 11:9–12) and endowed with the necessary structures for

---

8. The ESV translates Ps. 36:8 as "the river of delights," but the Hebrew word for "delight" is 'eden. On the Jordan River as the possible referent in these verses, see LeFebvre, "Adam Reigns in Eden," 39.

9. The "eastward" location of the garden in Gen. 2:8 is with respect to Eden, not the whole of Eden with respect to the world (i.e., Mesopotamia).

10. Alternatively, one could think the literal location of Eden was elsewhere (e.g., Mesopotamia), but the Eden-Canaan parallels are intentional for thematic or symbolic reasons. See more in Objection 2.

11. For example, Exod. 3:8; Num. 14:7; Deut. 1:25, 35; 3:25; 4:21, 22; 6:18; 8:7, 10; 9:6; 11:17; Josh. 23:15, 16; Judg. 18:9; 1 Kings 14:15; 1 Chron. 28:8.

12. Exodus 3:8, 17; 13:5; 33:3; Lev. 20:24; Num. 16:13, 14; Deut. 6:3; 11:9; 26:9, 15; 27:3; 31:20; Josh. 5:6; Jer. 11:5; 32:22; Ezek. 20:6, 15.

civilization (6:10–11). It was a promise Joshua revisited after Israel had begun taking possession of the land. God proclaimed, "I gave you a land on which you had not labored and cities that you had not built, and you dwell in them. You eat the fruit of vineyards and olive orchards that you did not plant" (Josh. 24:13). It was a land pre-readied for habitation. The promised land is thus a renewal, at least in part, of the original creation.[13]

Leading up to and during the exile, the prophets also spoke of a future restoration in terms of Eden. Zion's wilderness will be made "like Eden" and "like the garden of Yahweh" (Isa. 51:3; Ezek. 36:33–35; Joel 2:1–3). In Layer 5 ("Temple") we noted the parallel imagery of both Eden and the temple as the mountain of God, and both are referred to as a place where God would rest, dwell, walk, and reign.[14]

Collectively, these parallels speak strongly of at least a typological connection between the promised land and the original creation.[15] From here, we will move from the land to the inhabitants, Adam and Eve, as representatives of God's people.

ADAM AS ISRAEL

As we shift to the other subthemes, land will remain a prominent feature, as much of what takes place with Adam and with Israel has threads connecting back to the land. In this section, we will draw out parallels between the calling, instructions, covenants, and failings of Adam and those who would follow.

Of kings and priests

The functions of Adam and of Israel as kings and priests were subjects of Layer 4 ("Covenant") and Layer 5 ("Temple"). We revisit these themes briefly here as a reminder that kingly and priestly expectations of God's image-bearers continued beyond Eden. Israel, as God's chosen people, was to fulfill these roles, not just as individuals granted the titles of priest or king, but as the

---

13. LeFebvre, "Adam Reigns in Eden"; Postell, *Adam as Israel*, 88–92; Sailhamer, *Genesis Unbound*, 50–53.
14. Terje Stordalen catalogs at least thirty biblical references to Eden. Stordalen, "Heaven on Earth—Or Not?" See especially Ezek. 28:12–17; 47:1–12; Zech. 14:8–11; Joel 3:18; Ps. 65:9–13.
15. Sailhamer argues that Eden *is* Canaan, claiming support among medieval Jewish scholars (e.g., Rashi [Rabbi Shlomo Yitzhaki], a French rabbi from the eleventh century) and Christian interpreters (e.g., John Lightfoot from the seventeenth century) (see *Genesis Unbound*, 214–16). Sailhamer does provide a few specific quotes and citations of this earlier support, but not enough to discern how common it was.

entire nation (see table 11). The dual nature of the calling and the universal application is reflected in God's declaration that Israel was to be "a kingdom of priests" (Exod. 19:6).

TABLE 11. KINGLY AND PRIESTLY PARALLELS BETWEEN ADAM AND ISRAEL	
Adam and Eve (Genesis 1–3)	**Israel**
Kingly Roles	
commanded to fill the earth (1:28)	Abraham a father of nations (Gen. 17:4); blessing to the nations (18:18)
commanded to have dominion over creation (1:28)	kings to rise from Abraham (Gen. 17:6); dominion over Canaan (Deut. 9:1–6)
called image bearers (ANE expression of being steward-ruler under divine king) (1:27)	Israelite kings to serve under the authority of God (Deut. 17:14–20)
authority to name the animals (2:19–20)	God changed names (Gen. 17:5, 15; 32:28); kings gave names (Dan. 1:7)
Priestly Roles	
commanded to "work and keep" the garden (2:15)	warned against defiling the land (Jer. 2:7)
dwelled where God's presence was manifest (3:8)	dwelled in a land where God's presence was manifest (Lev. 26:12)
should have guarded against idolatry (snake) (2:15; 3:24)	guarding against idolatry (Lev. 19:4; 26:1)
dietary restriction from the fruit of a tree (2:16–17)	dietary restrictions from unclean animals (Lev. 11)
role as guardian replaced by cherubim (3:24)	cherubim guardians depicted in temple (Exod. 25:18–22; 26:1, 31; 36:8; 37:7–9; Num. 7:89)

Creation and Mount Sinai

Here again, much of the biblical territory identifying parallels between the creation story and Mount Sinai was covered in Layer 4 ("Covenant") and Layer 5 ("Temple"). We will spend a little more time reviewing those similarities as it builds toward additional parallels in the failures and future hope of God's people (discussed in the subsequent sections). For our comparisons, reference to "Mount Sinai" will include events and promises extending from Sinai to Israel's arrival in Canaan. An overview is provided in table 12, with expanded commentary in the text.

TABLE 12. PARALLELS BETWEEN CREATION AND ISRAEL'S EXPERIENCE (SINAI AND BEYOND)[16]		
	Creation/Eden (Genesis)	Sinai/Canaan
God prepares a special land ready for habitation	1–2	Deut. 8:7–10
People taken and placed into the land	2:9	Exod. 6:8
God rests and promises rest in the land	2:1–3	Deut. 12:8–11
Command to exert dominion	1:28	Deut. 7:1–5; 9:4
Warnings against disobedience (death/exile)	2:17	Exod. 22:20; Lev. 26:14–39
Symbols of idolatry	3:1–7 (snake)	Deut. 7:1–5 (Canaanites)
Sabbath and festivals	1:14; 2:1–3	Lev. 23
Fear of God's presence	3:10	Exod. 19:16; 20:18
Exile following disobedience	3:21–24	Num. 14:20–25

---

16. Postell, *Adam as Israel*, 124.

Placed in pre-readied land where God walks

For the six days of creation, God prepared a land that was fully nourished and ready for human habitation. Genesis 2:15 then says God took Adam and placed (rested) him in this preconditioned land. Eden was likewise an earthly place of God's rest: God walked in the garden (Gen. 3:8). In related fashion, Abraham, and later the nation of Israel, was taken from a distant land (Ur and Egypt) and brought to the land of Canaan, a land flowing with milk and honey, ready for habitation (Gen. 12:1; 13:1–18; Deut. 26:9). God walked and dwelled among Israel via the tabernacle during the wilderness journey, and promised to dwell among them in the land of promise (Exod. 29:46; Lev. 26:12).

Mandates and warnings

Mandates were given to Adam and to Abraham to multiply and fill the earth (kingly roles). To Adam and to Israel, commands were issued to subdue and exert dominion over the inhabitants of the land. For Adam, this dominion was over the creation and animals (Gen. 1:28). For Israel, it was taking possession of the land from the Canaanites (Deut. 7:1–5; 9:1–5). Adam and Eve were warned against eating from the tree of the knowledge of good and evil. The consequence of disobedience was said to be death (Gen. 2:17). Israel was warned against seeking to know and worship other gods. The consequence of disobedience was extermination from the land (Exod. 22:20; Lev. 26:14–39).

Temptations and idolatry

In the garden, Eve and then Adam were tempted into unfaithfulness by listening to the words of the snake, shifting their worship away from Yahweh (Gen. 3:1–7). Israel was told not to intermarry with the idolatrous Canaanites, as it would pull their hearts away from faithfulness to Yahweh (Deut. 7:1–5).[17] The snake, while a "beast of the field," is traditionally believed to represent a spiritual force opposing God—identified as Satan in the New Testament (Rev. 12:9). The comparison with the idolatrous temptations of the Canaanites has led some to speak of the snake as a "prototypical Canaanite."[18] Snakes are also the last animal mentioned in the list of dietary

---

17. Note the command was not a blanket prohibition to preserve racial purity, for marriage with a Canaanite convert was not condemned. Ruth, a Moabite woman, was not only accepted into Israel by God but also became the great-grandmother of David and is mentioned by name in the lineage of Jesus (Ruth 4:13–22; Matt. 1:5).
18. Postell notes several other relevant connections not detailed here. Postell, *Adam as Israel*, 109n31.

restrictions (Lev. 11:42), where we find the only other mention of the imagery of crawling on the belly (Gen. 3:14).

Sun, moon, and festivals

In Layer 6 ("Calendar"), we noted that Genesis 1:14 is worded in a curious way that suggests a forward-looking perspective. On day 4, the heavenly bodies are placed to be "for signs and festivals, and for days and years."[19] The grouping of phrases carries an indication that the sun, moon, and stars would prove useful not only for tracking the passage of days and seasons but also for marking the coming commemorative festivals. At Sinai, Israel was given multiple festival dates, all marked by the cycles of the sun and moon, to celebrate and commemorate God's provisions (Lev. 23).

Fear and nakedness

When Adam and Eve heard the sound of God walking in the garden, they hid themselves in fear (Gen. 3:10). At Sinai, the people heard the sound of God speaking from the mountain and retreated in fear (Exod. 19:16; 20:18). The concept of nakedness also appears in the context of the garden and Sinai. Adam and Eve hid, in part, because they became suddenly ashamed of their nakedness. At Sinai, multiple commands included warnings against uncovering nakedness (Lev. 18). To cover their nakedness, God made skins for Adam and Eve, and proscribed tunics for the priests of the tabernacle (Gen. 3:21; Exod. 28:42).

Sword at the entrance

Following sin, Adam and Eve were expelled from the garden, living in exile. Cherubim with a flaming sword took their place as guardian of the garden (Gen. 3:24). When Israel first approached Canaan and disobeyed, they were sent away into exile. When they changed their minds and tried to enter Canaan after the curse was issued, they met death at the swords of the people of the land (Num. 14:39–45).

We could add to this list the many functional and symbolic parallels between creation and the tabernacle described in detail at Sinai. For these, we refer readers back to Layer 5 ("Temple").

---

19. The ESV translates *mo'adim* as "seasons." See Layer 6 ("Calendar") for why we believe "festivals" is the preferred translation.

CERTAINTY OF ISRAEL'S FAILURE

If we expand on the previous section to focus on the failures of Israel, we find still more parallels. In one sense, it cannot be otherwise, for there is an unavoidable connection between temptation, sin, repentance or defiance, and consequences. There are no alternatives to this basic sequence. Still, there are noteworthy commonalities to many of the failures recorded in Scripture. As we consider examples, we will first draw from the Pentateuch (Adam, Abraham, Jacob, Israel entering Canaan) to consider the perspective of God's people in the Mosaic era. From there, we will move forward in time with examples from the era of the kings (David, Solomon, Israel divided).

At the broadest level, each story depicts the repeated theme of being called to follow God and falling short. Lives and histories are not complete failures, for there are notable occasions in Scripture where individuals are commended for their faith (e.g., Enoch, Noah, Abraham, Joseph, David),[20] and Israel experienced a time of great blessing under the reigns of David and Solomon. At the same time, all fell short of full obedience and faithfulness. Covenants were repeatedly made, renewed, and broken.

Failures inevitably start with listening to a tempting voice (explicit or implied) to accomplish God's intentions by human means. Adam and Eve sought understanding through the forbidden fruit (Gen. 3:6); Abraham attempted to fulfill God's promise of posterity through sex with his wife's maidservant (Gen. 16:1–4); Jacob looked for God's promise of material blessings through deceit (Gen. 27); and the first generation out of Egypt attempted to gain promised safety and provision through complaints, fear, trust in foreign gods, and unauthorized attack (Exod. 32; Num. 14). The Pentateuch comes to a close with the second generation out of Egypt back at the border of the promised land, where they nearly forfeited entry *again* by seeking to satisfy God's promises for good through the momentary and forbidden pleasures offered by Moabite women (Num. 25).[21]

The consequence of sin is exile, either as direct expulsion from the land of promise or a more abstract sense of exile from a condition of peace and bounty. Adam and Eve were expelled from the garden. Abraham's sin produced a son that not only introduced familial strife but also gave rise to nations that would

---

20. Gen. 5:24, 6:9; Rom. 4:3; 1 Sam. 13:14; Heb. 11.
21. There is much that could be said about the positive and negative aspects of human sexuality here as it relates to creation and the patterns of sins, but it lies beyond the scope of this layer.

be a constant threat to Israel (Gen. 21:18; 25:12–18).[22] Jacob's deception of his father Isaac and his brother Esau led to his exile from Canaan (Gen. 27:41–45). The sins of the first generation of the exodus resulted in forty years of exile and death in the desert (Num. 14:26–38). The same fate might have happened to the second generation if not for the zeal of Phineas and the repentance of Israel (Num. 25).

In each case, God did not ultimately abandon his people. He continued to preserve and care for a remnant, even in the midst of their punishment, with the promise of something better to come. If living at the time of the exodus, one might have reasonably thought that "something better" would finally be fulfilled with the possession of the promised land. This was the land where God would dwell with the people of Israel, a land of material bounty, a land free from fears of attack, and, finally, a land where they could fulfill the expectations of God and his covenant.

The Pentateuch dashes any such optimism. In Deuteronomy 32, a prophetic poem first reminds the nation that God found Jacob (Israel) in a desert land, in a howling waste, and encircled him, cared for him, and kept him as the apple of his eye. God provided for him like a mother eagle, feeding from the richness of the land. The words then turn dark, speaking of the future as if it had already occurred, declaring that Israel grew fat and sleek and forsook the God who made him, stirring God to jealousy with strange gods and provoking God's wrath.

That future proved true, again and again, through the generations of the judges and on through the kings. Our post-Pentateuch examples include even the most famous and blessed of the kings of Israel, David and Solomon. Each had moments or periods of their lives when they pursued material blessings by forbidden means. David took another man's wife (2 Sam. 11). Solomon took hundreds of wives and concubines from conquered lands and strayed after their gods (1 Kings 11). Each resulted in civil and familial strife, with the cumulative sins of subsequent kings leading to civil wars, defeat by external empires, and eventually to exile.

Theologically, exile is a reversal of Israel's covenant history and, thus, of God's original creational purposes. Exile is an anti-exodus, a "return to Egypt" (Deut. 28:68), which ironically includes the perpetuation of her idolatry: "there you will serve [other] gods" (Deut. 4:28; 28:64). The negative catalyst

---

22. Islam and portions of the Arab world trace their origins back to Ishmael, Abraham's son by Hagar.

becomes the consequence; what got them there will keep them there. Exile reverses the Abrahamic covenant: "Whereas you were as numerous as the stars of heaven, you shall be left few in number. . . . As Yahweh took delight in doing you good and multiplying you, so Yahweh will take delight in bringing ruin upon you and destroying you. And you shall be plucked off the land" (Deut. 28:62–68; cf. 4:27). The use of "death" language for exile (e.g., "perish," "be destroyed," "be annihilated")—a hallmark especially of Deuteronomy (e.g., 4:26; 28:63)[23]—recalls the original threat of death in Eden (Gen. 2:17), which turned out to be the original exile from a special land (Gen. 3:24). The exiles of Eden and Israel share the same exposed nakedness, dread, and rest-lessness (Gen. 3:7–19; Deut. 28:48–67). Thus the Pentateuch is shaped so that the beginning and end reflect each other.[24]

All this presents a rather dismal view of the message of Scripture. "Try hard, but know you will fail. Oh, and the consequences of that failure are really bad." Thanks be to God, there is more to this message, both within and beyond the Pentateuch. This brings us to the last theme—hope.

A FUTURE HOPE

This section is where the unity of the Pentateuch is seen at a higher level than in any previous layer. John Sailhamer (and Seth Postell) argues for several poetic seams inserted in the Pentateuch (Gen. 49; Exod. 15; Num. 24; Deut. 32–33) that point toward the solution to the problem of sin. The hope for redemption of the people of God, for a restoration and completion of the mission of Eden, is coming. It is not a return to the past, but a new exodus, a new covenant, a new creation—Eden not just as it was, but as it was intended to become. Life after exile. Life after death!

Three of the poems (all but Exod. 15) are messianic, centered on the phrase "in the end of days" (literal translation) (Gen. 49:1; Num. 24:14; Deut. 31:29), an expression that is forward-looking but also provides an arc back to the creation and the first sin.[25] We pick up this story with God's curse on the serpent:

---

23. On the "death" language of exile, see Turner, "Deuteronomy's Theology of Exile," 190–94 (the essay is a summary of the book titled *The Death of Deaths in the Death of Israel: Deuteronomy's Theology of Exile*).
24. We have focused on the big-picture connections. Space does not allow us to go into all the detailed lexical links and unique clusters between the beginning of Genesis and the end of Deuteronomy. See Postell, *Adam as Israel*, 136–37.
25. The Greek translation for "last" or "latter" (Hebrew *'akharit*, the opposite of *reshit* "beginning" [Gen. 1:1]) is the adjective *eschatos* from which we get our word *eschatology* (though it must be argued from context when *eschatos* connotes the theological sense).

I will put enmity between you and the woman,
>   and between your seed and her seed;[26]
he shall bruise your head,
>   and you shall bruise his heel.

(Gen. 3:15)

Traditionally, theologians have deemed this the "first gospel" (*protoevangelium*) because they see in it a prediction of Jesus's triumph over Satan.[27] Not all agree on this point, but if it is correct, we shouldn't jump straight to Jesus and skip over the Old Testament context. There is rich theological ground to till between Eden and the cross. As Sailhamer notes, the purpose of Genesis 3:15 is to raise the question, "Who is the seed of the woman?" rather than answer it.[28] For the original audience, the most obvious candidate was the offspring of Abraham—the nation of Israel. The Hebrew people were the recipients of Yahweh's covenant promises. The serpent and his seed were manifest in Israel's enemies (e.g., Canaanites). However, at every stage, Israel proved to be its own worst enemy. Even the best of its individual representatives and leaders (e.g., Abraham, Moses, David) came up short. God graciously forgave his people and renewed his covenant after each failed step, including the golden calf incident, the wilderness rebellion, and the exile. Still, God's creational and covenantal purposes remained unfulfilled.

In this context, we will consider the poetic interludes positioned strategically through the Pentateuch. The poems lay the foundation of what Israel should expect in the unfolding of God's plan.

Seam 1: Genesis 49—blessings of Jacob (Israel)

The book of Genesis ends with Jacob, whose name has been changed to Israel, pronouncing blessings on each of his sons. It is not just a series of hopes or dreams that a doting father wishes to pass on to his children. The blessings appear as an extended poem with prophetic overtones. The prophetic nature is seen most clearly in the words spoken to Judah.

---

26. The ESV has "offspring" in place of "seed," with note that the Hebrew word means seed.
27. The traditional reading is based on understanding that the serpent represents more than an animal (thus it exists throughout human history) and that the singular pronoun ("he") in line 3 of Gen. 3:15 intentionally refers to a singular referent of "her seed." (*Zera'*, "seed," is a collective noun, so it could be singular or plural depending on context). On the exegetical difficulties of Gen. 3:15, see Hamilton, *Book of Genesis*, 197–200.
28. Sailhamer, "Genesis," 91.

Judah, your brothers shall praise you;

> your hand shall be on the neck of your enemies;
>
> your father's sons shall bow down before you.

Judah is a lion's cub;

> from the prey, my son, you have gone up.

He stooped down; he crouched as a lion

> and as a lioness; who dares rouse him?

The scepter shall not depart from Judah,

> nor the ruler's staff from between his feet,

until tribute comes to him;

> and to him shall be the obedience of the peoples.

Binding his foal to the vine

> and his donkey's colt to the choice vine,

he has washed his garments in wine

> and his vesture in the blood of grapes.

His eyes are darker than wine,

> and his teeth whiter than milk.

(Gen. 49:8–12)

In this blessing, Israel is assured that the promise to Abraham shall still come to pass, that he will be a father to nations, that through him all the nations of the world will be blessed, and that kings will yet come from him (Gen. 17:6). A king will arise, the Lion of the tribe of Judah, who will reign forever over all peoples—a king whose hand shall be on the neck of his enemies. This will be a king who will finally accomplish the mission first given to Adam, to crush the serpent. Tribute and the fruit of the vine speak to a time, after the enemies are vanquished, of enjoying the bounty of the land in peace.

A human king was not outside of God's will for Israel, as one might infer from the story of Samuel and Saul (1 Sam. 8). In fact, it was part of God's redemptive plan. The criteria for establishing a king were provided at Sinai (Deut. 17:14–20).[29] The problem, when Israel did later ask for a king, was not the request itself, but their motivation to be like all the nations around them (1 Sam. 8:5, 20). It is noteworthy that the first king God gave Israel,

---

29. It is perhaps also significant that the two OT books that contain the most messianic prophecies (Psalms and Isaiah) also contain the most references to divine kingship (see Pss. 5:2; 10:16; 22:28; 24:8–10; 29:10; 44:4; 45:6; 47:2, 6–8; 68:24; 74:12; 84:3; 93:1–2; 95:3; 96:10; 97:1; 98:6; 99:1; 103:19; 145:1, 11–13; 146:10; Isa. 6:5; 24:23; 33:22; 37:16; 41:21; 43:15; 44:6; 52:7). Messianism allows divine and human kingship to coexist.

Saul, reflected their ill-conceived desire. The king that followed, David, reflected *God's* desire (1 Sam. 13:14; 16:1–13). An Israelite in the day of David might have wondered if this was the lion of the tribe of Judah. David was a man after God's own heart (1 Sam. 13:14), yet he was also subject to his own sin. One was still to come, a son of David, who would bring God's kingdom to earth (Isa. 11).[30]

Seam 2: Exodus 15—rescue from Egypt

Exodus 15 follows the miraculous rescue of Israel from the pursuing Egyptians. Pharaoh had a change of heart, regretting the release of his slaves and launching his army in pursuit. It was one last lesson God planned to demonstrate that he alone was God. The army was allowed to catch up to Israel, trapping the fleeing nation against the shores of the sea. God parted the waters to allow Israel to pass, holding the Egyptians at bay until Israel was safely across. The army pursued and perished as the waters collapsed over them. Exodus 15 is a song (poem) to commemorate God's salvation.

There is no explicit messianic message in the song, but it nonetheless speaks of a divine kingship that will endure forever. It sets the stage for what a true and godly kingship entails. The song ends with the following:

> You will bring [your people] in and plant them on your own mountain,
> > the place, O Yahweh, which you have made for your abode,
> > the sanctuary, O Yahweh, which your hands have established.
> Yahweh will reign forever and ever.
> > (vv. 17–18)

The song rejoices in far more than victory over an enemy or the confidence that Israel will be brought safely to Canaan. It anticipates a future in the land of promise where Yahweh will rest, walk, and abide with his people. The mountain of God—his sanctuary—is a clear allusion to Eden (see Layer 5, "Temple"). There will come a time when exile and wanderings are past, when God will redeem his people and bring them into a land where his presence dwells. The demonstration of his power over Egypt and its false gods provided all the assurance needed for Israel to know the day would indeed come.

---

30. In Isa. 11:1, a "shoot" or "branch" of Jesse (David's father) is a creative expression for a son of David.

God did bring his people to Canaan, slowly granting possession of the land and eventually sanctioning the building of a temple in Jerusalem. God filled the first temple with his spirit in a powerful display of his glory (2 Chron. 7). The reigns of David and Solomon provided glimpses of the promised kingdom, yet each was subject to the frailties of human sin. The kingdom proclaimed in Exodus 15 was still to come.

Seam 3: Numbers 24—the second generation

The third poetic seam does not come at the end of a book, but is nonetheless a major milestone in the story line. It appears in the transition from the first to the second generation of Israel in the wilderness. The first failed to enter the promised land as God commanded, resulting in forty years of wandering in the desert. At the close of those years, Israel is back at the border of the promised land. They nearly forfeit their opportunity again, as they repeat the sins of their fathers with grumblings, challenging authority, and even falling prey to a Moabite scheme to send women into the camp to draw Israel into sexual sins (Num. 20–21; 25).

God graciously intervenes through the zealous action of Phineas to bring sins to an abrupt end (chap. 25). Balaam, an enigmatic prophet hired by the king of Moab to curse Israel, is inspired to pronounce blessings rather than curses (chaps. 22–24). Three *blessings* are proclaimed, much to the Moabite king's chagrin. Each is proclaimed in poetic form. The final two carry a messianic message. The middle blessing (23:18–24) speaks of a king who shall rise from Israel, a seed from Jacob, who will be higher than any other, with horns like a wild ox, eating up the nations like a lion. Following this, Balaam tells the king of Moab what will happen to his people in the latter days ("the end of days").

I see him, but not now;
    I behold him, but not near:
a star shall come out of Jacob,
    and a scepter shall rise out of Israel;
it shall crush the forehead of Moab
    and break down all the sons of Sheth.
Edom shall be dispossessed;
    Seir also, his enemies, shall be dispossessed.
    Israel is doing valiantly.
And one from Jacob shall exercise dominion
    and destroy the survivors of cities!
(Num. 24:17–19)

Once again, a connection is drawn from the beginning to the end. The snake of Genesis 3 is represented in the idolatrous nations of Canaan. A snake whose forehead will be crushed by a future king who will bring all the earth into subjection beneath his feet;[31] a blessing to all who bless him, and a curse to all who curse him (v. 9). Balaam sees this kingdom as coming with all the power displayed by God against Egypt (v. 8), but "not now" and "not near." It will not come with the conquest of Canaan nor with the reign of earthly kings. The kingdoms of David and Solomon will serve as types of what is to come, but there is a future kingdom in mind that will fulfill Balaam's oracle.

Seam 4: Deuteronomy 32–33—future failure, future hope

The Pentateuch closes prior to entry into the promised land and new leadership under Joshua. Moses issues his final words to Israel as prophetic poems. The first is introduced with a sad declaration in Deuteronomy 31:29: "I know that after my death you will surely act corruptly and turn aside from the way that I have commanded you." Deuteronomy 32 then reminds the people of Israel of their election, providential care, and bounty in the promised land, followed by telling them of the evil that Israel will do to provoke God's wrath.[32] Yet in the future, God will vindicate his people and take vengeance on his adversaries (vv. 36–43). The final stanza (v. 43) carries a hint of the people of God expanding to peoples from all nations.[33] This segues into a positive poem in which Moses gives his final blessing on the tribes of Israel (Deut. 33). This parting message starts with praise of Yahweh, who met with Israel at Sinai. Yahweh is declared to be king in Jeshurun (Israel), and blessings are pronounced that mirror those of Jacob (Israel) at the end of Genesis (Gen. 49). Interestingly, the imagery of a lion is associated here with Gad and Dan (Deut. 33:20, 22), and majesty and strength of the wild ox are associated with Joseph (v. 17). Of Judah, Moses says,

---

31. The initial oracle in Num. 24 begins with a reference to Jacob/Israel (v. 5), but then references "his seed" (v. 7a). This draw on the collective noun "seed" (recall Gen. 3:15; 22:17–18) allows the shift in Num. 24:7b to the singular (i.e., the future king).

32. Postell makes a case for unique phrasing that appears only in Gen. 1–3 and in Deut. 32–33 as further evidence that the Pentateuch is an intentionally structured, unified text. Postell, *Adam and Israel*, 136–37.

33. This last point is based on a direct reading of the Hebrew: "Rejoice, O nations, his people" (Deut. 32:43). Some translations (e.g., ESV, NRSV, NLT) follow the Greek, which changes "peoples" to "heavens" (cf. v. 1). Most of the translations that read "nations" unfortunately add a preposition: "Rejoice, O nations, *with* his people." But this is unwarranted by the Hebrew and prophetic nature of this text; the redefining of "the people of God" to include the nations is attested elsewhere (e.g., Ps. 47:9; Isa. 19:24–25). See Sailhamer, *Pentateuch as Narrative*, 476.

Hear, O Yahweh, the voice of Judah,
  and bring him in to his people.
With your hands contend for him,
  and be a help against his adversaries.

(Deut. 33:7)

Though less explicit than other messianic passages, the blessing of Judah calls on people one day to listen to the voice of one who will come from the tribe of Judah and take up his cause. That coming king, we discover, will bring a message of salvation.

Last words of the Pentateuch

The Pentateuch records a profound history of God's interaction with his people from Adam to the time of Moses. The story of Adam becomes the story of Israel. God blesses a people with the promise of land under his sovereign reign and protection, calling them to serve as steward-kings and priests in his sanctuary. They fail and experience exile from the land, yet God is gracious and provides the means for redemption and restoration. His promises are sure.

Each of the four poetic seams discussed above provides assurance that a time is coming when God's kingdom on earth will be established, embracing the imagery and intention of Eden. It may thus seem odd that the *last* prophetic poem includes a lengthy pronouncement that Israel will fail yet again (Deut. 32). They will not just fail a little—they will fail spectacularly, becoming complacent and arrogant, chasing after foreign gods, and they will suffer the consequences of their rebellion. It is only after telling them of the certainty of their failure that Moses concludes with the assurance of God's faithfulness to provide a solution (Deut. 33).

But the message of the Pentateuch is not done with the last words of Moses. It finishes with his obituary. The very last words make a remarkable observation:

There has not arisen a prophet since in Israel like Moses, whom Yahweh knew face to face, none like him for all the signs and the wonders that Yahweh sent him to do in the land of Egypt, to Pharaoh and to all his servants and to all his land, and for all the mighty power and all the great deeds of terror that Moses did in the sight of all Israel. (Deut. 34:10–12)

These words were obviously not written by Moses. It is equally clear they were not simply added by Joshua, for the wording indicates the passage of many years and history with no other prophet arising to compare. There is textual evidence that these inspired words may date as late as the return from exile in Babylon.[34] This would mean the assessment was meant to apply to the entire Old Testament period from the conquest of Canaan forward.

The implication is profound, for it means that in all of Israel's postexodus history, no one arose who could ultimately solve Israel's heart problem or usher in the promised kingdom. Examples of great faith inspire, with notables such as Samson, Ruth, Samuel, David, Elisha, and Isaiah, yet all were subject to their own sin and frailties. No judge, king, priest, prophet, champion, or counselor could accomplish the mission of creation.

Centuries after Moses, long after judges and a dynasty of kings had ruled over the land, Israel found itself again in exile. The discouraging words of Moses in Deuteronomy 32 proved all too true, the pattern of sin and banishment repeated. The nation had looked to fulfill promises of peace and bounty through their own means, straying after foreign gods and abandoning God's commands. It is possible, or even likely, that this is the date of the inspired addendum to Moses's obituary. The Pentateuch thus ends in search of a leader more glorious and more faithful than Moses (cf. Heb. 3:1–6); someone who can offer more lasting "rest" than Joshua (cf. Heb. 4:8–10). It will need to be someone who can, once and for all, fix Israel's heart problem, so it can return to the land (Deut. 30:1–10) and complete its mission of mediating God's presence and will (Gen. 12:3; Exod. 19:5–6; Deut. 4:5–8; 26:19; 28:10). It is a king to whom prophets following Moses (after the Pentateuch) repeatedly looked with expectation and longing. The king of kings. The promised Messiah. The coming of King Jesus.

> For to us a child is born,
>> to us a son is given;
> and the government shall be upon his shoulder,
>> and his name shall be called

---

34. Phrases such as "before any king reigned over the Israelites" (Gen. 36:31) serve as indicators of updates by later scribes. At the more technical level, the Hebrew (e.g., orthography, grammar, syntax) of the Pentateuch matches the Hebrew of a much later period than Moses. All languages evolve over time. One of the obvious indicators of a time gap is to compare poetic texts (which tend to preserve older linguistic features) and narrative texts (e.g., contrast Exod. 14 with Exod. 15, or Judg. 4 with Judg. 5).

Wonderful Counselor, Mighty God,
    Everlasting Father, Prince of Peace.
Of the increase of his government and of peace
    there will be no end,
on the throne of David and over his kingdom,
    to establish it and to uphold it
with justice and with righteousness
    from this time forth and forevermore.
The zeal of Yahweh of hosts will do this.

                      (Isa. 9:6–7)

But he was pierced for our transgressions;
    he was crushed for our iniquities;
upon him was the chastisement that brought us peace,
    and with his wounds we are healed.

                      (Isa. 53:5)

And many nations shall join themselves to Yahweh in that day, and shall be my people. And I will dwell in your midst, and you shall know that Yahweh of hosts has sent me to you.

                      (Zech. 2:11)

CHALLENGES AND RESPONSES

Objection 1: Genesis 1 cannot describe the creation of the planet and Canaan.

The objection that Genesis 1 cannot be about both the earth and Canaan is similar to the earlier objection that the days of creation cannot be understood as both parallel (Layer 1, "Song") and sequential (Layer 2, "Analogy").[35] At one level, this concern can be addressed by recalling our mineral example from the Introduction. It may initially seem logical to insist that a single fluorite crystal that appears wholly pink cannot *also* be blue. Yet when actually viewed under different wavelengths of light, we discover that both colors are, in fact, exhibited. Genesis 1 may be understood with a focus on the whole of creation in one light, and with a more narrow focus on the land of promise in another light.

---

35. Layer 2, Objection 2.

If this seems like a weak defense, we may also note that for those living at the time of Moses, there wasn't really a difference between Eden-plus-surrounding-land versus all of the earth. The land of the ancient Near East and the heavens directly above was thought to be the entirety of the material world. They had no sense of living on a rotating sphere with additional continents beyond the seas. All of the biblical language describing the physical construction of the cosmos matches the common understanding of the time. This is not to suggest any error in Scripture, as there is no evidence that correction of any misconceptions about the structure of the cosmos was ever intended. Genesis was written to a people and a culture different from our own. We do the Bible a grave disservice when forcing it to fit the expectations of a culture far removed in time and space from the original audience.

Objection 2: Equating Eden with Canaan, and Adam with Israel, is a stretch.

Not all theologians agree that Eden was in Canaan or that Adam's story is Israel's story.[36] Geographical indicators may place Eden in another location within the region, and there are aspects of the two stories that are not directly comparable. As one example, Adam and Eve started sinless, the Hebrews did not.

Regarding the location of Eden, this layer is not dependent on Eden being physically in the same place as Canaan. Equating Eden with Canaan is principally a thematic or typological argument. There are remarkable parallels between what the land represents that do not ultimately hinge on the exact location. If they are different locations, it may be compared to the "mountain of God," which starts at Mount Sinai but is eventually moved to Mount Zion in Jerusalem (Ps. 68). They are thematically equivalent, even if not geographically in the same place.

The stories of Adam and Israel likewise do not need to be identical in all respects to serve as thematic equivalents. As David is a typological representation of the king to come (Jesus), so Adam is a typological representation of Israel. David is not the same in every respect to Jesus, nor is Adam the same in every respect to Israel. The ties between Adam's experience and Israel's is strengthened by the reminder that these stories were written at the same time, with the intention that each should be read in context of the other.

---

36. Some prefer the typology to run the opposite direction—Israel as Adam, not Adam as Israel. See Green, review of *Adam as Israel*.

DISCUSSION QUESTIONS

1. Why is there such a focus in Scripture on land? How is it used to connect the beginning to the end?

2. The Bible records a long list of failures by the people of God. Should this be a source of discouragement? What is the takeaway message?

3. How do the poetic seams of the Pentateuch point to a solution to the inevitability of human failings?

4. If God knows that we will fail, why does he still hold us accountable?

CONCLUSION

*T*he introductory chapters and seven layers covered a lot of theological ground. In this closing chapter, we offer short summaries of the main points or themes of each layer before addressing lingering questions readers may still have. Each summary includes an addendum that shows how the perspective points to or paves the way for the work and person of Jesus.

SONG: GOD AS ARTIST

God paints the days of creation in a unique literary genre found nowhere else in Scripture, blending elements of prose and poetry. Rhyming words, *tohu wabohu*, describe an initial state lacking light, purpose, or material things. Parallel sets of days first solve the issue of formlessness with the creation of the realms of light and dark, sea and sky, and dry land, followed by matching days of filling realms with heavenly bodies, fish and birds, and animals and man. The song of creation is completed with a day of rest, celebrating the artistry of God. As the message of the kingdom of God unfolds through the rest of the Old Testament, the divine Artist is ever present. God is a potter (Isa. 64:8). God's Spirit is the source of artistic talent in the construction of the tabernacle (Exod. 31:3; 35:31). And God inspired much of the Old Testament message to be communicated through poems and songs.[1]

Christ

John 1 tells us that Jesus, "the Word," was not only present at the beginning, but that "all things were made through him, and without him was not any thing made" (v. 3). The artistry of the Creator is obvious at every scale of study of the universe, from subatomic particles to the vastness of galaxies. The same artist is at work in the lives of his children. "For we are his workmanship,

---

1. More than one-third of the Bible is in poetic form. Duvall and Hays, *Grasping God's Word*, 346.

created in Christ Jesus" (Eph. 2:10). The Greek word for workmanship is
poiema—which is the origin of our English word *poem*.[2] We are not just made
by Jesus; we are his work of art.[3]

ANALOGY: GOD AS FARMER

Sequential days, separated by nights of rest and reflection, serve as models
for how our days should be lived and as insights into the work of God. Work
is good. Creativity is good. Rest and reflection are good. Each was part of the
original creation. Sin did not introduce work, but work, creativity, and rest
all are twisted when the creation mandate is ignored. Sabbath rest includes
thankfulness for the works of God and the gift of fruitful labor.

Christ

Jesus is portrayed as a divine Farmer in the parable of the sower, casting the
seed of the gospel message onto the soil of people's hearts (Matt. 13). His work
ran afoul of the Pharisees when he healed on the Sabbath. He challenged their
misconceptions of the Sabbath and work, asking whether any of them would
not lift a son or ox that had fallen into a well on a Sabbath (Luke 14:1–6). At
another time he answered more provocatively, saying, "My Father is working
until now, and I am working" (John 5:17). It was a twofold declaration, challenging their misconception of godly work and rest, and communicating his
authority to do so—equating himself with God (v. 18).

POLEMIC: GOD AS "I AM"

Contrary to pagan myths (old and new), no story is needed for the *origin* of
Yahweh. He alone brought the world into existence. He has no competition.
Creation was his intentional act and reflects his character—nature is orderly
and consistent, not a manifestation of capricious gods. Humans were not an
accident or made to ease the burdens of a pantheon of gods, but to commune
with God and serve as his image-bearers.

Christ

The nature and identity of God is captured powerfully in the simplicity of the
answer to a question Moses raised at the burning bush. Moses asked what

---

2. An insightful collection of quotes by theologians and pastors on *poiema* in Eph. 2:10 is
   found at preceptaustin, "Poiema—Greek Word Study."
3. Much more could be said about Jesus as an artist, including his rich use of storytelling to
   communicate the gospel message (e.g., Enns, "Jesus the Artist").

name he should use for God when going to the people of Israel. God's response was to tell them, "I AM has sent me to you" (Exod. 3:13–15). In a word, God is eternal, self-existent, and ever-present. Jesus stunned his Jewish audience when his authority was challenged by the Pharisees, declaring, "Truly, truly, I say to you, before Abraham was, I am" (John 8:58). Jesus was not a demigod or part of a pantheon of lesser gods. Jesus was the great I AM taking on flesh to walk among his people.

COVENANT: GOD AS SUZERAIN

Yahweh is a covenantal God, assuring his people of his sovereignty, care, and ability to bring his promises and warnings to fruition. Following the pattern of ancient Near Eastern treaties, God's covenant with his people is reflected in a suzerain-vassal relationship and the gifting of land over which he continues to reign. Breaking the covenant results in exile and separation from the presence of God. The first covenant was made not just with humans but also with the earth. Nature continues to declare the glory of God and to reflect its Creator. The curse is manifested where human interaction with nature brings harm.

Christ

Jesus did not erase the covenants made in the Old Testament. He is the fulfillment of those covenants. Jesus is the promised son of David, the righteous branch from the root of Jesse, who did and will yet take the throne as the great Suzerain—the King of kings (Isa. 11; Rev. 19). The royal land grant will one day be renewed and made permanent with a new heaven and new earth (Isa. 65:17–25).

TEMPLE: GOD AS PRESENCE

God's temple resides on his holy mountain, representing a place where God walks, dwells, rests, and reigns among his people. His resting presence was manifested in Eden and mirrored in the design and function of the tabernacle and later temple. Humans are called to serve as priests and stewards of God's temple, tending the garden and guarding against idolatry. God's temple presence was made flesh in the Messiah and continues now within believers. The original mission of Eden to expand the temple outward will be fully realized when the mountain of God—the new Jerusalem—fills the earth.

Christ

The temple presence of God is illustrated profoundly in the person of Jesus. In the same sense that Jesus was both man and God, he is described in Scripture as both priest of the temple and as the temple itself. His zeal for the temple in casting out the moneychangers fulfilled the priestly duty of protecting the temple from the profane (Matt. 21:12–13). The writer of Hebrews identifies Jesus explicitly as our Great High Priest, who serves as our intercessor before the throne of God (Heb. 4:14–16). Yet Jesus also declared himself to *be* the temple, saying to the Jews, "Destroy this temple, and in three days I will raise it up" (John 2:19). The final consummation of God's temple presence is depicted in the vision of John, in which the temple in the new Jerusalem is not a building but "the Lord God the Almighty and the Lamb" (Rev. 21:22).

CALENDAR: GOD OF SABBATH

The days of creation serve as a microcosm of each agricultural year—preparing the soil, planting, harvesting, and celebrating God's provision with feasts and holy days. The heavenly bodies of day 4 were provided to gauge the passing of days and seasons and, looking forward, to mark the times of worship and celebration. Harvest festivals and Israel's commemorative dates align with the agricultural calendar as reminders of God's sovereignty and care, emphasized each week by Sabbath rest and worship.[4]

Christ

The timing of specific aspects of Jesus's ministry on earth were aligned with the Jewish festivals and holy days. Jesus allowed his disciples to pick grain to eat and performed some healings openly on Sabbath days, inviting the outrage of the Pharisees. The ensuing challenges served as opportunity for Jesus to declare that he is "Lord of the Sabbath" (Mark 2:23–28; Luke 6:1–5). The Last Supper and the crucifixion were intentionally timed with the observance of Passover, commemorating the day when the firstborn of Israel were spared from the angel of death if the blood of a sacrificial lamb was found on their door (Exod. 12:23; Matt. 26:1–2, 17–19). History and holy days converged—the lamb in Egypt pointing forward to Jesus as the true Passover Lamb (1 Cor. 5:7).

LAND: GOD AS REDEEMER

The creation and story of Eden parallels the preparation of the promised land, Sinai, Israel's sin, and exile. Adam's story is Israel's story. The land of Canaan represents a typological return to Eden, a gift conditional upon obedience to God—a condition Israel did not live up to. It is a repeated pattern that speaks

---

4. This layer was not as amenable to a "God *as* . . ." summary title.

to the certainty of human failure, but it is coupled with an equally certain hope of a future restoration. Poetic seams within the Pentateuch point toward a coming King who will vanquish evil and dwell among his people.

Christ

The certainty of human failure even on the eve of Jesus's crucifixion is illustrated in the predicted denial by Peter. Peter's vehement insistence he would be faithful followed by his woeful failure is the story of the human race. Yet the promises of God are sure. The promises made to Abraham, Moses, David, Ezekiel, and others are solidified in Jesus. He is the second Adam who is finally able to meet the conditions where all others failed (Rom. 5:12–21). Jesus is the promised son of David, the righteous branch of the root of Jesse, who will put an end to suffering and evil, and draw God's people from among every nation to worship, spreading the kingdom of God to the ends of the earth. The mission of Eden will finally be fulfilled.

> I saw in the night visions,
> and behold, with the clouds of heaven
> there came one like a son of man,
> and he came to the Ancient of Days
> and was presented before him.
> And to him was given dominion
> and glory and a kingdom,
> that all peoples, nations, and languages
> should serve him;
> his dominion is an everlasting dominion,
> which shall not pass away,
> and his kingdom one
> that shall not be destroyed.
> (Dan. 7:13–14)

And one of the elders said to me, "Weep no more; behold, the Lion of the tribe of Judah, the Root of David, has conquered, so that he can open the scroll and its seven seals. . . ."

> And they sang a new song, saying,
> "Worthy are you to take the scroll
> and to open its seals,
> for you were slain, and by your blood you ransomed people for God

> from every tribe and language and people and nation,
> and you have made them a kingdom and priests to our God,
> and they shall reign on the earth."
>
> (Rev. 5:5, 9–10)

* * *

REVISITING THE MINERAL ANALOGY

Our analogy in the Introduction of a mineral radiating different colors when viewed under different light is fitting. A fluorite crystal continues to be fluorite, made from elements calcium and fluorine, regardless of the light in which it is viewed. Yet the colors displayed vary significantly under different wavelengths of light. Observing a fluorite crystal under different illumination does not undermine earlier identification of the mineral's name or composition. Discoveries under different light simply add to the richness of our understanding and appreciation of this mineral.

Approaching Genesis 1 from varying perspectives is to read it—metaphorically speaking—first under white light, again under shortwave radiation, yet again under longwave radiation, and maybe again after heating. Each reading brings out something that was always true, but only apprehended and appreciated when approached from a different angle. If read correctly, no new reading will undermine the central message of the text. Rather, each new light—each perspective—yields another layer of theological and artistic beauty. This is not to say that all understandings are valid or equally defensible. If a new understanding is proposed that applies inconsistent rules of biblical interpretation or that challenges core doctrines of the faith, it is likely wrong. In our mineral analogy, it would be akin to seeing a pink fluorite crystal turn blue under a different light and declaring it to be a quartz—a mineral made of entirely different elements.

The mineral analogy is applicable at another level (another layer!). Professional and amateur geologists have long known about fluorite and properties such as its crystal shape, hardness, density, and chemical composition, but some special properties were only discovered recently. Was the true nature of fluorite hidden from people for most of human history, only to be discovered and *genuinely* understood in these latter days? Not at all. People did not need to know of every possible property of fluorite to be able to identify it and appreciate how its known characteristics could be put to use. At the same time, appreciation—perhaps even wonder—simply increased as each new property was discovered.

The question of genuine understanding hidden from humanity for centuries may sound a bit silly applied to a rock, but what about Scripture? None of the layers presented in this book are entirely new, though the rigor, theological development, or connection with ancient Near Eastern manuscripts for some are recent. Would God have allowed a *full* understanding of Genesis 1 to be hidden from people for most of human history? Are we suggesting that no one *really* understood Genesis until this generation? The answer is the same as for our mineral analogy, though of much greater significance. People did not need to know of every conceivable property—every layer—of the creation story in order to understand its central theological themes of God's authorship and sovereignty over this creation, his relationship with humans as his image-bearers, separation from God because of sin, and the need for divine intervention and redemption. At the same time, our appreciation and wonder may yet grow as we discover that the text is deeper than we ever imagined. It is, indeed, a river in which a lamb can wade and an elephant can swim.[5]

WHAT IF I DON'T BUY INTO THEM ALL?

We would like to think that our presentation convinces you that all seven layers are valid understandings of the creation story, each perspective complementing the others and each yielding something unique. The overarching thesis, however, that there are multiple, overlapping layers of truth revealed in Genesis 1, is not contingent on acceptance of all seven.[6] Nor does it require that every element or defense of each layer be embraced. If one ultimately finds only three or four layers to be convincing, we still consider this a positive outcome, as it means recognition of the multifaceted nature of the text. There is not a solitary interpretational perspective that should be mounted and defended to the exclusion of all others. The scriptural river runs deep.

WHY NOW?

Some readers may recognize truth in the general assessment above, yet still struggle with the support for some layers being so new. In other words, why are some of these perspectives being fleshed out *now*, or at least only within the last century or so? There is a suspicious juxtaposition in time with scientific discoveries that have been used to challenge the veracity and relevance of the Bible. Is the flurry of new ideas about Genesis 1 really just

---

5. Gregory the Great, *Moral Reflections on the Book of Job*, 1:53.
6. We also make no claim our selection of layers is exhaustive.

an outgrowth of Christian angst, trying to find ways of making the Bible compatible with science?

This is a fair question—but one that we will answer with an emphatic *no*. In fact, we would argue for the exact opposite. The same God who shares his delight in his creation with humans who explore and make discoveries in his natural world also delights in providing his people with what they need from Scripture to meet the challenges of their time and place. In this context, it is noteworthy that the discovery of ANE libraries and their impact on biblical understanding has occurred within the same timeframe as scientific discoveries and challenges. Is the timing coincidental?

Consider this analysis. In the last two hundred years, scientific discoveries have raised particular questions about the truth and relevance of the Bible that no previous generation has faced. These challenges have driven introspective Christians back to the biblical text to see if there have been secondary assumptions made about the creation story, perhaps imposed on the text by our own cultural biases—assumptions never intended by the writer. Over the same period of time, archaeological discoveries have provided tools for that very assessment, tools that were not previously available—*nor previously needed*. Significantly, the application of these tools in every layer presented in this book *strengthens* the relevance of the text for the church today, enhances our wonder at the layers of theological truth, and opens doors for a greater sense of awe at God's natural creation. The timing is not a coincidence.

WHAT ABOUT SCIENCE?

It is natural and expected that some readers will get to this point in the book and ask, "What about science?" Where is the defense of a particular scientific understanding of the age or history of life on earth? How could *seven* layers of Genesis 1 be presented and not once weigh in on these questions? We can answer in two ways. First, the layers presented are not dependent on a particular understanding of natural history. People may hold differing opinions on science and still share an appreciation for the multi-layered message of the creation story.

A second, more substantive answer is that no specific scientific understanding is defended because the biblical text does not share this interest. The primary focus of the inspired writer is not on God's methodology but on God's character and his relationship with his human and material creation. Genesis 1 is about God and his kingdom.

This is not a new observation dreamed up to give science room or freedom to operate. Bible-believing theologians have long pondered the physical nature of the days of creation, with varied conclusions and speculations.[7] Uncertainty existed in the past and persists today, not because the Bible is unclear on exactly what a journalist on the scene would have recorded, but because this was not the purpose or intended focus.

This does not mean the creation story has nothing to say of relevance to science. There are layers, particularly the "Polemic" and "Covenant" layers (Layers 3 and 4), that have significant implications for what we should expect to see in nature. God's material creation reflects his own character. It is orderly and consistent in ways that make it amenable to scientific study. We can expect that nature is not designed to deceive because its Author is not capricious or deceptive. He created it good, and it continues to declare his glory. This means there is value in studying the natural realm to understand its workings and history. We should expect to be filled with wonder as we explore the intricacies and complexities of God's natural creativity. What we will not find is the details of natural history spelled out in advance in the pages of Scripture.

There is irony in the recognition above. In our increasingly secular culture, science has been elevated as the ultimate arbiter of truth. Rather than challenge this assertion directly, many Christians have unwittingly acquiesced and expressed agreement by forcing Genesis 1 to be a scientific text. The literary artistry and nuanced layers of its message are stripped away to make it fit within an anemic secular mold. We do no favor to the work of the kingdom when we defend the Bible by *secularizing* it. Sandra Richter offers a succinct assessment of the purpose of Genesis 1 and the errors of human interpretation in the opening of *The Epic of Eden*:

> The Bible, in all its parts, is intended to communicate to humanity the realities of redemption. Over the centuries, the church has stumbled when it has forgotten this truth, and has thereby, ironically, damaged the authority of the book from which it has drawn its life. Often the error has run in the direction of making this book less than it is—less than the inspired Word of God, less than the supernatural report of God's doings throughout the ages, less than the definitive rule for faith and practice among those who believe. But just as often, the error has run in the other

---

7. Robert Letham provides numerous examples of historical defenders of the Christian faith who argued against a literalistic reading of Gen. 1, including Origen (185–254), Basil the Great (330–379), Ambrose (339–397), Augustine (354–430), Bede (673–735), Anselm (1033–1109), Robert Grosseteste (1168–1253), Aquinas (1225–1274), and Martin Luther (1483–1546). Letham, "In the Space of Six Days." See also Allert, *Early Christian Readings of Genesis One.*

direction—attempting to make the Bible more than it is. Too often in our zeal for the worldwide influence of this book, we forget that it was not intended as an exhaustive ancient world history, or a guide to the biology and paleontology of creation, or even a handbook on social reform. We forget that this book was cast upon the waters of history with one very specific, completely essential and desperately necessary objective—to tell the epic tale of God's ongoing quest to ransom his creation.[8]

OUR HOPE

In the introduction, we stated a twofold hope for this book. The first is a greater appreciation for the grandeur and beauty of the creation story. It is not a monochromatic text. Multiple themes are interwoven into this amazing story, each complementing and enhancing the others, and all working toward the same mission of solving the problem of sin. It can be studied for a lifetime and its depths not fully plumbed.

The second hope is that this work will serve as a balm on the open wounds that Christians have inflicted on other Christians. The creation story should represent theological common ground for the people of God. Instead, it seems to be increasingly viewed as a battleground where an unholy war is being waged, pitting believer against believer. The attention of the church is distracted by unhealthy squabbles that undermine its mission. As the church begins to recognize and appreciate the multifaceted beauty of the creation story, our hope is that Christians will find themselves increasingly engaged in energetic, edifying discussions of their *favorite* layers (plural), rather than arguments over which preferred understanding (singular) should send all others into exile.

> Behold, how good and pleasant it is
> > when brothers dwell in unity!
> It is like the precious oil on the head,
> > running down on the beard,
> on the beard of Aaron,
> > running down on the collar of his robes!
> It is like the dew of Hermon,
> > which falls on the mountains of Zion!
> For there Yahweh has commanded the blessing,
> > life forevermore.

> (Ps. 133:1–3)

---

8. Richter, *Epic of Eden*, 15.

DISCUSSION QUESTIONS

1. The book started with a methodology that explored the genealogies of Jesus. What relationship is drawn between the opening of the Old and New Testaments?

2. How do you see the thesis of this book intersecting with science?

3. Is the timing of discoveries of ancient Near Eastern origin stories and treaties significant?

4. If Christians embrace the manifold beauty of Genesis 1 (all or a subset of these layers), how might conversations about Genesis or creation begin to change?

APPENDIX 1

An Unbroken Covenant with Nature

*T*he Covenant layer ended with the question of how an unbroken covenant with nature can be reconciled with animal death. Before engaging
this question, it is worth reiterating two points made in Layer 4. First,
recognition of the covenant message in Genesis 1–3 is not dependent on agreeing that the covenant with nature remains unbroken. It is not a trivial element
of the layer, but a covenant view does not critically hinge on this point. Second,
animal death prior to human sin is not offered here as an argument against a
literal reading of Genesis. The biblical defense for an unfallen material creation
is equally applicable within a literal six-day framework.

The objection to animal death before the first sin is based on a sentiment
that death and suffering of any kind are not good and therefore could not have
been part of the original creation. The most common verses cited in defense
of this view are from Genesis and Romans. God told Adam that eating from
the forbidden tree would bring about death (Gen. 2:17). The apostle Paul
follows in kind, saying that through Adam's sin, death spread to all people
(Rom. 5:12). Genesis 1:29–30 is offered as additional evidence of the absence
of death, at least among animals, as plants are specifically mentioned as food
for humans and all varieties of terrestrial creatures. It is not until the fall that
we read of animal death in order to make skin garments for Adam and Eve
(Gen. 3:21).

We address the objection in greater depth here than at the end of
Layer 4, though we will readily acknowledge that it is still not a thorough
or exhaustive response. Where we and others have addressed this subject

in other publications, the discussion fills many pages (or even books). For the purposes of this book, we will make a few salient observations and, for those wishing a more thorough analysis, recommend sources for further reading.

DEATH: HUMAN VERSUS EVERYTHING ELSE

Romans 5:12 is commonly used as a "prooftext" for death entering the world as a result of sin: "Therefore, just as sin came into the world through one man, and death through sin, and so death spread to all men because all sinned." If we take seriously the words of Scripture, we need to pay attention to how this verse ends. If the intention was that death in general was introduced by human sin, then the verse should have finished with "so death spread to all" or "so death spread to all creation." It says neither. The wording specifically says "so death spread to all men"—to all *humans* (plural of *anthropos*). The wording limits the scope of the curse of death to those with the capacity to sin—humankind.

This is consistent with the wording of Genesis 2:17, where Adam was warned, "Of the tree of the knowledge of good and evil you shall not eat, for in the day that you eat of it you shall surely die." Again, if we take the choice of words seriously, God did not say "*everyone* will surely die" or "you will bring death into the world." He declared, "*you* will surely die." The recipient of this death is specific to the one with the capacity for disobedience.

DEATH AND EXILE

The subject of death becomes complicated when we realize it is not simply a physical phenomenon. If it merely represented the cessation of biological function, then it would be hard to argue that a distinction could be made between animal and human death. But human death in the Bible is far more than biology. Death is often equated in Scripture with exile—separation from the abiding presence of God. It is for this reason that the curse of death on Adam and Eve was first manifest by being cast from the garden—exile. It is the same reason that Proverbs 12:28 can boldly declare,

> In the path of righteousness is life,
> > and in its pathway there is no death.

The righteous will, in fact, experience physical death; what they will not experience is separation from God. This threat of death is unique to humans.

DEATH: EFFICIENCY VERSUS WASTE

Within Christian circles, death is often spoken of as wasteful. So many creatures born only to die and decompose. The order once imposed on the land in the days of creation is believed to be working daily in reverse toward the unordered and unfilled pre-creation chaos. And yet, any actual study of nature reveals the opposite. It is an incredibly orderly system, with the products of death and decomposition serving as the sources of material and energy used by the next generation of life. The system God put into place is one of continuous recycling and rejuvenation. Nature may not always conform to our liking (our cursed experience with nature), but it is a beautifully crafted system.

Some may recognize the above but still protest that nature as a whole is subject to the second law of thermodynamics. The cosmos is in a constant state of decline into greater disorder. Is this not evidence of working back toward *tohu wabohu*? It is not, for the simple reason that the system of which creation principally speaks—the place of human habitation—is receiving a constant supply of order-enhancing energy. The combined sun-earth system experiences a net increase in disorder as the sun works toward its long burnout, but the earth, as beneficiary of the sun's light, constantly experiences localized increases in order. Just consider the transition from seed to tree, larva to butterfly, or fertilized cell to human baby. All represent incredible increases in order, happening in billions of organisms even now. It is a system designed to last far into the future, with no fear of running out of juice before the return of Christ and final redemption.

CARNIVORY AND "PLANTS AS FOOD"

The fact that Eden had boundaries, and getting kicked out was bad, means conditions inside and outside the garden of Eden were not the same. It is possible that the description of plants for food was the condition inside the garden. Carnivory outside the garden could have existed without posing any threat to Adam and Eve. Being cast out did not change nature, but placed humans in an environment where protections were now less certain—comparable to finding oneself on the wrong side of a glass barrier at the tiger exhibit.

CARNIVORE DESIGN

Finally, consider the design of predators. They are exquisite creatures, fashioned in intricate detail for their place in the ecosystem. Claws, fangs, talons, mandibles, fast-twitch muscles, digestive systems, and much more all work together to ensure that prey can be captured, rendered, and digested. In carrying out their role in nature, they ensure that herbivores do not overrun the planet, wiping out plant life.

At what time did carnivores attain their designs and roles? And who was responsible? If one were to suggest they were made this way from the start but initially only ate plants, this means they were poorly designed for life until sin came along. Alternatively, if one were to suggest their bodies morphed into carnivorous forms at the fall, this would make sin, or perhaps Satan, a master creator on par with God. Neither of these options fit with what we find in Scripture, where God delights in feeding lions their prey and the sporting of Leviathan in the seas—with every indication it was so from the start.

RECOMMENDED BOOKS

Reading Genesis Well: Navigating History, Poetry, Science, and Truth in Genesis 1–11 by C. John Collins. Grand Rapids: Zondervan, 2018.

Friend of Science, Friend of Faith: Listening to God in His Works and Word by Gregg Davidson. Grand Rapids: Kregel, 2019.

God's Good Earth: The Case for an Unfallen Creation by Jon Garvey. Eugene, OR: Cascade, 2019.

Death before the Fall: Biblical Literalism and the Problem of Animal Suffering by Ronald E. Osborn. Downers Grove, IL: IVP Academic, 2014.

APPENDIX 2

Excerpts from Ancient Near East Origin Myths

L ayer 5 ("Temple") summarized temple and creation language found in ancient Near Eastern tablets. Selections below draw attention to the ancient Near Eastern concept of an earthly temple, made at the time of creation, as a place of rest for the gods.

The first excerpt is from the fifth and sixth tablets of Enuma Elish, a seven-tablet Babylonian creation epic.[1] Brackets indicate missing portions from a tablet. In the fifth tablet, Marduk created the earth and heavens from the body of Tiamat, the defeated chaos sea goddess. Babylon was created as the terrestrial counterpart to Esharra, abode of the gods in heaven. The sixth tablet addresses the creation of humans, and revisits the creation of Babylon and temple.

Tablet V, lines 117–139
Marduk opened his mouth to speak
And addressed the gods his fathers,
"Above the Apsû, the emerald (?) abode,
Opposite Ešarra, which I built for you,
Beneath the celestial parts, whose floor I made firm,
I will build a house to be my luxurious abode.

---

1. Excerpts taken from "Enuma Elish" in *Babylonian Creation Myths*, trans. W. G. Lambert (Eisenbrauns, 2013), reproduced at the ETANA archive, http://www.etana.org/node/581.

Within it I will establish its shrine,

I will found my chamber and establish my kingship.

When you come up from the Apsû to make a decision

This will be your resting place before the assembly.

When you descend from heaven to make a decision

This will be your resting place before the assembly.

I shall call its name "Babylon," "The Homes of the Great Gods,"

Within it we will hold a festival: that will be the evening festival.

[The gods], his fathers, [heard] this speech of his,

[. . .] they said,

"With regard to all that your hands have made,

Who has your [. . .]?

With regard to the earth that your hands have made,

Who has your [. . .]?

In Babylon, as you have named it,

Put our [resting place] for ever.

[. . .] let them our bring regular offerings

Tablet VI, lines 51–57

"Let us make a shrine of great renown:

Your chamber will be our resting place wherein we may repose.

Let us erect a shrine to house a pedestal

Wherein we may repose when we finish (the work)."

When Marduk heard this,

He beamed as brightly as the light of day,

"Build Babylon, the task you have sought."

From the preamble to a prayer connected to the founding of Eridu, one of the earliest cities in southern Mesopotamia:[2]

No holy house, no house of the gods, had been built in a pure place;

No reed had come forth, no tree had been created;

No brick had been laid, no brickmold had been created;

No house had been built, no city had been created;

No city had been built, no settlement had been founded;

---

2. Foster, *Before the Muses*, 488. After quoting this text, Walton (*Lost World of Genesis One*, 79) observes, "Then Marduk settles the gods into their dwelling places, creates people and animals, and sets up the Tigris and Euphrates."

Nippur had not been built, Ekur had not been created;

Uruk had not been built, Eanna had not been created;

The depths had not been built, Eridu had not been created;

No holy house, no house of the gods, no dwelling for them had been created.

All the world is sea,

The Spring in the midst of the sea was only a channel,

Then was Eridu built, Esagila was created.

From an Akkadian prayer dedicating the foundation brick of a temple:[3]

When Anu, Enlil, and Ea had a (first) idea of heaven and earth,

They found a wise means of providing support of the gods:

They prepared, in the land, a pleasant dwelling,

And the gods were installed (?) in this dwelling:

Their principal temple.

From the Temple Hymn of Keš (Sumarian):[4]

House . . . inspiring great awe, called with a mighty name by An;

house . . . whose fate is grandly determined by the Great Mountain Enlil!

House of the Anuna gods possessing great power, which gives wisdom to the people;

house, reposeful dwelling of the great gods!

House, which was planned together with the plans of heaven and earth, . . . with the pure divine powers;

house which underpins the Land and supports the shrines!

From an Egyptian (Memphis) creation text:[5]

So has Ptah come to rest after his making everything and every divine speech as well,

Having given birth to the gods,

Having made their villages,

Having founded their homes,

Having set the gods in their cult places,

---

3. This is part of a prayer dedicating the foundation brick of a temple. Clifford, *Creation Accounts in the Ancient Near East*, 61.

4. Temple Hymn of Keš 4.80.2, D.58A–F, Electronic Text Corpus of Sumerian Literature, https://etcsl.orinst.ox.ac.uk/cgi-bin/etcsl.cgi?text=t.4.80.2#.

5. From the Egyptian cosmology Memphite Theology (Hallo and Younger, *Context of Scripture*, 1:15).

Having made sure their bread-offerings,
Having found their shrines,
Having made their bodies resemble what contents them.

BIBLIOGRAPHY

Alexander, T. Desmond. *From Paradise to the Promised Land: An Introduction to the Pentateuch*. 2nd ed. Grand Rapids: Baker Academic, 2002.

Allert, Craig D. *Early Christian Readings of Genesis One: Patristic Exegesis and Literal Interpretation*. BioLogos Books on Science and Christianity. Downers Grove, IL: IVP Academic, 2018.

Allis, Oswald T. *The Five Books of Moses*. Eugene, OR: Wipf & Stock, 2001.

Andersen, Francis I., and David Noel Freedman. *Hosea*. Anchor Bible 24. New York: Doubleday, 1980.

Anderson, Bernhard W. "From Analysis to Synthesis: The Interpretation of Genesis 1–11." *Journal of Biblical Literature* 97, no. 1 (1978): 23–39.

Augustine of Hippo. *The Confessions of Saint Augustine*. Translated by E. B. Pusey. Mount Vernon, VA: Peter Pauper, 1940–1949.

———. *The Literal Meaning of Genesis*. Translated and annotated by John Hammond Taylor. 2 vols. Ancient Christian Writers 41–42. New York: Newman, 1982.

Averbeck, Richard E. "A Literary Day, Inter-textual, and Contextual Reading of Genesis 1–2." In *Reading Genesis 1–2: An Evangelical Conversation*, edited by J. Daryl Charles, 7–34. Peabody, MA: Hendrickson, 2013.

———. "Tabernacle." In *Dictionary of Old Testament: Pentateuch*, edited by T. Desmond Alexander and David. W. Baker, 807–27. Downers Grove, IL: InterVarsity, 2003.

Bartor, Assnat. "Narrative." In *The Oxford Encyclopedia of the Bible and Law*, edited by Brent A. Strawn, 2:125–33. Oxford: Oxford University Press, 2015.

Beale, G. K. "Eden, the Temple, and the Church's Mission in the New Creation." *Journal of the Evangelical Theological Society* 48, no. 1 (2005): 5–31.

———. *The Temple and the Church's Mission: A Biblical Theology of the Dwelling Place of God*. New Studies in Biblical Theology 17. Downers Grove, IL: InterVarsity, 2004.

Beale, G. K., and Mitchell Kim. *God Dwells among Us: Expanding Eden to the Ends of the Earth*. Downers Grove, IL: IVP Academic, 2014.

Beall, Todd S. "Reading Genesis 1–2: A Literal Approach." In *Reading Genesis 1–2: An Evangelical Conversation*, edited by J. Daryl Charles, 45–59. Peabody, MA: Hendrickson, 2013.

Beckman, Gary M. *Hittite Diplomatic Texts*. 2nd ed. SBL Writings from the Ancient World Series 7. Atlanta: Scholars, 1999.

Ben-Dov, Jonathan. "Calendars and Festivals." In *The Oxford Encyclopedia of the Bible and Law*, edited by Brent A. Strawn, 1:87–93. Oxford: Oxford University Press, 2015.

Blocher, Henri. *In the Beginning: The Opening Chapters of Genesis*. Downers Grove, IL: InterVarsity, 1984.

Block, Daniel I. *Covenant: The Framework of God's Grand Plan of Redemption*. Grand Rapids: Baker Academic, 2021.

———. "Eden: A Temple? A Reassessment of the Biblical Evidence." In *From Creation to New Creation: Biblical Theology and Exegesis; Essays in Honor of G. K. Beale*, edited by Daniel M. Gurtner and Benjamin L. Gladd, 3–29. Peabody, MA: Hendrickson, 2013.

Bouma-Prediger, Steven. *For the Beauty of the Earth: A Christian Vision for Creation Care*. Grand Rapids: Baker Academic, 2001.

Boyd, Steven W. "Statistical Determination of Genre in Biblical Hebrew: Evidence for an Historical Reading of Genesis 1:1–2:3." In *Radioisotopes and the Age of The Earth: Results of a Young-Earth Creationist Research Initiative*, edited by Larry Vardiman, Andrew Snelling, and Eugene F. Chaffin, 2:631–734. San Diego, CA: Institute for Creation Research, 2005.

Carmichael, Calum. *The Spirit of Biblical Law*. The Spirit of the Laws Series. Athens: University of Georgia Press, 1996.

Cassuto, Umberto. *A Commentary on the Book of Genesis*. Part 1, *From Adam to Noah*. Translated by Israel Abrahams. 3rd ed. Jerusalem: Magnes Press, 1961.

Clements, Ronald E. "Sacred Mountains, Temples, and the Presence of God." In *Cult and Cosmos: Tilting Toward a Temple-Centered Theology*, edited by L. Michael Morales, 69–84. Biblical Tools and Studies 18. Leuven: Peeters, 2014.

Clifford, Richard J. *The Cosmic Mountain in Canaan and the Old Testament*. Harvard Semitic Monographs 4. Cambridge, MA: Harvard University Press, 1972. Reprint, Eugene, OR: Wipf & Stock, 2010.

———. *Creation Accounts in the Ancient Near East and in the Bible*. Catholic Biblical Quarterly Monograph Series 26. Washington, DC: Catholic Biblical Association, 1994.

———. "The Temple and the Holy Mountain." In *The Temple in Antiquity: Ancient Records and Modern Perspectives*, edited by Truman G. Madsen, 107–24. Provo, UT: Religious Studies Center, Brigham Young University, 1984.

Cohen, Mark E. *The Cultic Calendars of the Ancient Near East*. Bethesda, MD: CDL Press, 1993.

Collins, C. John. "Adam and Eve in the Old Testament." *The Southern Baptist Journal of Theology* 15, no. 1 (2011): 4–25.

———. *Did Adam and Eve Really Exist? Who They Were and Why You Should Care*. Wheaton, IL: Crossway, 2011.

———. *Genesis 1–4: A Linguistic, Literary, and Theological Commentary*. Phillipsburg, NJ: P&R, 2006.

_____. "Reading Genesis 1–2 with the Grain: Analogical Days." In *Reading Genesis 1–2: An Evangelical Conversation*, edited by J. Daryl Charles, 73–92. Peabody, MA: Hendrickson, 2013.

_____. *Reading Genesis Well: Navigating History, Poetry, Science, and Truth in Genesis 1–11*. Grand Rapids: Zondervan, 2018.

Copan, Paul, and Douglas Jacoby. *Origins: The Ancient Impact and Modern Implications of Genesis 1–11*. Nashville: Morgan James Faith, 2018.

Coppes, Leonard J. "Of C. John Collins and the Analogical View." In *OPC Report of the Committee to Study the Views of Creation*, 329–42. Willow Grove, PA: Orthodox Presbyterian Church, 2004. https://www.opc.org/GA/creation.html.

Currid, John D. *Against the Gods: The Polemical Theology of the Old Testament*. Wheaton, IL: Crossway, 2013.

_____. *Ancient Egypt and the Old Testament*. Grand Rapids: Baker, 1997.

Davidson, Gregg. *Friend of Science, Friend of Faith: Listening to God in His Works and Word*. Grand Rapids: Kregel, 2019.

Davis, John. *Biblical Numerology: A Basic Study of the Use of Numbers in the Bible*. Grand Rapids: Baker, 1968.

Dean, Signe. "Not So Unique? A Key Feature of the Human Brain Has Just Been Found in Monkeys." *Science Alert*, May 26, 2017. https://www.sciencealert.com/scientists-have-found-a-network-in-monkey-brains-that-exclusively-deals-with-social-interactions.

DiMattei, Steven. *Genesis 1 and the Creationism Debate: Being Honest to the Text, Its Author, and His Beliefs*. Eugene, OR: Wipf & Stock, 2016.

Dumbrell, William J. *Covenant and Creation: An Old Testament Covenant Theology*. Rev. ed. Milton Keynes, UK: Paternoster, 2013.

Duvall, J. Scott, and J. Daniel Hays. *Grasping God's Word: A Hands-On Approach to Reading, Interpreting, and Applying the Bible*. 2nd ed. Grand Rapids: Zondervan, 2005.

Eichrodt, Walther. *Theology of the Old Testament*. Translated by J. A. Baker. 2 vols. Old Testament Library. Philadelphia: Westminster Press, 1961–1967.

Enns, Peter. "Jesus the Artist." *BioLogos*, September 28, 2012. https://biologos.org/articles/jesus-the-artist.

Estes, Douglas C. *The Temporal Mechanics of the Fourth Gospel: A Theory of Hermeneutical Relativity in the Gospel of John*. Biblical Interpretation Series 92. Leiden: Brill, 2008.

Fee, Gordon D., and Douglas Stuart. *How to Read the Bible Book by Book: A Guided Tour*. Grand Rapids: Zondervan, 2014.

Fleming, Daniel, "By the Sweat of Your Brow: Adam, Anat, Arthirat and Ashurbanipal." In *Ugarit and the Bible: Proceedings of the International Symposium on Ugarit and the Bible Manchester, September 1992*, edited by G. J. Brooke, A. H. W. Curtis, and J. F. Healey, 93–100. Ugaritisch-Biblische Literatur 11. Neukirchen-Vluyn: Neukirchener, 1994.

Foster, Benjamin R. *Before the Muses: An Anthology of Akkadian Literature*. 3rd ed. Bethesda, MD: CDL Press, 2005.

France, R. T. *The Gospel of Matthew*. New International Commentary on the New Testament. Grand Rapids: Eerdmans, 2007.

Futato, Mark. "Because It Had Rained: A Study of Gen 2:5–7 with Implications for Gen 2:4–25 and Gen 1:1–2:3." *Westminster Theological Journal* 60, no. 1 (1998): 1–21.

Garvey, Jon. *God's Good Earth: The Case for an Unfallen Creation*. Eugene, OR: Cascade, 2019.

Gentry, Kenneth L., Jr. *As It Is Written: The Genesis Account, Literal or Literary?* Green Forest, AR: Master Books, 2016.

Gentry, Peter J., and Stephen J. Wellum. *Kingdom through Covenant: A Biblical-Theological Understanding of the Covenants*. 2nd ed. Wheaton, IL: Crossway, 2018.

Godfrey, Robert W. *God's Pattern for Creation: A Covenantal Reading of Genesis*. Phillipsburg, NJ: P&R, 2003.

Gonzales, Robert, Jr. "The Covenantal Context of the Fall: Did God Make a Primeval Covenant with Adam?" *Reformed Baptist Theological Review* 4, no. 1 (2007): 5–32.

Green, Peter. Review of *Adam as Israel*, by Seth Postell. *For Christ and His Kingdom* (blog), April 9, 2013. https://wheatonblog.wordpress.com/2013/04/09/review-adam-as-israel-postell.

Greenwood, Kyle. *Scripture and Cosmology: Reading the Bible between the Ancient World and Modern Science*. Downers Grove, IL: IVP Academic, 2015.

Gregory the Great. *Moral Reflections on the Book of Job*. Translated by Brian Kerns. 3 vols. Collegeville, MN: Liturgical Press, 2104.

Grudem, Wayne. *Systematic Theology: An Introduction to Biblical Doctrine*. Grand Rapids: Zondervan, 1994.

Guillaume, Phillip. *Land and Calendar: The Priestly Document from Genesis 1 to Joshua 18*. Library of Hebrew Bible/Old Testament Series 391. New York: T&T Clark, 2009.

Guillermo, Gonzalez, and Jay Richards. *The Privileged Planet: How Our Place in the Cosmos Is Designed for Discovery*. Washington, DC: Regnery, 2004.

Habig, Brian C. "Hosea 6:7 Revisited." *Presbyterion* 42 (2016): 4–20.

Hallo, William W., and K. Lawson Younger Jr., eds. *The Context of Scripture*. 3 vols. 2nd ed. Leiden: Brill, 1997.

Hamilton, Victor P. *The Book of Genesis Chapters 1–17*. New International Commentary on the Old Testament 1A. Grand Rapids: Eerdmans, 1990.

Hasel, Gerhard F. "The Polemic Nature of the Genesis Cosmology." *Evangelical Quarterly* 46 (1974): 81–102.

———. "The Significance of the Cosmology in Genesis 1 in Relation to Ancient Near Eastern Parallels." *Andrews University Seminary Studies* 10 (1972): 1–20.

Herder, Johann Gottfried. *The Spirit of Hebrew Poetry*. Translated by James Marsh. Burlington, VT: Edward Smith, 1833.

Hill, Carol A. "Making Sense of the Numbers of Genesis." *Perspectives on Science and Christian Faith* 55, no. 4 (2003): 239–51.

Hill, William Ely. "My Wife and My Mother-in-Law." *Puck* 78 (1915): 11.

Hoekema, Anthony A. *Created in God's Image*. Grand Rapids: Eerdmans, 1986.

Hogenboom, Melissa. "Humans Are Nowhere Near as Special as We Like to Think." *BBC Earth*, July 3, 2015. http://www.bbc.com/earth/story/20150706-humans-are-not-unique-or-special.

Hopkins, David C. *The Highlands of Canaan: Agricultural Life in the Early Iron Age*. The Social World of Biblical Antiquity Series 3. Sheffield: JSOT Press, 1985.

Hummel, Charles E. "Interpreting Genesis One." *Journal of the American Scientific Affiliation* 38, no. 3 (1986): 175–85.

Hyers, Conrad. *The Meaning of Creation: Genesis and Modern Science*. Atlanta: John Knox, 1984.

———. "The Narrative Form of Genesis 1." *Journal of the American Scientific Affiliation* 36, no. 4 (1984): 208–15.

International Council on Biblical Inerrancy. "The Chicago Statement on Biblical Hermeneutics." 1982. https://library.dts.edu/Pages/TL/Special/ICBI_2.pdf. Articles reprinted in *Journal of the Evangelical Theological Society* 25, no. 4 (1982): 397–401.

———. "The Chicago Statement on Biblical Inerrancy." 1978. https://library.dts.edu/Pages/TL/Special/ICBI-1978-11-07.pdf.

Irons, Lee. "The Framework Interpretation: An Exegetical Summary." *Ordained Servant* 9, no. 1 (2000): 7–11.

Irons, Lee, and Meredith G. Kline. "The Framework Interpretation." In *The Genesis Debate: Three Views on the "Days" of Creation*, edited by David G. Hagopian, 217–56. Mission Viejo, CA: Crux Press, 2001.

Jenson, Philip P. "Temple." In *Dictionary of the Old Testament Prophets*, edited by Mark J. Boda and J. Gordon McConville, 767–74. Downers Grove, IL: IVP Academic, 2012.

Keller, Timothy. *The Reason for God: Belief in an Age of Skepticism*. New York: Penguin, 2008.

Kenneally, Christine. "So You Think Humans Are Unique? Six 'Uniquely' Human Traits Now Found in Animals." *New Scientist*, May 21, 2008. https://www.newscientist.com/article/mg19826571-700-so-you-think-humans-are-unique/.

Kitchen, K. A. *Ancient Orient and Old Testament*. Downers Grove, IL: InterVarsity, 1966.

Kline, Meredith G. "Space and Time in the Genesis Cosmogony." *Perspectives on Science and Christian Faith* 48, no. 1 (1996): 2–15.

———. *Treaty of the Great King: The Covenant Structure of Deuteronomy: Studies and Commentary*. Grand Rapids: Eerdmans, 1963.

"Lausanne Covenant." First International Congress on World Evangelization, 1974. https://www.lausanne.org/content/covenant/lausanne-covenant#cov.

LeFebvre, Michael. "Adam Reigns in Eden: Genesis and the Origins of Kingship." *Bulletin of Ecclesial Theology* 5, no. 2 (2018): 25–57.

———. "Cracking the Code of Cadence: The Genre of Genesis." *BioLogos*, September 26, 2019. https://biologos.org/articles/cracking-the-code-of-cadence-the-genre-of-genesis.

————. *The Liturgy of Creation: Understanding Calendars in Old Testament Context.* Downers Grove, IL: IVP Academic, 2019.

Leichty, Erle. *The Omen Series Šumma Izbu.* Texts from Cuneiform Sources 4. Locust Valley, NY: J. J. Augustin, 1970.

Letham, Robert. "'In the Space of Six Days': The Days of Creation from Origen to the Westminster Assembly." *Westminster Theological Journal* 61, no. 2 (1999): 147–74.

Levenson, Jon D. *Sinai and Zion: An Entry into the Jewish Bible.* New Voices in Biblical Studies. San Francisco: Harper & Row, 1985.

Lewis, C. S. *The Magician's Nephew.* London: The Bodley Head, 1955.

Lewis, Geraint F., and Luke A. Barnes. *A Fortunate Universe: Life in a Finely Tuned Cosmos.* Cambridge: Cambridge University Press, 2016.

Longman, Tremper, III. *How to Read the Psalms.* Downers Grove, IL: InterVarsity, 1988.

————. *Genesis. The Story of God Bible Commentary*, edited by Tremper Longman III and Scot McKnight. Grand Rapids: Zondervan, 2016.

————. "What Genesis 1–2 Teaches (and What It Doesn't)." In *Reading Genesis 1–2: An Evangelical Conversation*, edited by J. Daryl Charles, 103–28. Peabody, MA: Hendrickson, 2013.

————. *Confronting Old Testament Controversies.* Grand Rapids: Baker Books, 2019.

Lyons, Jeremy D. "Genesis 1:1–3 and the Literary Boundary of Day One." *Journal of Evangelical Theological Society* 62, no. 2 (2019): 269–85.

McCabe, Robert V. "A Critique of the Framework Interpretation of the Creation Week." In *Coming to Grips with Genesis: Biblical Authority and the Age of the Earth*, edited by Terry Mortenson, 211–50. Green Forest, AR: New Leaf, 2008.

McCaul, Alexander. "The Mosaic Record of Creation." In *Aids to Faith: A Series of Theological Essays*, edited by William Thomson, 189–236. London: John Murray, 1861.

Mendenhall, George, and Gary A. Herion. "Covenant." *Anchor Bible Dictionary* 1:1179–1202. New York: Doubleday, 1992.

Middleton, J. Richard. *The Liberating Image: The* Imago Dei *in Genesis 1.* Grand Rapids: Brazos, 2005.

————. *A New Heaven and a New Earth: Reclaiming Biblical Eschatology.* Grand Rapids: Baker Academic, 2014.

Miglio, Adam E., Caryn A. Reeder, Joshua T. Walton, and Kenneth C. Way, eds. *For Us, but Not to Us: Essays on Creation, Covenant, and Context in Honor of John H. Walton.* Eugene, OR: Pickwick, 2020.

Millar, J. Gary. *Now Choose Life: Theology and Ethics in Deuteronomy.* New Studies in Biblical Theology 6. Downers Grove, IL: InterVarsity, 2000.

Miller, Johnny V., and John M. Soden. *In the Beginning . . . We Misunderstood: Interpreting Genesis 1 in Its Original Context.* Grand Rapids: Kregel, 2012.

Moo, Douglas J., and Jonathan A. Moo. *Creation Care: A Biblical Theology of the Natural World.* Biblical Theology for Life. Grand Rapids: Zondervan, 2018.

Mortenson, Terry. *Searching for Adam: Genesis & the Truth about Man's Origin*. Green Forest, AR: Master Books, 2016.

Murray, John. "The Adamic Administration." In *Collected Writings of John Murray*. Vol. 2, *Systematic Theology*, 47–59. Edinburgh: Banner of Truth, 1977.

Noordtzij, Arie. *Gods Woord en der Eeuwen Getuigenis*. Kampen: Kok, 1924.

Origen. *De Principiis*. Vol. 4, *Ante-Nicene Fathers*. Edited by Alexander Roberts, James Donaldson, and A. Cleveland Coxe. Translated by Frederick Crombie. Buffalo: Christian Literature Publishing, 1885.

Osborn, Ronald E. *Death before the Fall: Biblical Literalism and the Problem of Animal Suffering*. Downers Grove, IL: IVP Academic, 2014.

Oswalt, John N. *The Bible among the Myths: Unique Revelation or Just Ancient Literature?* Grand Rapids: Zondervan, 2009.

Patterson, Todd. "Genesis 1:1–2:3 The Creation Account as Hebrew Poiesis." Todd Patterson personal website, January 21, 2010. https://www.toddjana.com/genesis-11-23-the-creation-account-as-hebrew-poiesis/.

Peterson, Brian Neil. *Genesis as Torah: Reading Narrative as Legal Instruction*. Eugene, OR: Cascade, 2018.

Piper, John. *Rethinking Retirement: Finishing Life for the Glory of Christ*. Wheaton, IL: Crossway, 2009.

Polak, Frank H. "Poetic Style and Parallelism in the Creation Account (Genesis 1.1–2.3)." In *Creation in Jewish and Christian Tradition*, edited by Henning Graf Reventlow and Yair Hoffman, 2–31. Journal for the Study of the Old Testament Supplement Series 319. London: Sheffield, 2002.

Postell, Seth D. *Adam as Israel: Genesis 1–3 as the Introduction to the Torah and Tanakh*. Eugene, OR: Pickwick, 2011.

preceptaustin (blog). "Poiema—Greek Word Study." September 24, 2012. https://preceptaustin.wordpress.com/2012/09/24/poiema-greek-word-study.

Presbyterian Church in America. "Report of the Creation Study Committee." 28th General Assembly. Studies and Actions of the General Assembly of The Presbyterian Church in America. 2000. https://www.pcahistory.org/pca/digest/studies/creation/report.pdf.

Rankin, John C. *Genesis and the Power of True Assumptions*. West Simsbury, CT: Theological Education Institute, 2013.

Richter, Sandra L. *The Epic of Eden: A Christian Entry into the Old Testament*. Downers Grove, IL: IVP Academic, 2008.

Ridderbos, Nicolaas Herman. *Is There a Conflict between Genesis 1 and Science?* Grand Rapids: Eerdmans, 1957.

Rochberg-Halton, Francesca. "Calendars, Ancient Near East." *Anchor Bible Dictionary* 1:810–14. New York: Doubleday, 1992.

Rorison, G. "The Creative Week," in *Replies to "Essays and Reviews,"* 277–346. London: J. Henry and J. Parker, 1862.

Ross, Hugh. *The Fingerprint of God: Recent Scientific Discoveries Reveal the Unmistakable*. 2nd ed. Orange, CA: Promise, 1991.

Rudolph, David J. "Festivals in Genesis 1:14." *Tyndale Bulletin* 54, no. 2 (2003): 23–40.

Russell, Emmet. "Genealogy of Jesus Christ." In *The Zondervan Pictorial Bible Dictionary*, edited by Merrill C. Tenney, 304–5. Grand Rapids: Zondervan, 1967.

Ryken, Philip G. *Art for God's Sake: A Call to Recover the Arts*. Phillipsburg, NJ: P&R, 2006.

Sailhamer, John H. "Creation, Genesis 1–11, and the Canon." *Bulletin for Biblical Research* 10, no. 1 (2000): 89–106.

———. "Exegetical Notes: Genesis 1:1–2:4a." *Trinity Journal* 5, no. 1 (1984): 73–82.

———. "Genesis." In *Expositor's Bible Commentary*, edited by Tremper Longman III and David E. Garland, 1:21–331. Rev. ed. Grand Rapids: Zondervan, 2008.

———. *Genesis Unbound: A Provocative New Look at the Creation Account*. Sisters, OR: Multnomah, 1996.

———. *The Making of the Pentateuch: Revelation, Composition and Interpretation*. Downers Grove, IL: IVP Academic, 2009.

———. "The Mosaic Law and the Theology of the Pentateuch." *Westminster Theological Journal* 53, no. 2 (1991): 241–61.

———. *The Pentateuch as Narrative: A Biblical-Theological Commentary*. Library of Biblical Interpretation. Grand Rapids: Zondervan, 1992.

Schreiner, David B. "Zerubbabel, Persia, and Inner-biblical Exegesis." *Journal for the Evangelical Study of the Old Testament* 4, no. 2 (2015): 191–204.

Schreiner, Thomas R. *Covenant and God's Purpose for the World*. Short Studies in Biblical Theology. Wheaton, IL: Crossway, 2017.

Shetter, Tony L. "Genesis 1–2 in Light of Ancient Egyptian Creation Myths." *Bible.org*, April 22, 2005. http://www.bible.org/page.php?page_id=2966.

Shirley, Steve. "How Many Pagan/False Gods Does the Bible Mention?" *JesusAlive*. Accessed January 29, 2021. https://www.jesusalive.cc/ques220.htm.

Sleet, J. Matthew. *Serve God, Save the Planet: A Christian Call to Action*. Grand Rapids: Zondervan, 2007.

Stek, John H. "Covenant Overload in Reformed Theology." *Calvin Theological Journal* 29, no. 1 (1994): 12–41.

Stern, Sacha. *Time and Process in Ancient Judaism*. The Littman Library of Jewish Civilization. Oxford: Oxford University Press, 2003.

Stordalen, Terje. "Heaven on Earth—Or Not? Jerusalem as Eden in Biblical Literature." In *Beyond Eden: The Biblical Story of Paradise (Genesis 2–3) and Its Reception History*, edited by Konrad Schmid and Christoph Riedweg, 28–57. Tübingen: Mohr Siebeck, 2008.

Thomas Aquinas. *Summa Theologica*. Translated by the Fathers of the English Dominican Province. 2nd ed. 1920. http://www.newadvent.org/summa.

Turner, Kenneth J. "Deuteronomy's Theology of Exile." In *For Our Good Always: Studies on the Message and Influence of Deuteronomy in Honor of Daniel I. Block*, edited by Jason S. DeRouchie, Jason Gile, and Kenneth J. Turner, 189–220. Winona Lake, IN: Eisenbrauns, 2013.

———. "Exodus." In *What the Old Testament Authors Really Cared About: A Survey of Jesus' Bible*, edited by Jason S. DeRouchie, 80–101. Grand Rapids: Kregel, 2013.

_____. "The Kind-ness of God: A Theological Reflection of Mîn, 'Kind.'" In *Genesis Kinds: Creationism and the Origin of Species*, edited by Todd C. Wood and Paul A. Garner, 31–64. Center for Origins Research in Creation. Eugene, OR: Wipf & Stock, 2009.

_____. Review of *Against the Gods: The Polemical Theology of the Old Testament*, by John D. Currid. *Journal of Baptist Studies* 7 (February 2015): 83–86.

Van Goudoever, Jan. *Biblical Calendars*. 2nd ed. Leiden: Brill, 1961.

Van Leeuwen, Raymond C. "Cosmos, Temple, House: Building and Wisdom in Mesopotamia and Israel." In *Wisdom Literature in Mesopotamia and Israel*, edited by Richard J. Clifford, 67–92. Society of Biblical Literature Symposium Series 36. Atlanta: Society of Biblical Literature, 2007.

Vasholz, Robert I. Note on Hosea 6:7. In *ESV Study Bible*, edited by Lane T. Dennis and Wayne Grudem. Wheaton, IL: Crossway, 2008.

Vogels, Walter. "The Cultic and Civil Calendars of the Fourth Day of Creation (Gen 1, 14b)." *Scandinavian Journal of the Old Testament* 11, no. 2 (1997): 163–80.

Waltke, Bruce K., with Cathi J. Fredricks. *Genesis: A Commentary*. Grand Rapids: Zondervan, 2001.

Waltke, Bruce K., with Charles Yu. *An Old Testament Theology: An Exegetical, Canonical, and Thematic Approach*. Grand Rapids: Zondervan, 2007.

Walton, John H. *Ancient Israelite Literature in Its Cultural Context: A Survey of Parallels between Biblical and Ancient Near Eastern Texts*. Library of Biblical Interpretation. Grand Rapids: Zondervan, 1994.

_____. "Creation." In *Dictionary of the Old Testament: Pentateuch*, edited by T. Desmond Alexander and David W. Baker, 155–68. Downers Grove, IL: InterVarsity, 2003.

_____. *Genesis 1 as Ancient Cosmology*. Winona Lake, IN: Eisenbrauns, 2011.

_____. *Genesis*. NIV Application Commentary. Grand Rapids: Zondervan, 2001.

_____. *The Lost World of Genesis 1: Ancient Cosmology and the Origins Debate*. Downers Gove, IL: IVP Academic, 2009.

Walvoord, John F., and Roy B. Zuck, eds. *The Bible Knowledge Commentary: Old Testament*. Colorado Springs: David C. Cook, 1985.

Weeks, Noel K. "The Bible and the 'Universal' Ancient World: A Critique of John Walton." *Westminster Theological Journal* 78, no. 1 (2016): 1–28.

Weinfeld, Moshe. "Sabbath, Temple, and the Enthronement of the Lord—the Problem of the *Sitz im Leben* of Genesis 1:1–2:3." In *Mélanges Bibliques et Orientaux en l'honneur de M. Henri Cazelles*, edited by A. Caquot and M. Delcor, 501–12. Alter Orient und Altes Testament 212. Neukirchen-Vluyn: Neukirchener, 1981.

Wenham, Gordon J. "The Coherence of the Flood Narrative." *Vetus Testamentum* 28, no. 3 (1978): 336–48.

_____. *Genesis 1–15*. Word Biblical Commentary 1. Waco, TX: Word, 1987.

_____. "Sanctuary Symbolism in the Garden of Eden Story." In *Proceedings of the Ninth World Congress of Jewish Studies, Division A: The Period of the Bible*, 19–25. Jerusalem: World Union of Jewish Studies, 1986.

Westminster Confession (1646). Bible Presbyterian Church. https://bpc.org/
  wp-content/uploads/2015/06/D-ConfessionOfFaith.pdf.

Widengren, George. *The King and the Tree of Life in Ancient Near Eastern Religion
  (King and Saviour IV)*. Uppsala Universitets Arsskrift 4. Uppsala, Sweden: Lund-
  equist, 1951.

Williamson, Paul R. *Sealed with an Oath: Covenant in God's Unfolding Purpose*. New
  Studies in Biblical Theology 2007. Downers Grove, IL: InterVarsity, 2007.

Wirzba, Norman. *From Nature to Creation: A Christian Vision for Understanding and
  Loving Our World*. Grand Rapids: Baker Academic, 2015.

Wright, N. T. "Paul's Gospel and Caesar's Empire." In *Paul and Politics: Ekklesia, Israel,
  Imperium, Interpretation; Essays in Honor of Krister Stendahl*, edited by Richard
  A. Horsley, 160–83. Harrisburg, PA: Trinity Press International, 2000. https://
  ntwrightpage.com/1998/01/01/pauls-gospel-and-caesars-empire/.

———. *What Saint Paul Really Said: Was Paul of Tarsus the Real Founder of Christianity?* Grand Rapids: Eerdmans, 1997.

Wyatt, Nicolas. "A Royal Garden: The Ideology of Eden." *Scandinavian Journal of the
  Old Testament* 28, no. 1 (2014): 1–35.

———. "When Adam Delved: The Meaning of Genesis 3:23." *Vetus Testamentum* 38,
  no. 1 (1988): 117–22.

Young, Davis A. "The Contemporary Relevance of Augustine's View of Creation."
  Perspectives on Science and Christian Faith 40, no. 1 (1988): 42–45.

Young, Edward J. *Studies in Genesis One*. Phillipsburg, NJ: P&R, 1999.

AUTHOR INDEX

SUBJECT INDEX

SCRIPTURE INDEX